This writing is inspired by my soul calling to embody Ayni, the principle of respect and reciprocity. It's about coming into right relationship with self, others and Earth. In this journey, I've learned that there is no destination, only a process of learning.

Authentic Collaboration: A Bridge to Meaningful Connection
Copyright © 2023 by Elizabeth Soltis

Info graphics and book cover designed by INHOUSE Productions Ltd.
Author photos taken by Theresa Chalmers Limitless Photography.
Earth-Hands image by Mario Lopes, dreamstime.com
Dedication page image by Somrak Jendee.

All rights reserved. No part of this publication may be reproduced, distributed, or transmitted in any form or by any means, including photocopying, recording, or other electronic or mechanical methods, without the prior written permission of the author, except in the case of brief quotations embodied in critical reviews and certain other non-commercial uses permitted by copyright law.

Tellwell Talent
www.tellwell.ca

ISBN
978-0-2288-8235-0 (Paperback)
978-0-2288-8236-7 (eBook)

Thank you Owen and Laura for the beauty of your hearts! ♡
Elizabeth

This book is dedicated to all the heart-centered bridge-builders in the world.

May those who practice authentic collaboration
for the benefit of all beings
experience great love, joy and peace.

*"Our ability to reach unity in diversity will be the
beauty and the test of our civilization."
Mahatma Gandhi*

TABLE OF CONTENTS

Acknowledgments vii
Introduction ix
Prologue xvii
Chapter 1: Bridge-Building with Authentic Collaboration 1
               Ayni: Coming into Right Relationship with All 2
Chapter 2: Relating with Self, Others and Earth 18
Chapter 3: Unpacking Conventional Collaboration 33
               Illustrating Collaboration Distinctions 55
Chapter 4: Envisioning Authentic Collaboration as a New Paradigm 59
               Illustrating Authentic Collaboration with a Bridge Metaphor ... 67
Chapter 5: Exploring the Nature of Relationships 85
Chapter 6: Reflecting on Why Authentic Collaboration Matters 102
Chapter 7: Examining Collaboration Blocks and Enablers 123
               I) Victim-Thinking Block: Enabler of Empowerment (Self) 126
               II) Conflict Block: Enabler of Sharing Power (Culture) 135
               III) Hierarchy Block: Enabler of Co-creating Vision (Systems) .. 146
Chapter 8: RELATE Guiding Principles and Practices
               R = Respond by Balancing Giving and Receiving 157
               Practice the Principle 170
Chapter 9: E = Empathize by Connecting with Heart 177
               Practice the Principle 188
Chapter 10: L = Listen by Uncovering Feelings and Needs 193
               Practice the Principle 206
Chapter 11: A = Appreciate by Welcoming Different Perspectives 211
               Practice the Principle 226
Chapter 12: T = Trust by Speaking Authentically 231
               Practice the Principle 245
Chapter 13: E = Equalize by Valuing Process with Outcome 249
               Practice the Principle 263
Chapter 14: Flying on the Wings of Inner Growth and Outer Engagement. 269
Notes 288
Additional Resources 302
About Elizabeth 303

ACKNOWLEDGMENTS

Writing this book felt like a pilgrimage. The creative process was a soul-expanding journey in exploring my own authentic truth. On every level, I was challenged and renewed. So, my first expression of gratitude is for my guides, both seen and unseen. They accompany and uplift me in extraordinary ways. Thanks to these precious relationships, and the mysterious power of Earth, my path was illuminated with grace.

During my lifetime, I have received the blessing of many teachers, edge-walkers, authors, thought-leaders and mentors who supported my odyssey of unlearning and relearning. I acknowledge their gifts of wisdom and caring service. With an inspired heart, I bow to their light in facilitating my healing and growth. This includes my family and friends, who remind me that the quality of our lives depends on the quality of our relationships.

Since we are a culmination of our experiences born through relationship, I feel thankful for each person who has danced with me to the music of Life. From them, I gained understanding about the nuances, beauty and possibility of collaborative relationship-building. Be it pleasant or unpleasant, every encounter offered insights. Each person contributed to my unfoldment. Many loved me into being.

Some of my stories are included herein. While indebted to my co-journeyers, I've chosen to omit their names and identifier locations for privacy. Those details are insignificant compared to the lessons learned. May each chronicle of collaboration point you to the understanding that all beings primarily seek love and peace.

I appreciate the generosity of those who offered editorial feedback. Through dialogue, these insightful and kind-hearted people helped me craft this bridge-building vision. It felt good to weave collaborative energy into these pages. I also drew from amazing indigenous and non-indigenous wisdom sources. For reading ease, I reference those people and resources in the Notes section, followed by a list of recommended reading in Additional Resources.

AUTHENTIC COLLABORATION

Lastly, I have abundant gratitude for you, dear reader. Thank you for showing up to reflect on your relationships. Soon they will take center stage before your front-row seat. In this theatre of inquiry, drama is inherent in the play. Stay tuned for a lamenting of past regrets and a celebration of triumphs. The crucible of relationships holds the full gamut of Life. Whatever this production holds for you, I hope the process of gentle discovery enables you to see the magnificence of who you truly are.

INTRODUCTION

It's time for a new relationship narrative.

When I first put pen to paper, this was the thought foremost in my mind. As I wrote, my heart felt heavy with the weight of separation that typifies modern society. Too many of us live with the archetype of the universal orphan—cut off from Mother Nature, others and even our own hearts. Despite widespread online connectivity, loneliness, alienation and isolation are rampant. I feel this pain deeply. This book was thus born at the intersection of relational grief, a need for meaningful connection and a desire for inner coherence.

As my heart healed, the book evolved. It began to write *me*. I started to wonder, *what would our world look like if people learned how to hold all needs with care?* This question had me brushing up against the paradox of separation and connection. Humans yearn for sovereignty *and* belonging. We need autonomy *and* community. Our Western culture exudes this push-pull dynamic; we foster individualism while our spirit desires togetherness.

In our increasingly polarized world, separation underpins the "us-versus-them" mentality. We seek unity, yet our behavior speaks to protective self-distancing. We long for intimacy yet armor up with a mask. Harmony is preferred, but at the slightest hint of perceived threat, rivalry grips the mind. Bridge-building toward shared interests takes a back seat to self-interest. Personal gain overrides the greater good. The "either-or" conversation trumps an "and-both" stance. Individualism and connection sometimes feel irreconcilable. Our life journey is an ongoing balancing act between self-focus and other focus. In every relationship interaction, the pendulum swings back and forth.

For the past twenty-five years, I've played with this dichotomy as an organizational development practitioner, learning facilitator, leadership coach and team-builder. During some of those years, I served the United Nations (UN). As its name suggests, I saw this multilateral organization as an ideal space to experiment with unifying ways of relating—on many levels. Yet, after working with countless leaders and groups around the world, I noticed the same patterns as I do in business, government and the social service sector. Despite positive intentions, well-meaning professionals and impressive work, collaboration is often sacrificed at a table designed for competition. The "we" spirit of collaboration becomes secondary to hidden agendas, one-upmanship and strategic gamesmanship. Hierarchy supersedes co-creation. Powering-over outflanks power-sharing. Being polite displaces authentic truth-telling. Turf protection goes unchecked. Marginalization persists. Rarely do I—and likely others—experience a sense of mutual gain in the workplace. The "unity" in comm*unity* is lost. Diversity and inclusion are touted as important values, but do we *really* appreciate difference?

Beyond the workplace, long-held dissension and division are also experienced in our families and communities. Regardless of culture, generation or gender, the suffering of separation abounds. Common behaviors include judgment, exclusion and passive-aggressiveness. These coping strategies bring about the tendencies to distrust, dismiss and label others. It's a slippery slope into dehumanizing ways of relating. With our limited sensory experience, our perspective has built-in borders. When we're attached to certain beliefs, we post a guard at each border station. We close ourselves off from exploring the frontier of Life, of people and of the rich terrain of relationships. We even see ourselves as separate from Earth. By disconnecting from our source, we perpetuate the climate crisis and the extinction of innumerable species.

Pause for a few minutes and consider the impact of separation on your life. How do these behaviors play out in your home, at work and in community?

If separation is the root cause of relational dis-ease, the antidote is meaningful connection. This is what lies at the heart of relationship. Meaningful connection and respectful relationship-building go hand in hand. When our stated goal is peace, love, prosperity, sustainability, equity, communal belonging, staff engagement, talent management or strong team performance, the underlying unexpressed desire is *healthy relationships. This is the means to any viable end.* For many of us, this is what we are truly seeking as the elusive promised land.

AUTHENTIC COLLABORATION

In the realm of healthy relationship-building, I see skillful collaboration as the approach that holds the most potential. It's the only approach with a "win-win" mindset or a mutual-gain ethos. The challenge is becoming aware of *how we* collaborate. From my vantage point, the conventional approach is steeped in power struggles, discord, blaming and adversarial thinking. Conscious or unconscious habits of domination, criticism and manipulation can easily usurp the process. We *say* that we're collaborating when, in truth, we don't address the real aspirations nor oppositional dynamics at play. When differences arise, we skirt around them and try to cooperate. Collectively, it seems that we have assumed or forgotten the nuances of true collaboration.

Authentic Collaboration: A Bridge to Meaningful Connection attempts to reimagine this story. This book asserts that collaboration is a practice that extends beyond people working together and tolerating differences. To elevate this paradigm, this book offers a holistic, integrative model that honors the beauty of interdependence. At its finest, it calls forth the best within and among us. It aims to advance the concept of collaboration with a new vision, a bridge-building framework, support tools and practice exercises. Authentic collaboration is a synonym for healthy relationship-building. With a respect-for-all foundation, this approach begs honest, meaningful connection. It's not only the basis of authentic collaboration, we need this closeness to thrive. Indeed, heart-centered connection has the power to transform even the toughest interactions. In this caring space, separation converts into unity: relating becomes a joyful, productive exchange.

Furthermore, this holistic model of authentic collaboration is explored at the levels of self, others and Earth. Each relationship mirrors the other two. In the deepest sense, there is no separation because we live in an interconnected web of Life. We are each a unique expression of the universe being projected within itself as a path to self-realization. In our essence, everything and everyone is in each of us. One could say that we are each on a path of individuation toward oneness. Relationship implies the coming together of seemingly separate entities and inner aspects. Differentiation helps us see the interlacing parallels. For example, the degree of trust we have in others reflects how we trust ourselves and Earth or Life. How we separate from others reveals how we distance from the natural world. Case in point: Do you see yourself living *in* nature or being *from* nature? In our shared Earth home, how connected do you feel with other living beings?

By offering this vision of authentic collaboration, my wish is for us to experience greater vitality in our relationships: to realize the potential of who we are as a valued member of the whole. Together, we can grow beyond personality to wiser Self, from personhood to community and from ego-centrism to eco-centrism. We can see all Life forms through the eyes of reverence. This is the bridge urging us to cross. It's the story waiting to unfold.

We live in a unique time in history. Crisis and possibility have us navigating deep change. In the face of these shifting tides, effective collaboration is key. Plain and simple, we need each other. As the old industrial growth model begins to die, mindful bridge-building is the predominate leverage opportunity for humanity to discover sustainable ways to live, work and play. Learning the generative practice of collaboration is crucial to harnessing creativity and collective wisdom. Responding to complex issues such as war, poverty, refugee migration, organizational transformation, biodiversity loss, environmental degradation, discrimination and violence is a call to re-examine how we perceive and relate to ourselves, others and our beloved planet. More of the same is not an option. Dare I say, collaboration is the most essential skill of the twenty-first century.

To that end, my intention is to encourage us to co-create the conditions for effective collaboration by exploring cultural norms, revisiting our systems and building our relational muscle. The journey starts with self. For support, I've included more than forty exercises to expand awareness and skills. An array of disciplines has been taken into account such as behavioral science, systems thinking, complexity theory, indigenous wisdom, emotional intelligence research, relational neuroscience, anthropological and ecological studies, positive psychology and evidence-based change frameworks. Whatever field of inquiry resonates with you, I hope you find some golden pearls that motivate and empower.

As we're hardwired for connection, I assume that people *want* to develop healthy relationships. We want to be seen, heard and appreciated for who we are, as we are. We are social beings in need of our tribe. Because our tribe depends on how we connect with ourselves and Earth, the study of collaboration is core to our survival. To flourish, it's imperative that we learn how to harmonize with others and realign with nature's laws. This reflection calls for courageous truth-telling.

When I've reflected on my relationships, I've been taken to the mountaintop and to the valley of despair. At times, this messiness, confusion and suffering left me bereft, and on my knees in humility. I questioned at one point whether to write about the topic of collaborative relationships, given some of my cringe-worthy painful experiences. But I realized that my love for people and Earth were my qualifications. I saw that healing may be the fruit of this writing if a sincere heart-rendering was offered.

With this in mind, note that this is *not* an advice-giving book but an invitation to walk together on this learning journey. This is but one map of millions, reflective of my own struggles and edges. I suggest that we are all students immersed in the curriculum of relationship-building. Our growth comes from failure and success, misery and rejoicing, anger and love, hurt and belonging. Perhaps for us all, the breadcrumbs on this lesson trail will be collected until our last breath.

While this book was written to support people who want to learn and practice collaborative relationship-building in all domains of life, I especially hold change-makers near and dear. Change-makers are those people who strive to make a positive difference. They intend to be of service at work, at home and wherever Life takes them. They understand that success depends on nurturing relationships. I assume this is your aspiration as well, whatever your mission. During this time of immense change, I believe that we are all being called to step up and out as change-makers.

Whether you self-identify as a change-maker or not, the practice of healthy relationship-building is all-inclusive. Meaningful connection is a universal need, regardless of title, position or socioeconomic circumstance. I bow to each person as a wisdom-holder in their own right.

AUTHENTIC COLLABORATION

This offering is for those who:
- desire a deeper sense of belonging and connection with self, others and Earth.
- feel frustrated with the current way of collaborating, sensing that another path is possible.
- value respectful collaboration as a route to conscious engagement, co-owned decisions and sustainable outcomes.
- want to skillfully respond to conflict, exhausted from reactivity and divisive bad-othering.
- are curious about reciprocity, power-sharing and vulnerable truth-telling.

Whatever your intention, note that relationship intelligence holds different cultural flavors around the world. What constitutes a "best practice" is in the eye of the beholder. Context matters. While I have my own biases, I attempt to use a global lens to acknowledge relationship acumen from diverse cultures. As a global citizen, I honor all the diverse customs that uphold the principle of mutual respect.

With *your* unique cultural and personal lens, you are invited to examine your relationship history, beliefs and communication habits. This is the space to explore your growing edges, those places within that are contracted, hidden or suppressed. Unravel the knots. Embrace your inner skeptic: all parts of self want to be warmly received. If resistance arises, stay open and get curious. Some ideas presented are meant to be counterculture and evocative. I've purposefully gone against the grain of mainstream consciousness to stimulate reflection. Draw upon your own life experience, for you undoubtedly hold great insight from your own relationships. Consider this writing to be a friendly portal to further realize, release and refine.

As you read, I hope that you will start new conversations about relationships in general and collaboration specifically. Experiment with new ways of thinking and interacting. Hold these conversations with tender compassion, as a parent holds a child. With collaboration, the full spectrum of Life appears in technicolor, with all its sweetness and pain. Invite others to join this growing movement of conscious bridge-builders. Anyone with a pioneering spirit is

AUTHENTIC COLLABORATION

welcome, for we have all been on the "other side." Growing a network of kindred spirits is how we manifest the vision of authentic collaboration.

May this book inspire you to develop the art and skill of collaboration. May the ideas, principles and exercises support you in co-creating extraordinary relationships to build a better world. Digest the material slowly. Peruse with a sense of wonder. Drink it in and savor the taste. Most importantly, read from your heart.

Like a farmer tending to the soil of the collective soul, I throw vision-seeds into the wind. I trust the universe to germinate as it will. May the harvest be nourishing for all.

Namaste,

Elizabeth Soltis

Namaste is a Hindu greeting that means "I honor the light in you and me, for we are one."

PROLOGUE

"There is an eagle [and condor] in me that wants to soar."
Carl Sandburg

The prophecy of the eagle and condor

In ancient times, Native Americans spoke of the eagle and the condor prophecy. They foretold the split of human society into two paths, beginning in the late fifteenth century. Symbolically, this split was characterized by two powerful birds: the eagle and condor. The eagle of the North represented the masculine, the mind, industry and technology. The condor of the South carried the feminine, the heart, nature's wisdom and intuition. It was predicted that a severe wintertime would last five hundred years. This season would see a prolonged period of colonization, greed, war and injustice. At the hands of the invading people of the North, the people of the South would near extinction. This societal separation would generate great suffering.

When this dark winter came to an end, spring would blossom. The birth of a new human consciousness would be revealed. The prophecy states, "When the eagle of the northern hemisphere flies with the condor of the south, the spirit of the land will awaken." The people of the North, with abundant material wealth yet spiritual impoverishment, will reconnect with their hearts. The people of the South, with spiritual wealth yet material impoverishment, will regain their power and voice. With the joining of these magnificent birds, the mind and the heart will integrate. The masculine and feminine will embrace into wholeness. Collective injury and intergenerational trauma will begin to heal. Compassion will cauterize wounds. Human beings will once again realize that we are all Children of the Sun. People will shift out of self-focus and into unity, understanding that all belong and are free in the ring of Life. Together, they will "write on the huge page in the sky the sacred word of liberty." In this expanded consciousness, interdependence will become our birdsong.

AUTHENTIC COLLABORATION

Now is the time for the eagle and the condor to reunite.

These awe-inspiring bird totems symbolize not only an illuminated vision but also a heightened responsibility for the power of becoming. Our becoming. The multilayered issues in our families, communities and organizations are beckoning us to unite and evolve. Our climate crisis, racism, food insecurity, homelessness, pollution and gender violence are but a few issues that warrant collaborative action. Civilization teeters at the precipice. To respond, we need to work together differently.

Our current polarizing habits and practices are ineffective, tearing apart the very fabric we need to survive and thrive. It's important that we call upon the spirit of eagle-condor to widen our lens so we can truly see the value of divergent perspectives. To switch into a sustainable way of living, it matters that we collaborate anew. It's time to pool our intelligence across cultures and sectors. This is our moment to reconfigure our relationship to diversity: welcoming differences is at the heart of peaceful coexistence. Earth is giving us wake-up calls to re-evaluate our societal norms. The long-term well-being of all planetary inhabitants is at stake.

> "The interdependence of humankind, the relevance of relationship, the sacredness of creation is ancient, ancient wisdom."
> Rebecca Adamson

Given the complex challenges in our world, there is great relevance for eagle-condor unity. We need to rise together and fly into a greater awareness of how we relate. It's essential to realize that everything and everyone exists within an interconnected web of relationships. We live in an ecological community which, in fact, has no outsider. Each living being is bound by the law of interdepedence. The potential for synergy is ever-present. Any goal that humans want to achieve is done for, because of and with others. Whether acknowledged or not, our relationships with self, others and Earth are the bedrock of Life. This is our universal shared reality.

The Alaskan Aleut people of the sea lion understand this truth. As one of the oldest indigenous cultures in North America, they have an enlightened way of greeting others. Upon meeting, they say, "Aang Waan." This means "Hello, my other self." They live the axiom; we are all of the same spirit, just in different disguises. They realize that nature only knows inclusion. When we embrace interdependency, our tendency to judge and ostracize dissipates. The pain-inducing behaviors of name-calling and finger-pointing during conflict decrease. We start to entertain ways to balance power, actively listen and express from a deeper part of our being. Our relationship template begins to transform.

In the vessel of relationship, collaboration is an ideal fulcrum point to develop our human potential. Compared to other strategies, collaboration is the only approach that upholds interdependence as an underlying principle. Yet, our conventional collaboration norms do not reflect this principle. The practice, as it stands, is insufficient as a viable path forward. The us-versus-them mindset produces astonishing divisiveness. The societal fracture amplified during from the pandemic—coupled with the uncertainty, volatility and ambiguity in our world—is now our rallying call. We need to reconnect, relate and respond with courage and fortitude. It's time to galvanize a new conversation: to stretch beyond our comfort zone, reclaim our power, repair the rupture and co-learn through group wisdom.

Inherent in authentic collaboration is an opportunity to co-create with inspiration. By tapping into the intelligence of the eagle, we can explore new ways to open communication channels. By unleashing the compassion of the condor, we can rediscover how to repair relationship hurt and mistrust. We can raise the bar to collaborate by declaring that all living beings are sacred. This mutual respect paradigm enables us to experience a deeper sense of belonging. Indeed, authentic collaboration offers a powerhouse approach to Life-affirming relationships for the people of the North, South, East and West. Immense strength comes with solidarity. It's a portal to enter a new era, surrender our resistance to the interdependent flow of nature, solution-find with renewed creativity and fulfill the eagle-condor prophecy.

The uniting of eagle-condor acknowledges the dualism of Life while healing dualistic thinking. Authentic collaboration is thus a platform to expand consciousness and unify opposites. For instance, an "and-both" mindset can replace an "either-or" approach. We all carry so-called good and bad aspects. We can step beyond inferior-superior thinking to see "me" in "you." We can stop othering and embrace our profound interconnection. We can celebrate our autonomy *and* experience heart-opening connection. Self-sovereignty can sit

AUTHENTIC COLLABORATION

alongside interdependence. The living beings in a forest know how to hold this paradox. They are masterful collaborators. Just as a forest would never want a maple tree to become an evergreen, we too can accept others as different.

By the same token, we can acknowledge our flaws *and* accept the fullness of who we are. Building esteem comes from embracing *both our shadow and light.* We can create space for both materialism *and* spirituality. Science and indigenous traditions can *both* be held as sources of wisdom. It's not necessary to battle one over the other as a repository of truth. We can agree to disagree. Yes, we can even appreciate people's unique life experiences while recognizing the fundamental sameness of all. This understanding helps us reconcile the primordial paradox of separation and unity. Every relationship is an opening to transcend division and experience wholeness.

Attuning to the noble spirit of eagle-condor reminds us that we're all in the same nest of togetherness. When we embody their vigor, valiance and perseverance, we unlock our individual and collective greatness. More becomes possible. The phrase *embracing diversity* takes on a whole new meaning. At home, we can bravely mend our hearts and grow closer.

> *"We are eagles of one nest... the nest is in our soul."*
> Led Zeppelin

At work, we can engage, motivate and retain talent with joyful teamwork. In community, we can respect differences by supporting those in need. All this is achievable in our shared crusade toward well-being. The wisdom we seek is found within and between. Allow this knowing to be the spark in re-imagining the art of collaboration. Wingtip to wingtip, let us fly together with the uplifting vision of relational peace.

In essence, the authentic collaboration vision is in service to this prophecy. The co-joining of eagle-condor symbolizes, in this interpretation, what healthy relationship-building means. The extraordinary power of collaboration is waiting to be unbridled. Consider this to be a collective rite of passage. As we grow our relationship awareness and skill, we pass this legacy on to future generations. On the other side of this evolutionary threshold lies a world with greater equanimity.

AUTHENTIC COLLABORATION

The message of eagle-condor is powerfully simple: meaningful connection not only fosters healthy relationship-building, it's the key to sustaining life on this planet. As a bold declaration, activating this potentiate is humanity's foremost mission.

Are you willing to fly on the updraft of eagle-condor to soar into a new tomorrow?

Life is waiting for your unequivocal yes.

CHAPTER 1

BRIDGE-BUILDING WITH AUTHENTIC COLLABORATION

*"Understanding is the bridge between two minds;
love is the bridge between two souls."*
Matshona Dhliwayo

Ayni: Coming into Right Relationship with All

Have you ever traced back to a decision that changed your relationship with Life? Twelve years ago, I made a pivot-turn by choosing to step onto the path of shamanism. In doing so, I adopted a whole new mind-bending worldview. Shamanism is an ancient, cross-cultural spiritual practice, dating back 100,000 years. As healers, the word "shaman" directly translates into "one who sees in the dark." With extraordinary vision, indigenous shamans can pierce the veil of mystery to uncover profound insights about sacred living and interconnection. It's said that we all have ancestral roots in shamanism, given its long history and widespread impact throughout the world. For me, this empowering, Earth-loving philosophy transformed my life in miraculous ways.

Over the years, I've had the privilege of studying the Laika wisdom tradition of Peru. The Laika, also known as Earthkeepers, are the medicine men and women who fled to the high Andes long ago to avoid persecution from the Spanish conquistadors. As such, they kept their teachings intact. In 1950, these high-shamans descended back into society to begin sharing their insights. Their intention was and is to support humanity in navigating these challenging times. They foresaw that the coming generations would give birth to a new world.

Through the Laika teachings, I learned about the eagle-condor prophecy. I felt moved by this oracle and the potential it holds for positive change. Intuitively, I sensed that my raison d'etre would support this vision. I now realize that the coming together of people is beautifully expressed through authentic collaboration. Consider this approach to be a starting block on the track toward unity. In service to this prophecy, I feel inspired to grow the conditions for meaningful connection with self, others and Earth.

> *Ayni means sacred reciprocity. By extension, it's about coming into right relationship with all living beings.*

Early in my shamanic studies, the Quechua word *ayni* (pronounced "i knee") piqued my interest. Directly translated, ayni means "today for you, tomorrow for me," implying that giving and receiving are indelibly intermixed. The Peruvian Laika shamans hold ayni as the practice of *sacred reciprocity*. By balancing giving and receiving, we create the foundation for coming into "right relationship" with all our relations on this planet. It's a profound practice in interdependent living. My soul purpose marinades in the desire for ayni.

Ayni is central to shamanism because it acknowledges the equal value of every living being, our co-creative capacity and the beauty of sharing. On another level, the concept means owning our power while in service to community. When we contribute to the greater whole, we acknowledge our gifts and value. We lift ourselves up, along with all Life forms. Intrinsic to ayni is the paradox that giving to others is, in fact, a compelling pathway to receive love and respect.

Even now, ayni remains in the Andean culture. The people of that region see Pachamama, or Mother Earth, to be ever-present as a creative power. They understand that the nature of reality is interrelated and abundant. They contend that peace, love and joy derive from living in right relationship with all. In Western culture, we hold the opposite platitude. We're taught to pursue our own happiness, hoping that healthy relationships follow from this feeling. Ironically, in our land of plenty, many people are raised with the mindset of scarcity and separation. With this comes a focus on individual gain. Thus, competition, overconsumption, craving and greed have become commonplace. This motivates people to take more from each other and nature than needed. Evidence of this is the scale to which human beings use worldwide resources. The choices we make about what we eat, the products we use, and the extent of our travel has left a heavy ecological footprint. A great deal of suffering, loss and dis-ease has resulted from this disparity. By consequence, our happiness is also dwindling.

Ayni is the opposite of this imbalance. The spirit of ayni is learning to live in eagle-condor harmony, to share our gifts, take what we need, waste nothing, express gratitude for what we take and respect the symbiosis inherent in ecology.

For insight, we can look to plants and animals. In the chain of interconnection, they understand the role and purpose of other species in their midst. An ocean, for example, contains diverse marine sea life, coral, kelp forests, salt marshes and rocky shorelines. All exist in right relationship with one another. While whales feed off phytoplankton, their waste also provides phytoplankton with nutrients such as iron, nitrogen and phosphorus. Giving and receiving operate in a unified field of exchange. This is but one example of nature showing us what interdependency looks like.

Reciprocity in human relationships is intended to be as ease-filled as the act of inhaling and exhaling. When done mindfully, the exchange is transformational rather than transactional. In the giving, we are refashioned. In the receiving, we are made pliable for healing. In every interaction, we see how much we need each other. The effect ripples throughout our planet in ways beyond our comprehension. With ayni, we think of our own personal well-being and that of others as one and the same. We can liken this to barn-raising in Amish communities. It's presumed that, if the need were to arise, communal help would be reciprocated. We each have a stake in the flourishing of all.

> *"We are all one drum.*
> *We need each other."*
> *Indigenous teaching*

If this book was summarized in a word, it would be ayni. It has the power to anchor us into a wider connecting arena of both self-empowerment *and* belonging. In this space, we realize that we are never "A Lone" but rather "All One." Rather than tolerate each other in attempting to coexist, we learn to live in right relationship with all beings. As members of the Earth tribe, what homes us, togethers us. This writing is dedicated to realizing this possibility. It's a notion that does not call for a hard cognitive understanding but a soft heart knowing. When we live in ayni and honor all Life forms, we transcend separation and relate with a loving heart.

Introducing authentic collaboration

Since ayni revolves around relationships, let's explore the term further. The word *relationship* derives from the Latin *relatus*, which comes from *referre*, "to bring back or restore." While a challenging path, healthy relationship-building does have the potential to restore the essence of our humanity. Relating, as a moment-to-moment transmission of energy, can be restorative to our mind, body and spirit. As social beings, we gleam with the sweetness of caring connection. As language evolved in the seventeenth century, *relationship* came to mean "to stand in some relation; have reference or respect." Our ancestors knew that respect had to be brewed into the definition.

> *Authentic collaboration is a respect-for-all relationship intelligence practice.*

Given this backdrop, authentic collaboration is a new relationship-building vision with an old meaning: it's a practice that comes full circle to restore respect in relationship yet with a wider holistic and integrative lens. I define *authentic collaboration* as respecting self *and* others while working towards a shared goal.

With this descriptor, *and* is the key differentiator as the whirl of the mind often brings us into either-or thinking. In relationship, patterns of behavior fall on a spectrum. On the one end, people tend toward self-focus as their default way of relating. Here, they display a strong ego and narcissistic characteristics. On the other end, people have a penchant to be other-focused. As such, they deny their own feelings and needs. Self-interest is secondary. With various relationships, we tend to repeat our patterns toward one end *or* the other of this spectrum, trying to find a middle ground. In the realm of mutual respect, however, we expand our ability to relate from the center, simultaneously connecting with self *and* others to balance both sets of needs.

Compared to the conventional practice of collaboration, the paradigm of authentic collaboration fosters a different quality of communication. The latter is a hope-infused exercise in reciprocity, whereas the former is suffused with mistrust, cynicism and enemy images. The practice of authentic collaboration rises above this tendency and holds interconnection as an accepted maxim. Mutual benefit overrides competition. A people-centric, friendly culture evolves with mindful communication. Values and assumptions are explored because the process of dialogue is valued as much as the outcome. Empathetic listening is generously offered. Diverse viewpoints are expressed without fear of reprisal and rejection. Co-creation turns my story into our story. Just as a rose slowly unfurls its petals, emotional safety is cultivated so vulnerability has space to flower. When we communicate with an open heart, courage, curiosity and compassion arise. Trust grows, along with a desire to learn and find common ground. In brief, authentic collaboration is an expression of ayni.

These features of relating allow meaningful connection to develop. Connection occurs when we feel another person while feeling the other feeling us. As Dan Siegel explains, "When we attune with others, we allow our own internal state to shift, to come to resonate with the inner world of another. This resonance is the important sense of 'feeling felt' that emerges in relationships." From this space, we feel cared for. New insights and creative possibilities surface. We relax into being seen and feel encouraged to reveal more of who we really are. When people experience interconnection, there's a solid foundation to uphold the practice of authentic collaboration. This way of interacting is simple to understand, profound in impact, yet not easy to do.

> *"A focus on interconnectedness increases serendipitous encounters, unexpected insights and deep friendships."*
> Kare Anderson

Three principles to support authentic collaboration

To further elaborate on the authentic collaboration vision, I offer three intertwining ideas. Each will be introduced here to set the stage and then unpacked in the chapters ahead.

1. Authentic collaboration as a bridge metaphor
2. Authentic collaboration as a holistic passageway
3. Authentic collaboration as an integrative whole-person practice

Proposing a bridge metaphor

Consider the bridge metaphor to visualize the paradigm of authentic collaboration. The structure of a bridge connects seemingly disconnected parts, spanning that which separates. As such, a bridge is a powerful link that allows us to travel to new landscapes. Similarly in relationship, a bridge assists us to cross over and discover different perspectives, ideologies, personalities and ideas. Bridge-building reduces isolation, enabling us to join together in spite of differences. Just as all the parts of the bridge are necessary for the thoroughfare to be functional and strong, all aspects of self and others serve a purpose when collaborating. When we mistreat people, and burn the relational bridge, it takes a concerted effort to meet in the messy middle section to repair the relationship. In every culture, the bridge is a mighty symbol for connection and shared understanding.

> *"The moment to bridge the chasms that divide us has come. The time to build is upon us."*
> Nelson Mandela

Bearing this in mind, let's glimpse the authentic collaboration bridge with its tied-arch design. Its overall purpose is to bridge the chasm of diversity so we can meaningfully connect. This bridging occurs not in spite of but in celebration of our differences. Starting with the undergird, this bridge has three supporting towers to sustain the deck. These towers are referred to as "power pillars" representing empowering self, sharing power and co-creating vision. Each power pillar is grounded in acceptance of self *and* others. As such, the roadway is paved on a respect-for-all deck. It's constructed with an attitude of "I'm okay, you're okay." To maintain the bridge's relational traffic load, six vertical ties distribute the weight. In this vein, the weight of collaborative relationships is supported by six guiding principles. Each tie is embedded across the span of the bridge with letters forming the acronym RELATE. Practicing a mindful way to RELATE enables meaningful connection.

On this pedestrian-friendly bridge, there is a degree of mystery. For there is always more to discover in every relationship. As we cross over to unknown terrain, we can pluck our fearlessness to receive people for who they are in that moment. We can sink into our shaky, tender heart to let go of othering. Under the archway of interdependence, we can open to otherness while saying yes to the synergistic flow of Life. Even when difficult, unpredictable relational dynamics arise, we can choose to respond with care for self *and* others. With mutual respect weaved into this bridge architecture, our life*span* supports affirming collaborative relationships.

For a sneak peak, you'll find an illustration of this authentic collaboration bridge in Chapter 4 (see page 67).

The authentic collaboration bridge as a holistic passageway

As Albert Einstein taught, "No problem can be solved from the same level of consciousness that created it." In the context of authentic collaboration, expanding consciousness includes appreciating our relationship with self, other people and Earth. In our interconnected world, each relationship informs and affects the others. Even though we often do not collaborate by actively considering Earth, the natural world is in everything and everyone. By ramping up consciousness of all our relations, this holistic perspective alters both our path and the outcome of any collaboration.

> *The bridge to healthy, sustainable relating is built by honoring self, others and Earth—all in equal measure.*

As noted, authentic collaboration espouses an attitude of respect for self and others. *Others* includes Earth or Life. These words are used interchangeably because Earth *is* Life. Authentic collaboration is thereby a win-win-win holistic proposition. As a foundational ethic, it's about valuing both humans and non-human beings. In the circle of Life, we are never outside the ring. With this awareness, even the effect of hierarchy can transform so that diverse voices are welcomed and held with care. Embodying this mindset brings the beauty and power of ayni into our everyday life.

Many of us narrow our focus to respect only important and immediate relationships. Family and friends are central in our world, ranking as a priority. In government and business, people at the so-called "top" are often given extra attention and support. We see those who wield financial wealth as having more power. What would it look like to expand respect to include strangers, neighbors and those who sit at the "bottom" of our social hierarchy? In the eyes of Life, we are all residents of Earth first and foremost. Dust to dust, we come from this terrestrial planet, and one day our bodies will return. Earth is the great equalizer.

Since Earth is our constant source of sustenance, it serves us well to discern how we relate with her. When we deeply appreciate and immerse ourselves in nature, we elicit greater sensory awareness. We activate the wild wisdom within. By acknowledging the intricacy, richness and beauty of the natural world, we gain understanding about relationships overall. Beyond the self, Earth is an animated, sacred being, deserving of care for her own sake. Accordingly, the full human experience of collaboration ought to include consideration for all who carry the breath of Life.

> "The plants already breathe, while we still ask ourselves how to speak to each other, without taking breath away from them."
> Luce Irigaray

Taken further, consider that each aspect of self, others and Earth is a *mirror* to the other two. In the shamanic world, it is well-understood that our words and actions toward people are a projection of how we relate to self and Earth. Our relationships are but a reflection of how we think. When we change, people reflect that back to us with their behavior. In shifting our attitude, our outer circumstances begin to transform. Unwittingly, we produce an ongoing cycle of feedback. Every interaction is an opportunity to know ourselves more so.

Ponder the following examples. If we feel cut off from our heart, this separation will, on some level, show up in how we relate to nature and to other people. We may find ourselves communicating from the neck up rather than bringing forth our full-body truth. If we power-over Earth in overconsuming her resources, we can see how this translates into collective patterns of oppression and force. Culturally, we see evidence of abuse, rejection and violence. And, we also notice micro-aggressions such as interrupting people, issuing commands or stuffing our feelings. I see these behaviors as different mirror facets. The looking glass reflects the wound of separation—within and between.

> "[Because] all life is interrelated, we are caught in an inescapable network of mutuality; tied in a single garment of destiny. Whatever affects one directly affects all indirectly."
> Martin Luther King Jr.

Conversely, if we respect and understand the symbiosis of the natural world, we also bring this reciprocating energy to our relationships.

When we advocate for our precious biodiversity, we take a stand for the value of all beings on Earth—including ourselves. In the system of Life, nothing exists in isolation. Our outer reality and inner subjective world are interwoven into the same fabric. Each relationship is a fractal image of the whole.

With this in mind, the authentic collaboration bridge road has three lanes dedicated to self, others and Earth. Consciously and unconsciously, we pass in and out of these lanes every day, as each one guides and sustains the others. In practicing authentic collaboration, each lane has the potential to generate a desirable outcome: the lane of self builds confidence, the lane of others engenders belonging and the lane of Earth brings forth harmony. As a way of enriching and uplifting our lives, this three-lane journey is well worth exploring.

Authentic collaboration as an integrative whole-person practice

This bridge has one more feature of significance. It's designed to be an integrative whole-person passageway. Consequently, all aspects of self are welcomed on this bridge. The invitation is to express our full humanity at home, at work and in community. This includes the notion that we are spiritual beings in a physical form. So, whenever possible, the collaboration space ought to respect all five dimensions of being human: mental, physical, emotional, energetic and spiritual.

Given the complex challenges in our midst, it's imperative that we bring the fullness of who we are to the table. This is how creativity unfurls. With remote work, this can be especially challenging. Collaborating virtually or in hybrid meetings changes the group dynamics and inhibits full, spontaneous expression. Online meeting etiquette needs to evolve to recognize the multi-dimensionality of our humanity—not as a sideline action but to support the process of valuable discourse. On a practical level, this includes prioritizing rapport-building conversation, co-creating emotional safety, noticing body language, slowing down to fully breathe, checking in for understanding, taking stretch breaks, monitoring turn taking and inviting people to share how they really feel.

Whether we're connecting virtually or in-person, an integrative approach involves the whole-person experience. This means taking the long journey from the head to the heart and gut. All three connection points help us access bodily wisdom. For many, this is the road less traveled. It takes courage to blend the focus of the mind with the compassion of the heart and the intuition of the gut. It's a process that can slowly rejig our personality to be in service to our heart. As a daily practice, this is inner bridge-building at its best.

The cojoining of mind, heart and gut intelligence helps us be resourceful in responding to complex issues. We're learning that the mind alone is insufficient. In fact, the mind can spin us in circles, believing that we're addressing issues when we're actually reinforcing underlying conditions. This is seen when people react to issues with the same mindset that underlies the issue itself. A problem-oriented mindset can generate more of the same. Case in point, if we perceive and label someone as a "problem," this will shape how we interact with this person. Our interpretation molds and limits how we communicate.

Sometimes, the best approach is to empty the mind. For knowledge can suffocate and memory can distort. It's helpful to recognize that we don't know what we don't know. Our intelligence is more than mental intellect. Collaborating effectively involves balancing reason with love. It also entails reconciling our mind with our feelings. When we discount our heart and emotional guidance, we disregard insight from our body, ancestors and nature.

> *"Mind creates the abyss, the heart crosses it."*
> *Sri Nisargadatta Maharaj*

Contrarily, if we rely only on our heart, and neglect our mind and gut wisdom, we may have compassion without the impetus to act. Some people are overwhelmed and paralyzed with sadness when they feel compassion. If we heed our gut instinct with no heart, we may act hastily without due regard for the process of learning. Our heart tells us to slow down and be sensitive to the needs of others. If our mind and heart say "act" but we ignore our gut intuition, our action may be futile. For our gut holds the big picture in scanning the whole environment around us. That's why the phrase "trust your gut" is a commonly known axiom. Many of us learned to suppress our gut intuition as children for the sake of connection. Yet, working against our gut can lead to subconscious self-sabotage. I know this pattern all too well. Collaborating with the mind, heart and gut is akin to relating with full-body acumen. When our mind and gut bow to the bridge of our heart intelligence, we begin to expand from me to we, from separation to unity consciousness. New possibilities arise.

Consider this example. Our climate crisis is often said to be a by-product of excessive greenhouse gas emissions. While this is accurate at the mind level, there's a deeper truth to be found when we surrender our ego to our heart center. If we see through the eyes of our heart, we feel the pain of our disconnection from Earth. We start to understand how this converts into systems and policies that harm the natural world. When we merge our cognitive reasoning with our heart wisdom, we see how our outer ecology reflects our inner ecology. In connecting these dots with a system-thinking lens, our response to climate change will include reconnecting with ourselves and Earth. With new awareness, different choices will take shape. Regenerative practices, which take inspiration from nature, will advance. Integrative whole-person collaboration grows understanding, energizes creativity and spawns innovation.

Harnessing full-body resourcefulness

> *"When the brain is whole, the unified consciousness of the left and right hemispheres adds up to more."*
> Roger Wolcott Sperry

Authentic collaboration, as an integrative practice, also rebalances our brain's logical-left and relational-right hemispheres. The left brain is associated with linear, mathematical and analytical capabilities, whereas the right brain is intuitive, creative, emotional and big-picture-oriented. Both sides serve a purpose. They naturally interrelate. Our brain's ability to collaborate between the left and right to process neural information is what produces clear perception. If we become left- or right-brain dominant, our way of thinking is skewed and compromised. It's important to synchronize the brain to improve focus, mental clarity and emotional health. To effectively respond to our fast-changing world and the challenges before us, it's advantageous to value and integrate both aspects.

Whole-brain unified thinking has been demonstrated by exceptional artists, philosophers and great inventors who can simultaneously use both brain hemispheres. This is why many people engage in brain exercises like learning a new language, swimming cross-laterally, solving puzzles, playing imaginative games and strategizing. It's an active attempt to stimulate the corpus callosum

AUTHENTIC COLLABORATION

to engage the nerve fibers of both the logical and creative hemispheric sides of the brain. By increasing this synaptic connection, our brain can develop complex functions while expanding awareness and generating empathy. This neurological bridge allows the brain to function as a whole.

To uphold many bridges, the strong binding material of concrete is used. Concrete is a mixture of cement, water, air, sand and gravel. Figuratively, the authentic collaboration bridge is made from blending the raw materials of our full personhood; namely, a curious mind, a caring heart, an intuitive gut, an analytical left-brain and a compassionate right-brain. For extra good measure, let's throw in the courageous action of our masculine and the gentle nurturing of our feminine. If any of these are missing, we risk interacting in an unbalanced way or at the surface level. Dialogue narrows and contracts. This can leave us wanting more in how we collaborate and relate overall.

When all these elements are integrated, the binding potential of collaboration strengthens. Developing full-body resourcefulness augments our sense of empowerment. When dialogue flows from a space of inner coherence, a deep reservoir of potential creativity is found. Integrity becomes a felt experience. Speech becomes succinct, clear and on point. Our listening produces a rare, uplifting quality of connection. Conflict is met from our center. We can more readily see beyond what's visible to the eyes. We can trust and feel safe in the arms of another. Personal transformation is ripe to unfold. Innovative solutions come forth. By combining our astute mental clarity with heart sensitivity, our sixth-sense gut intuition and both brain hemispheres, we become a powerhouse amalgam.

> *"The great solution to all human problems is individual transformation."*
> Vernon Howard

When this metaphoric bridge is upheld by these crucial elements *and* the spirit of ayni, authentic collaboration becomes a lever for growing a culture of mutuality. In my own life, incorporating these elements in my relationships has given me greater insight, adaptability and agency. When I consciously transverse this bridge, I feel enthused and challenged to get real about how I relate. I feel inspired to reflect on when I close to defend and how I open to love. My commitment to self-growth expands in discovering my darkest shadows, highest gifts and greatest power. When I let go of fear and touch the depth of my true nature, I experience what it means to be fully human.

Join me in further exploring this bridge. Let's take each other by the hand and cross over with a beginner's mind. The spirit of eagle-condor will be our guide.

A Peruvian bridge story to braid these threads together.

Each June, four indigenous communities in Peru come together to literally bridge-build over the Apurimac River. They live the principle of ayni while bridge-building in a holistic, integrative manner. During this three-day festival, the annual Q'eswachaka bridge-building reconstruction is celebrated as a special ritual that dates back five hundred years to the Inca Empire. At that time, the bridge served as a vital passageway for trade in the high Andes. Amazingly, this 124-foot-long suspension fibre bridge, with a twig-based platform, continues to have a load-bearing capacity of fifty-six people. Now a UNESCO heritage site, this handmade bridge connects tradition and culture while demonstrating the art of communal authentic collaboration.

The Peruvians see this bridge-building process as a spiritual custom, symbolizing the importance of social bonding and mutual care. They understand that the act of relationship-building is an ongoing investment of effort. Even if this grass-made bridge does not need to be torn down every June, they do so anyway to begin again. The harsh elements deteriorate the bridge in ways seen and unseen. Similarly, this exercise is a reminder that relationships also move through abrasive elements over time, generating the need for repair. They recognize that the thread of conflict weaves through the landscape of every human being. It's healthy to let go of the past. Starting anew with a fresh attitude fortifies our connection with those we care about. Integrating our mind, heart and gut creates novel ways of relating. The indigenous people understand that relationships are impermanent, and bridges are temporary. Meaningful connection requires ongoing care, time and attention.

Just as the Q'chewa-speaking people twist and braid the grass into strong bridge cables, we too can see ourselves as collaborative bridge-keepers in weaving together our talents, skills and compassion. In the same manner as each Peruvian household creates ninety feet of braided cord, we too can bear responsibility for how we contribute to and affect our family, organizations and community. It is a lifelong quest to balance giving and receiving with self, others and Earth. A holistic approach sees the value of all three interwoven strands. Braids, by definition, represent interdependency.

As this Peruvian bridge cannot be patched up but must be made wholly new, it serves us well to widen our perspective and look at the net of our relationship patterns. Rather than patching past hurts with band-aid words, we can choose to heal our relationships on a deeper level. We can honestly examine the themes of our relational story to disrupt habits and break cycles. With their covenant of reciprocity, these communities honor their ancestors and Mother Nature. In thanks, they offer food and coca leaves to Earth. They also exchange food and gifts when meeting in the middle of the bridge. For the privilege of living in community, we too need to routinely express our gratitude for the gift of each other. Mutual appreciation is the joy of ayni.

> *"We are each other's harvest."*
> Gwendolyn Brooks

This amazing story weaves together these three idea strands into another braid: the bridge metaphor, the holistic self-others-Earth passageway and the integrative whole-person substructure. The Peruvian indigenous people model the art of collaborative bridge-building—literally and figuratively. By amicably working together year after year, they achieve extraordinary outcomes.

Framing this writing with the power of questions

Whether you're a team player, change-maker, family bridge-builder, community leader, activist, entrepreneur, artist, business manager, development practitioner or innovator, authentic collaboration can inspire you to see the art of relationship-building with the wonder of childlike eyes. As an experiment, set aside any jaded thoughts you may have and open yourself to new ways of interacting with those in your circle. Even on a smallscale, the revaluation of relationship can have a far-reaching ripple effect.

Ten questions are offered to support your reflection and to frame this writing.

Ten Questions to Spark a New Way to Collaborate

How can we...
1. meaningfully connect in the face of polarizing behaviors?
2. bridge-build with an and/both mindset?
3. work creatively with distressing behaviors?
4. hold competing perspectives with care and curiosity?
5. feel safe and deepen trust when experiencing judgment?
6. have nurturing conversations that foster courageous expression?
7. transform powerlessness and overwhelm while expanding resiliency?
8. mindfully interact in a reactive culture?
9. collaborate with greater ease, impact and love?
10. holistically collaborate with self, others and Earth?

With this in mind, you are encouraged to enter the "cave of inquiry." Be sure to question, tease apart and try on new ways to relate. Study what resonates and discard that which is unhelpful. As you can see from this line of inquiry, this book does not dissect the structure and strategy of collaboration. Rather, these pages are devoted to exploring the art, skill and science of collaborative relationship-building. So bring forth your queries, confusion, pain and heart longing. All of you is treasured.

> *"The cave we enter holds the treasure we seek."*
> Joseph Campbell

Because this writing is a guide to learning, it includes principles, stories, tools and skill-building exercises. It's a response to the *what, why and how* questions that often accompany any new model. In parallel, this book addresses the three most common reasons why people do not create or embrace change.

1. They don't know *what* the desired change looks like.
2. They don't understand *why* there's a reason to change.
3. They aren't clear on *how* to create the conditions for change.

The RELATE section, in particular, offers a response to each reason. Chapters 8 to 13 explains the *what, why* and *how* of each guiding principle. The *what* speaks to the meaning of the principle, the *why* pertains to its relevancy and the *how* offers exercises to apply the principle. After all, it's one thing to *know* the value of collaborative relationships, yet an entirely different matter to *do*. This is where the rubber meets the road.

> *"I am always doing that which I cannot do, in order that I may learn how to do it."*
> Pablo Picasso

Closing the knowing/doing gap is the sincere aspiration held in these pages. These exercises are an opportunity to delight in the practice of collaborating with self, others and Earth. Perhaps we may once again view people not as a means to an end, a way to meet needs or achieve something, but rather as a wayshower to truly RELATE and experience comm*union*.

An invitation to cross the bridge as we build it

As we walk across this bridge, imagine this is a communal process. Others around the world are likely engaged in a similar inquiry—they too may be drawn in by the magic of meaningful connection. Know that you are not alone as you dream from a quiet inner creative space. Every mindful interaction you take on this journey is a stone thrown in the river below, cascading out waves of positive change.

Every social change movement is started by one conversation. The conversation of this book revolves around the building blocks of authentic collaboration. This includes trust, openness, mindful speaking, emotional intelligence, vulnerable honesty, assertive boundary-setting and active listening. Let's gently untie the knots of power grabs, bullying, ostracizing and emotional withdrawal. Let's play with the cadence of respectful dialogue and enter the enigma of interdependence. Together, let's stay in the in-between state of not knowing, musing over questions such as "What inspires us to bridge-build?" "What do we think is on the other side?" and "Why cross at all?"

On this journey, allow the principle of ayni to be our chaperone. You might say that coming into right relationship with all is the water underneath this bridge: the very reason why a bridge is needed. In action, ayni is the uniting of people via sacred reciprocity. In spirit, ayni is the updraft under eagle-condor and the wind under our own wings. If we deeply listen, we will hear the whisper of ayni calling us to greater love. In every culture, love is the bridge between souls.

With the intention of ayni, the pull toward personal mastery will soon be felt. It will spur us to fine-tune the most important instrument we have to offer—self. We will be reminded that intrapersonal development is an investment in self-empowerment, while interpersonal development co-creates a more peaceful, just world. With ayni as our bridge-building escort, greater connection, aliveness and fulfillment will wave us over. Another exciting world of possibility awaits.

> *"Another world is not only possible, she is on her way. On a quiet day, I can hear her breathing."*
> Arundhati Roy

CHAPTER 2

RELATING WITH SELF, OTHERS AND EARTH

"Most people believe that successful relationships are about finding the right people and doing the right things. Yet how we relate to others is a reflection of how we relate to ourselves. The outer mirrors the inner. We can only be as open, trusting and present with others as we are with ourselves."
John Welwood

Living under the umbrella of relationship

The human story is that of relationships, with all its joys and sorrows. Our relationships form the umbrella of our lives. The umbrella spokes hold every experience—moments of kindness, creativity, belonging as well as pain, anguish and loss. We are born in relationship to our mothers, and we die in relationship to our bodies. In between cradle and grave, relationships nourish and deplete us on every level, in all facets of life. We are separate beings yet entirely interconnected. Even our soul stardust signals our relationship with the cosmos. All 70 trillion cells of our humanity are ignited by the fire of kinship. Every being spins in the energetic vortex of relationship.

> *"The most important thing in life is relationship."*
> *Jiddu Krishnamurti*

Psychologists tell us that our sense of who we are is not activated until we are witnessed by another. Our identity develops through relationship with another. Connecting is primal to our well-being. We are preordained for community. Relationship-building is foundational to developing a team, healing families, forging alliances, expanding a network, catalyzing movements, inspiring a community, improving procedures or evolving an organizational culture. Indeed, relationships are how stuff gets done. Because human beings are neurobiologically wired for connection, we intuitively know that a joyful and prosperous existence lies on the other side of affirming relationships.

When Harvard Medical School conducted a seventy-five-year longitudinal study on life satisfaction, the findings spoke to the power of relationships. As it turns out, the greatest indicator of happiness depends on the quality of meaningful relationships we form. Our physical health and longevity are correlated to warm, caring relationships. The conclusion was clear: happiness is love. Full stop. There's no escaping the potent role of relationships in our lives.

Healthy relationship-building as a life quest

In 2003, I fulfilled a long-held wish to serve as an AIDS hospice volunteer in sub-Saharan Africa. For two months, I witnessed the significance of relationship. While bathing, feeding and dressing patients, I listened to their stories. Day after day, I was transfixed by the depth of authentic heart-sharing. These beautiful people needed to be heard as they reflected on issues of love, family, conflict, forgiveness, abandonment, loss and gratitude. Each person's story was both unique and universal. Their stories reminded me that matters of the heart matter the most. Some people carried regret and felt as though they were drowning in a well of sadness. Others were lit up by love as they regaled me with tales of sweet heart connection. It seemed ironic that during these raw, tender conversations about relationships, the dying came alive. When we face death, our truth has a profound way of being expressed. This experience kindled an awakening within me.

> "What you leave behind is not engraved in stone monuments, but what is woven into the lives of others."
> Pericles

During these two months of hospice service, I also underwent a death of sorts. A part of myself let go so another part could open and blossom. I surrendered my heart to Life for the first time. My old habit of striving to reach an elusive "there" suddenly seemed pointless. I realized that "here" is the "there" I was seeking. The reins of control slackened as I felt the supportive flow of Life in a new way. My affinity with each patient inspired me to relax into the preciousness of each moment. As I held their fragile hands and looked into their eyes, I felt a joining of our souls. Like a raindrop returning home to the ocean, I felt a merging of myself with others.

Slowly, the veil of separation lifted, and I began to touch the deep waters of connection. I saw that the condition of our lives is intimately intertwined with the richness of our relationships. I noticed that we are all brothers and sisters in a global community. The words of Rumi sprung to mind: "Death is a coming together. The tomb looks like a prison, but it's really release into union." The peace of the last exhale gave me a window into our interconnected universe. I understood that how we feel supported by others reflects the tone of our relationship with self and Earth. It was at this time that I decided to explore healthy relationship-building and the art of collaboration as a life mission.

> *"When we feel supported for who we are at our deepest level, it fundamentally changes the tenor of our relationships."*
> Marianne Williamson

Expanding our relationship frame of reference

Often, when people think about relationships, they tend to refer to other human beings. It's easy to forget that the most crucial relationship we have in our life is with ourselves. The person we speak to the most is ourselves. Furthermore, we tend to discount the importance of relating with Earth or Life, even though Earth is our vital Life force. In Sanskrit, this vitality is referred to as *prana vayus*. The word *vayu* comes from *wind*. With the wind of Life coursing through our veins, we are Earth personified. In every conceivable way, people are nurtured by her constant giving. Our relationship with nature is indispensable.

Consider that self, others and Earth are three interrelated aspects, with each playing a distinct role in how we function. All three forms of differentiation exist in the relational hoop of Life.

To acknowledge the multidimensionality of relationship, I offer a holistic relationship frame that's inspired by the pioneering work of Ken Wilber. As a world-renowned philosopher and systems thinker, Ken Wilber developed a powerful conceptual model called integral theory. In this theory, Eastern and Western philosophy is blended, along with the physical and spirit worlds. This model is a unified construct with four dimensions: inner, outer, self and other. It translates into inner/self (beliefs), outer/self (behavior), inner/other (culture) and outer/other (systems) for an all-embracing worldview. Similarly, this holistic frame reveals the multifaceted nature of relationships.

A Holistic Relationship Frame	
Inner Domain Our relationship with our beliefs, feelings, needs, values and consciousness. *Reflection:* *What motivates me in my life?*	**Outer Domain** Our relationship with how we speak, listen and behave. *Reflection:* *How do I describe my communication style?*
Self Domain Our relationship with our mind, heart, gut, body and soul. *Reflection:* *How do I connect my mind with my heart?*	**Other Domain** Our relationships beyond self, including Earth. *Reflection:* *How supported do I feel by Earth or Life?*

Because the nature of relationship is dynamic and organic, the interplay of all four domains is continually in motion, changing one day to the next. This holds true even if we carry the misperception that people never change. In a long-term relationship, for instance, people may believe that the other is the "same" as when they met, yet the body, mind and heart are ever-evolving. When we join a work team, our contribution adapts and grows with experience. Long-lasting friendships morph at every age and stage. In government, the populace mindset shifts the sands of policymaking. Even at a cellular level, atoms are never static. We epitomise evolution. As we reflect on the ever-changing terrain of relationship, keep this holistic frame in mind to tease apart the subtleties.

Relating is a delicate inner-outer interweave

> "Other [people] are lenses through which we read our own mind."
> Ralph Waldo Emerson

Let's look at the inner-outer interweave, starting with the domain of self. How we view the world is an echo of our inward gaze. How we observe, judge and reason reflects the interaction within. On the flip side, our brain's neuronal firing, the tumble of thoughts and the flutter of feelings affects how we move in the world and connect with others. The messages we hold about ourselves influences how we collaborate with others. For example, the degree to which I depend on myself is correlated to how I depend on others. If I display frequent bouts of impatience with myself, rest assured this pattern will also be apparent in my relationships. If I prioritize self-care, this will be seen in my ability to set healthy boundaries. Projection is, by definition, self-originating. Our external reality is but a manifestation of our internal reality.

As mentioned, people are our mirror. They offer a reflection as to what we think, love, critique and appreciate. If we find it challenging to love and accept others, consider how this speaks to our inner discourse—even if it's subconscious. People help define our identity, chipping away our esteem or nurturing our sense of self. On a practical level, we can learn a great deal about ourselves by how we perceive and react to others. This is because everything we see is subjective. Our view of others is always about self. At the Johns Hopkins University Perception and Mind Lab, researchers conducted a series of experiments to learn how people detect objects under various conditions. They concluded that "a person cannot see an object in a way that is entirely separate from their point of view." When we try to see the world as it is, we cannot discard our own perspective.

In relationship with others, this tie-back to self is revealed daily. If we feel triggered by someone, this person helps us see that we likely have an unresolved issue. If we experience someone as tranquil and laid-back, this aspect is already alive within. If we feel impoverished by our circumstances, we may be challenged in receiving the richness of Life. Since relationships show us our blind spots, people bring to light that which is hidden to our eyes.

As psychologists remind us, we don't respond to what happens, we respond to our *perception* of what happens. When we understand this point of origin, we clearly see that it's far more beneficial to focus on self-discovery than fault-find. Anything and everything we do is supported by others and Earth, whether acknowledged or not.

> *"We see things not as they are but as we are."*
> Anais Nin

A concept that expresses the profound interconnection between people is *Ubuntu*. This South African Nguni term means "I am what I am because of who we all are." It's a sentiment that speaks to relational interdependence. Ubuntu is rooted in humanist African philosophy, where community is one of the building blocks of a healthy, vibrant society. It's about de-centering the self so the focus is on the lattice of community. Ubuntu also points to the reverberation inherent in relationship.

A self-love wedding…until death do us part

I came to a new understanding of this inner-outer interweave when I read this quote: "Marry yourself and promise to never leave you." This quote came to me as I began my year-long solo travel adventure around the world in 1999. I was struck by the idea that we are our own beloved, the one we've been waiting for. This turned my outer-seeking for a partner inward. So I decided to move this sentiment into action by performing a marriage ritual with myself as the couple, officiant and witness. It was an opportunity to heal self-betrayal and recommit to my heart. To prepare for this ritual, I reflected on how I wanted to self-relate during this travel experience and beyond. Who did I want to become as an expression of my best self? My vows sprung from those core values.

In Israel, I chose a special sacred site for the ceremony. On the day of my wedding, Mother Earth provided exquisite flowers and spectated with a gentle breeze. I initiated the ritual by lighting a candle and honoring my ancestors and those of the land. When I read my vows out loud, the words rang with beauty and authenticity. As a part of my self-love promise, I committed to balanced relating, respecting my feelings and needs as equally important as those of others. As a life quest, I pledged to compassionately accept, integrate and unify all parts of myself. I then placed a silver ring on my finger, kissed my hand and quoted Shakespeare: "To thine own self be true."

All these years later, my self-love relationship continues to grow. I still have that ring as a symbol of infinity. I've discovered that a healthy marriage with self is as much of a daily commitment and practice as it is with a mate. Perhaps, on the deepest level of marriage, whereupon two become one, we are continually marrying ourselves.

> *"How you love yourself is how you teach others to love you."*
> *Rupi Kaur*

Our partner allows us to meet ourselves, like it or not. Both matrimony and self-love offer an opportunity to occasionally renew our vows. I tend to upgrade my vows because the words change as I change. My heart has become my arbiter of truth. As it turns out, learning to unconditionally accept ourselves is a never-ending spiral staircase of growth. Respect for all of who we are is the quintessential act of authentic self-collaboration. It shape-shifts every relationship we have.

The habit of othering

Even if we intentionally cultivate self-love, we still experience disconnection in the outer/other domain of relationship. In our collective narrative, disconnection shows up with our habits of analyzing, judging and classifying people. While these ego-driven habits are primal survival strategies, they also generate a pattern of "othering" in perceiving people as fundamentally different or even alien. It's a common social and cultural construct—perhaps for some an unconscious default state of mind.

Othering is about attributing negative characteristics to individuals and groups. It's a perception that's rooted in projection as our judgments reveal more about us than another. When we assess that people do not fit into social norms, some form of ostracizing or rejection takes place. This starts the process of dehumanization, concluding that others are a threat—not "one of us." This reaction is a reflection of our own insecurity. Othering is at the root of all oppression.

> *You don't see me.*
> *You see me in you.*

With this thinking, intergroup bias can spring forth. This is the act of evaluating and favoring people based on superficial criteria. We see intergroup bias in our media. Politicians use this as a mechanism to divide and conquer. Rhetoric is taken as the truth. The labelling effect separates people. Attempts to collaborate become laden with the pain of *isms*—racism, sexism, ageism and so on. This mind noise impedes meaningful connection. Our hope rests in turning this habit around. As Harville Hendrix reminds us, "we are born in relationship, we are wounded in relationship, and we can be healed in relationship."

A team I worked with informed me that their goal was to develop healthy relationships with other departments for a seamless client experience. The word *collaboration* was said to be a core value in their culture. When I began to explore what was happening vis-à-vis their aspiration, it became clear that the relational field was steeped in othering. During interdepartmental team meetings, rather than look for mutual gain and reciprocating support, the conversations were exclusionary and self-focused. I observed micro-aggressions such as name-calling, interrupting the speaker and withholding information. Some people dominated the dialogue while others advocated for change by pushing colleagues to accept an uncomfortable decision. In focus groups, people remarked that staff turnover was high because team punishment followed lack of performance. Contrarian viewpoints were dismissed. Mistrust converted into cynicism. Colleagues did not feel a sense of belonging to the organization. The team needed to realign the work culture with their stated values. The concept of collaboration had become an empty buzzword.

In the face of othering, what would bridging across differences look like in your world? What actions would you take to restore meaningful connection?

Relating with Earth or Life

As another nuance, how we relate with self and others is a reflection of our relationship with Earth. If this idea is foreign, take a few minutes to become aware of your natural environment and your place in it. How would you describe your connection with nature, your Life source?

Earth's elements and minerals are intrinsic to our physiology. We breathe in the oxygen produced by trees and marine plants and drink the water in our regional ley line. Literally and poetically, we cry and sweat the sea. Just as the rivers carry water into nature, our blood system circulates her nutrients in our body. In fact, our body is largely comprised of Earth's elements: oxygen, hydrogen, nitrogen, carbon, calcium and phosphorus. We depend on Earth and a healthy biosphere for essentials such as food, water, shelter, clothing and transportation. Earth's gifts are ubiquitous. When we are fully present with nature, we can no longer look at Earth as inert. She's a pulsing, breathing, feeling, sensing being. We can't help but give thanks.

> *"Please shake me into wakeful gratitude as I remember how to merge with you."*
> Clare Dubois

As an expression of Life, Earth is a continually changing organism. Every pebble, wave, leaf, insect, mammal, mountain and human being is inextricably linked to the entirety of matter. Quantum mechanics proves the interconnection inherent in Life. As physicist David Bohm concluded, "The universe is *one whole*, as it were, and is in some sense unbroken." To underscore this point, Bohm asserts that "our separateness is an illusion." He argues that, at a deeper level of reality, we are one and indivisible. This includes the particles that make up matter. Literally, Earth is the ground of Life.

This interconnection obligates us to revise our long-held conceptual frameworks of nature. For example, many people believe that there is an ontological separation between humans and non-humans. Subsequently, people are seen to be more important than our non-human relatives. With this hierarchical perspective, it stands to reason that Earth is for human convenience, profit and comfort: to satiate our hunger for "more, better, best." These anthropocentric values are steeped in an attitude of superiority. It's a mindset that leads to dangerous choices, with people rationalizing overconsumption to fulfill material desires. Contrary to this thinking, consider that all Life forms on Earth have value, regardless of their worth to human beings. Given that we are *of* the natural world, it is our destiny to harmoniously coexist with nature.

> *"Man's heart, away from nature, becomes hard... lack of respect for growing, living things soon [leads] to lack of respect for humans."*
> Chief Luther Standing Bear

The upshot of eco-disconnection

If interconnection is our essential nature, why do human beings experience widespread eco-disconnection? Understanding this reality starts with unloading long-held societal beliefs. One prominent belief is that isolated acts of harm won't negatively affect the natural world, nor us by extension. For example, we have no idea how toxic landfill chemicals, including nuclear waste disposal, will leach into our groundwater. We are oblivious as to where our single-use throwaway plastic bottles will end up. When planes spray pesticides on crops, we are naive about the long-term consequences. We are ignorant as to how razing huge swaths of the Amazon rainforest will impact thousands of species, including human beings.

AUTHENTIC COLLABORATION

This separation-based belief system positions Earth as a competitor. It's another form of othering. In many cultures, we pit jobs against eco-conservation. Economy trumps ecology. Housing and commercial development overrides the ecosystem. Our relationship with Earth has become a confrontational either-or dynamic rather than a collaborative and-both discovery. The everyday actions of gas fracking, oil drilling and mining extraction are an attempt to plunder the environment to benefit our lifestyle. It's a control strategy gone amok. Too often, there is little or no consideration of long-term ramifications.

> "The planet's life force begs us to set down our devices and social constructs and remember the warm blood that pulses through our veins."
> Kim Krans

In our urban-scape, eco-disconnection is normal. People spend most of their time indoors. In just two generations, we've become fixated on electronics. Our go-to source of entertainment is found on a screen rather than in the magic of nature. Children can name more video games than names of trees and flowers. For many, technology has replaced outdoor recreation. This disconnection from nature produces inner imbalance, showing up as anxiety, depression, grief, sadness and restlessness. It's as though we know in our gut that something is missing. Intuitively, we sense that this feeling of lack can't be satiated with stuff.

Our separation from Earth, by extension, affects our relationships. When we disassociate from nature, it impacts how we protect her, ourselves and others. In dominating Earth, we dominate and control others. Case in point, we control people with intimidation, criticism, gaslighting and keeping score. Demands are issued out of frustration. We feign agreement rather than speak up. We ignore bullying instead of safeguarding people who are ridiculed. When people commit a crime, we lock them away in prison without rehabilitation support. We forget that "they" are "us."

With the paradigm of eco-disconnection, it's easy to discount our ancestral wisdom: we forget that the roots of all living things are entangled. The rhizome of our interconnection is forever intertwined.

A serious wake-up call: a snapshot picture of Earth science

As every year passes, more alarming research points to how disconnected we are from Earth. The Stockholm Resiliency Centre conducts research on how human beings impact our planet using a framework that measures nine planetary boundaries: climate change, ozone depletion, biogeochemical loading, biodiversity loss, ocean acidification, global freshwater use, land system change, chemical pollution and atmospheric aerosol loading. As of 2022, three of these nine boundaries are at extreme risk: biodiversity loss, biosphere integrity and toxic chemical emissions. Land system change is also at a precarious level of disruption, with massive degradation and deforestation. Since Earth is a complex, self-regulating interdependent system, when some planetary aspects are out of balance, a negative effect vibrates throughout the chain of Life. Learning how to respectfully relate with Earth is not a pie-in-the-sky ideal but a stark necessity.

> *"Humans are causing the sixth mass extinction both directly and indirectly."*
> Gerardo Ceballos,
> National Autonomous University of Mexico

Even though we live in the Anthropocene era in which human beings are seen as the primary force of change, we can no longer act as though Earth carries infinite resources. It is a gross misperception to use, enjoy and discard precious resources as though the planet is a bottomless pit. It's shocking to realize that by 2019, human beings consumed 1.75 planets' worth of resources. The Global Footprint Network measures this overshoot by calculating how the demand of human consumption exceeds Earth's regenerative capacity. By 2032, it's estimated that we will need *two planets* to maintain our current rate of consumption. To state the obvious, this is unsustainable.

The fact that we now release 419 parts per million tonnes of carbon into the atmosphere, as reported by NOAA's Mauna Loa Atmospheric Baseline Observatory on January 15, 2023, is proof that our way of relating with Earth is not working. With the climate crisis, humanity is dealing with the most existential threat to ever face civilization. Regardless of whether you believe the climate science or not, there has never been more need to revisit how we relate to Earth as a mirror to self.

If you find yourself doubting the science and the causes of global warming, I invite you to move beyond politics. It's a debate that can deaden the spirit. Besides, Mother Earth reminds us that partisan division is not the cloak she wears. Instead, focus on how you can protect the basics of clean air, water and land. If not for you, then for future generations. What does your relationship with source *want from you*? Listen for her guidance. Make it personal and urgent. Every action you take at the local level makes a difference. By activating Earth care, you strengthen your ability to collaborate with a respect-for-all approach.

Healing our disconnection by partnering with Earth

In our Western culture, it's a course turn to consider our shared mother—Mother Earth—as a significant relationship. The upshot validates the web of Life and all the unique, separate nodes that are contained therein. As we steward Earth, we attune to the music of the seasons, the navigational pull of the night-sky stars, the warm life-giving energy of the sun, the refreshing caress of a breeze, the revitalization of water, the cleansing fierceness of a windstorm, the soothing peace of a forest, the inspiring beauty of a hummingbird and the gentle kiss of moonlight. Drinking in this enchantment nurtures our mind, body and soul. Accordingly, Earth responds to our human thoughts, actions and consciousness in ways that science will never fully understand. This ayni dance is the ultimate cosmic collaboration.

> "Earth has music for those who listen."
> William Shakespeare

As our indigenous neighbors teach us, we walk on holy ground. If we treat the land as an extension of our body temple, and we hold self-respect, we will naturally live with a lighter footprint. Our relationship with Earth will become a sacred trust pact. We will begin to understand that we don't own the land, the land owns us. We are borrowing beneficiaries. As Sam Mickey suggests, it's time to adopt Whole Earth Thinking, which is "thinking of, by and for the Earth community." This mindset supports not only the interdependence of human-Earth relations but benevolence toward all.

Shifting to healthier, productive ways of relating is our viable path forward. Returning home to our emotion-filled body enables us to experience the *body of Earth in and as our own*. By growing our connection to the natural world, we adopt an Earth-respect mindset that informs new practices, laws, policies and systems. By listening to the ancient voice of Earth and our fellow citizens, creative solutions arise. With fresh resiliency, we can better adjust, innovate and govern the commons.

Meaningful connection with self, others and Earth is the gift that keeps on giving, regardless of whether you are a city-, suburb- or country-dweller. The more value we ascribe to Earth, the more we see the preciousness of humanity. The more we recognize the intelligence of animals, the more we see our own gifts. The more we hold all Life forms in high regard, the more we lubricate the conditions of authentic collaboration. The more we reposition people as a part of creation, the more humility we have as a partner to Life. We need to remember the wilderness, from where we came, to embrace our humanity. This idea is the foundation on the authentic collaboration bridge roadway.

> *"Every animal is a gateway to the phenomenal world of the human spirit. What most fail to realize is that what they think of animals reflects the way they think of themselves."*
> Ted Andrews

The Great Turning: Expanding relationship consciousness

This is the time to consider how we relate with ourselves, others and Earth because we are living during a time of great change and disruption. As our living systems collapse, "business as usual" can no longer be our motto. A massive societal shift is now upon us. The industrial growth model is dying and a life-affirming, sustaining civilization is waiting to birth.

In David Korten's book, *The Great Turning: From Empire to Earth Community*, the author claims that we are moving through an "epic passage" from an Era of Empire to a new Era of Earth Community. While Empire arranges human relationships by dominator hierarchy, Earth Community adopts the notion of partnership characterized by mutual caring and accountability. In the 1990s, eco-activist, author and thought pioneer Joanna Macy popularized the phrase "the Great Turning." She describes our ecological and social challenges as hinge points of this shift. Joanna's impactful work in deep ecology is about transforming the consciousness of despair and fear into active hope. This involves facing our shadow, mobilizing resources for self-healing and sensing into what *coexistence with Earth* really means.

AUTHENTIC COLLABORATION

During this Great Turning, we have an immense opportunity to reconfigure how we want to holistically collaborate. Countless issues can serve as an entry-point. In our collective field, we're dealing with gender inequality, social injustice, complex health challenges, urban sprawl, irresponsible consumption and production, fossil fuel addiction and plastic pollution, to name a few.

To respond to these issues and others, the United Nations developed the Sustainable Development Goals (SDGs) as a universal call to action. In 2015, 193 signatory nations agreed to protect the planet, end poverty and improve people's lives. By adopting this nationally owned, country-led SDG framework, the world's leaders acknowledge that the status quo cannot continue. Exclusive, win-lose collaboration can no longer be a defining feature of our geo-political landscape. We need to find new ways to tackle these challenges by bridge-building across cultures, nation-state lines, sectors and disciplines. Cooperation is a necessity.

Expanding our collaboration consciousness also means leaning into the tension of diversity. For the preconditions for collaboration are never perfect. Differences are expected. Conflict is inevitable. We need to develop the capacity to presence what is. To inhale our fear and exhale our resolve to transform. To appreciate the talents in the room even if we don't like people's behavior or agree with what's said. We need diverse perspectives to better understand our systems.

> *"The most radical thing any of us can do at this time is to be fully present to what is happening in the world."*
> Joanna Macy

Collaboration requires co-learning. It means considering new ways of operating with what's available. Co-learning involves being open to critical thinking and cross-cultural insights. This includes recognizing that our perspective is limited. Knowledge, by definition, is incomplete. Waiting for a fail-proof plan of action is futile. Every action produces an effect which, in turn, becomes our teacher. Experimentation and adaptation are crucial.

With a holistic lens, we see how the inner/self domains of collaboration influence the outer/other domains. The micro, meso and macro levels are all knit together. When we harness the courage to open our hearts, we celebrate our successes and learn from the fallout of our choices. By grieving, we begin to heal our wound of separation. We remember that anger begets more anger whereas a peaceful heart begets peaceful relations. When we befriend and hold our tender emotions with compassion, we transmute our anxiety, frustration, powerlessness and overwhelm into wisdom. We realize that the only way to heal is to feel. In doing so, we start to change the cultural narrative about how to collaborate. New choices arise as we reorient to a wider skyline of possibility.

It's said that an ocean liner only needs to pivot two degrees in another direction to end up in a different port. Authentic collaboration is the ultimate rudder to turn around our Lifeboat—our Earth-boat. Our ability to survive and thrive depends on it.

CHAPTER 3

UNPACKING CONVENTIONAL COLLABORATION

*"Nothing is perfect. Life is messy. Relationships are complex.
Outcomes are uncertain. People are irrational."*
Hugh Mackay

Collaboration history and triumphs

Collaboration dates to the Stone Age, approximately 200,000 years ago, when Homo sapiens hunted game and gathered wild plant food. Living in small nuclear-family groups, our early ancestors worked together to make simple huts or tepees, along with basic stone and bone tools. These hunter-gatherers had to cooperate to successfully migrate from one location to another. With the advent of agriculture about 10,000 years ago, people began to pool resources and barter food to feed larger tribes. As people developed complex, unique language skills, they started to exchange new ideas. Problem-solving occurred around communal fires. Reciprocity supported the greater good. For thousands of years, the seeds of collaboration have been watered. You might say it's in our cellular memory and DNA endurance genes.

Throughout history, human beings have tremendous lived experienced with collaboration. Consider the following success stories. These achievements in past decades reveal extraordinary teamwork and innovation in advancing human development.

"Alone we can do so little; together we can do so much."
Helen Keller

AUTHENTIC COLLABORATION

Celebrating Collaboration Successes

- In 1969, *Apollo 11* made history with the first lunar landing. The crew of three astronaunts were over the moon happy. One small collaboration step by NASA produced one giant leap for humanity.

- In 1975, Steve Jobs and Steve Wozniak co-developed the first pre-assembled personal computer. With this collaborative technology-advancing effort, the world was forever changed.

- In 1987, 197 countries around the world signed the Montreal Protocol, a treaty that banned ozone-depleting chemicals. It was the first UN treaty to receive universal ratification.

- The Jubilee 2000 global campaign resulted in the cancellation of over $100 billion of debt owed by the poorest thirty-five countries. This collaborative coalition engaged millions of people around the world.

- In 2017, twelve boys and their soccer coach were brought to safety from a flooded cave in Thailand, thanks to the collaboration of rescuers from around the world.

- In 2021, the largest orchestra ever assembled, consisting of 8,573 musicians, performed in Venezuela. Awe-inspiring melodies resulted from this collaboration.

- In 2021, over 1 million people planted 250 million saplings in India's Uttar Pradesh state to support an annual mass tree-planting campaign to mitigate climate change.

- Film sets are collaborative artistic think-tanks. Ground-breaking cinema starts with writing a great story, yet is brought to life by directing, cinematography, set design, costumes, lighting and editing talents.

- The Red Cross collaborative response to natural disasters has a long, impressive track record. Multidisciplinary teams quickly form so those in need receive aid and emergency support.

Acknowledging the challenges of collaboration

Even with countless collaboration success stories over many millenia, this effort does not always produce the desired outcome. In many instances, collaboration falls short of expectations. The process can be flat-out hard work. Even the word itself underscores this reality. The Latin root of *collaboration* comes from *com*, which means "with, together or jointly," and *laborare*, which means "to labor." This description of labor, which often translates into effort, toil and struggle, aptly characterizes how many of us experience collaboration. It's not uncommon to hear people say that collaboration is laborious and difficult, especially when strong opposing viewpoints are evident.

> *Collaboration translates into "laboring together"—an apt description for the conventional approach.*

Over the centuries, collaboration has had its fair share of dysfunction. At home, at work and in community, attempts to collaborate have produced the tragedies of armed combat, revolution, economic collapse, unjust systems, exclusion and poverty. In these circumstances, an us versus them mindset was activated, whereupon the interests of the whole become secondary to the interests of a group. Clashing viewpoints generated right/wrong/good/bad thinking such that people were negatively perceived. In some cases, individuals and groups were labelled as enemies. Even if collaboration was said to be at play, competition won the day. Rather than observe the plurality of traditions and values, differences were seen as problematic. As a distinction, these patterns will be referred to as *conventional collaboration*.

A signature element of conventional collaboration is the challenge of power imbalance. Power-over/power-lose dynamics are due to many factors such as greed, personal over public interest, unequal distribution of authority, denial of human rights and favoritism based on caste, religion, age or gender. When differences arise, force energy tends to leach into the dynamic. It can be as subtle as ignoring contrarian perspectives, invalidating feelings or pushing people into a fast decision. Bullying others to gain power is as common as losing power by remaining silent. The imbalance of power in our relationships extends to how we relate with Earth. In many corporate towers or government halls of decision-making, the well-being of Earth is disregarded. A hierarchy of needs takes over: profit overrules planetary considerations.

Power imbalance is common in relationships. Many people struggle with this dynamic and its varied iterations: namely, emotional distancing, push-pull interactions, passive-aggressive tendencies and attack-defend habits. I certainly do. When I'm facilitating an important collaboration with stakeholders across departments or sectors, I often sense nervousness, anxiety and stress. A group may start the dialogue with polite friendliness. Yet, the real test of collaborative skill occurs when people deal with a lack of shared purpose, mistrust, groupthink, apathy, unskillful feedback and misunderstandings. This is when communication breakdown can happen. Collaboration can devolve into a protracted conflict, particularly if one individual or group attempts to dominate the others. Contradicting priorities can easily result in a power imbalance as expressed by criticism, demands, threats and unilateral rule-setting. Throw in an assortment of personalities and relationship-building becomes a labor-intensive exercise. Collaboration is rarely a simple and straightforward practice. It's often a relationship minefield.

> "The single biggest problem in communication is the illusion that it has taken place."
> George Bernard Shaw

This is not to say that conventional collaboration can only be described as dysfunctional, as many functional elements are held within this paradigm. Instead, consider collaboration as a spectrum, with every interaction demonstrating fluctuating degrees of respect, connection and mutuality. Each collaboration reveals different aspects of our humanity and skill levels—some of which produce positive results in serving the intended purpose while some do not.

Unpacking the concept of collaboration

There's a myriad of opinions as to what the concept of collaboration really means. Because we collaborate continually in every aspect of our lives, many people do not think about it as a "thing". Like the wallpaper, it's there but invisible. For those who do reflect on this highly nuanced way of relating, collaboration assumes a win-win approach. The prevailing attitude is that collaboration is a communication process to explore a mutually acceptable outcome for all parties.

While many people say they are collaborating, and believe they are doing so, many relational patterns do not constitute a win-win approach.

Examples of so-called collaboration include:

- politicians who offer a cursory opportunity for civic engagement.
- parents who consistently impose their will on teenaged children.
- partners who over-appease or over-accommodate with a bitter aftertaste.
- teams who rely on rules with no bend or flex.
- managers who ask for feedback but override the input.
- entrepreneurs who sell to clients by pushing a self-gain agenda.
- a mediator who favors one party over the other.
- stakeholders or end users who are excluded from a decision-making process that affects them.

It's a misnomer to call these examples of relating *collaborative*.

In the same vein, the word *collaboration* is sometimes used interchangeably with *cooperation* and *coordination*. Yet, as humans evolve, so does language. Note these distinctions as you reflect on your use of these terms.

Collaboration	Cooperation	Coordination
• To co-create something new together • Implies a sharing of vision, power, ownership and accountability	• To support each other toward a shared purpose, regardless of ownership • May not be collaboration if one person carries most of the responsibility	• To plan and arrange a set of tasks together • May not be collaboration if there's no commitment beyond managing tasks

I realized this distinction between collaboration, cooperation and coordination when I led a group of volunteers in an empowerment project. Our shared commitment was to support people in a developing country to access their own creative solutions in response to their challenges. In our group of twelve volunteers, I was the one carrying the bulk of responsibility. Yes, we cooperated over two years and coordinated tasks with African village leaders, but the execution consistently fell on my shoulders. This was a painful awakening for me to acknowledge that we were not actually collaborating. Despite my best efforts to share leadership, deepen the group commitment and disperse the workload, there was very little co-ownership in our work process.

These distinctions also hold true in the workplace, yet people often collapse the terms. For example, the spirit of collaboration erodes when goals are mandated by senior management versus self-generated. When people lack a voice in decision-making, this is contrary to co-creation. If people's input is solicited yet they are not contributing to nor determining the course of action, this is a feedback request, not collaboration. Making these distinctions is not an exercise in semantics but important for clear communication and managing expectations.

More distinctions to consider

At home, work and in community, the process of collaboration has several phases. This includes agreements to:

- explore a shared interest or challenge,
- decide how to work or live together,
- understand each other's values, beliefs and other relevant information,
- co-create a vision or define a problem to set a shared goal, and
- co-develop a strategy and commit to an action plan.

In each of these phases, differences can and do arise. When tension or conflict surfaces, there are five relationship strategies commonly used: avoidance, competition, compromise, accommodation and collaboration. All are valid. The appropriateness of each approach depends on the situation. While each has pro and con aspects worth noting, collaboration is the only win-win strategy.

TRY THIS: As you review this list, consider the strategy you most often use in your relationships.

- What are the patterns that show up with your work colleagues?
- What are your go-to habits with your family and friends?
- How does each strategy affect your connection with people?
- Which strategies do you want to use less and more?
- How might you practice collaboration with a win-win mindset?

AUTHENTIC COLLABORATION

STRATEGY	PROS	CONS
Avoidance Lose-Lose	• Saves time/energy with low priority issues • Pause allows for reflection and healing • Permits space for wise discernment	• Signals lack of caring, connection suffers • Low investment and no resolution • Cannot explore the issue to learn
Competition Win-Lose	• Positive intent (new job, a gold medal) • Can lead to high performance • Can be motivating, fun and playful	• Can drive a wedge between people • Dualistic thinking (right-wrong/good-bad) • Pursuit of "top dog" status = tension
Accommodation Lose-Win	• Can be a one-way approach to harmony • Fast, easy way to cooperate • Accommodators perceived as easygoing	• May be a distorted way of valuing peace • Can produce resentment in the long run • May indicate low self-esteem/worth
Compromise Lose-Lose	• Faster negotiation to make a concession • Easier if issue is relatively unimportant • Perception that both people are satisfied	• Issues glossed-over, slow burn of anger • Significant needs may be forfeited • Can compromise relationship integrity
Collaboration Win-Win	• Intention is a mutually agreeable outcome • Integrative strategy that welcomes difference • The discovery process can produce synergy	• Expanded consciousness and skill needed • Requires time and commitment • True co-ownership takes mindful communication

Discerning if collaboration is an appropriate strategy

> *While collaborative relationships are consistently desirable, a collaborative strategy is not always fit for purpose.*

Even if collaboration offers the highest *quality* of win-win interaction, it's important to recognize that this approach may not always be the best course of action. For instance, sometimes a government must decide unilaterally via executive rule if national safety is at stake. Or, if timing is critical and a fast decision is needed in an organization, leaders must take the wheel. Managers may need to use a directive approach in declaring the team direction—especially in the case of an emergency or crisis. With a high-functioning group, situations may arise when the ideal solution to a problem seems obvious, and collaboration is not necessary. In a family, there are times when parents need to assert and take action rather than negotiate interests with their kids.

Whatever the context, there are no absolute right or wrong ways to work and live together. There are only pros and cons to consider and manage. Discerning the most appropriate decision-making process is an enabling skill in and of itself.

When deciding if collaboration is an appropriate strategy at work, notice if the soil is ripe for the seeds of collaboration to be planted. For example, does an organization encourage people to take risks, experiment with new ideas and brainstorm for innovation? Is failure allowed? Is information readily shared? Will the opportunity cost be too high and thus negate the value gained? Will cross-departmental collaboration produce significant budget overruns or delay bringing a product to market? Have employees been fired or sidelined for speaking out and expressing contrarian views? To what extent is conflict avoided?

On occasion, I work with organizational leaders who perceive themselves to be collaborative, but staff have an entirely different viewpoint: they describe the culture as autocratic and authoritative. If supervisors act like a parent-administrator in micromanaging and enforcing rigid rules, they may not see the effect of controlling behaviors. If staff are forced to heed top-down dictates, the fallout may be a feeling of powerlessness or even sabotage. Compliance may seem like it makes good business sense, but it may come at the cost of stamping out creativity. If punishment follows failure, the pump will not be primed for a power-sharing dialogue. Not everyone is equipped to skillfully collaborate.

Another way to assess if a work culture has been groomed for collaboration is to inquire about beliefs and assumptions. Does change automatically start with a new policy or program instead of exploring the landscape of relationships? Some managers assume that change will only "stick" if it's imposed. Alternatively, notice how people are incentivized. Are individuals or teams rewarded and, if so, for what? This speaks volumes about what management values. Notice the beliefs that managers have about motivating people as revealed by their behavior. If people are believed to be primarily driven by a paycheck, then involving staff in a collaborative work improvement process is unlikely. If people are perceived to care about work quality, efficiency gains, client service and decision-making, then collaboration is a viable prospect. If leaders are encouraged to act as a facilitator or coach in supporting people talent, this relationship can offer ample dividends. Any type of engagement strategy that empowers people generates favorable conditions for collaboration. A telltale sign of a healthy collaborative work culture occurs when leaders and teams broadcast the message that results *and* relationships matter.

> *A collaboration success indicator is a balanced focus on relationships and task.*

If, at this point, you realize that your workforce may not have the skills to effectively collaborate, and you're curious about *how* to address this gap, continue reading. We will later explore how to turn this around. Practical suggestions abound in the chapters ahead.

Assumptions that strain conventional collaboration

The field of conventional collaboration contains a heap of assumptions. Many are not communicated, adding potential stress to the relationship turf. For instance, it may be assumed that people naturally have an ability to productively collaborate. Yet, this skillset is a learned capacity that requires support. Without enabling conditions, many group collaborations become an exercise in aggravation.

Another set of assumptions pertains to conflict resolution. When personality clashes or competing interests arise, many people resort to the behaviors of

AUTHENTIC COLLABORATION

> *"Perhaps all so-called bad behavior is a cry for love."*
> *Unknown*

attack, defend, argue or retreat. This presupposition has people face off with the weapon of judgment. Distrust festers. Some may demonize people, while others dig in their heels to resist change. If polarizing positions become cemented, rigidity leads to exasperation and weariness. In some cultures, this equates to hiding behind devices, not answering emails or phone calls and disengaging. It's easier to avoid the creative tension inherent in collaboration.

Moreover, some people assume others *want* to collaborate. But, if people feel the sting of past hurt or fear of reprimand, collaboration may be undesirable and unproductive. Communication can choke on the residue of emotional pain. It's easy to sense when people disengage and their heart is not in the discussion. If there's insufficient rapport and goodwill, authentic dialogue will come to a grinding halt. Collaboration is painful when it's dry, banal or argumentative. Relationships suffer greatly when people lie, over-explain, hide their mistakes or manipulate. Often, we assume that people will agree with the "logic" of our perspective. Or, that what is said is accurate. The boat of true collaboration can only sail if the wind of honesty blows.

Do you hold any of these assumptions?

- Collaboration is long and arduous.
- Collaboration takes too much time and effort.
- It's uncomfortable if we venture into a touchy-feely zone.
- I want to do it my way. It's easier to do the task myself.
- We need to focus on results, not relationship-building.
- Until I see the behavior I want, I can't trust people's words.
- I'd rather just tell people what to do.
- People don't care if they are involved with decision-making.
- It's too risky or costly to collaborate.
- People are deceptive. I don't want to be hurt.

Further to this reflection, notice how attached you are to your way of thinking. To what extent are you open or closed to different ideas? Do you have a repulsion, distaste or bias that prevents you from effectively collaborating? The more truthful we are about how we relate, the more we can take steps to address that which no longer serves.

The landscape of conventional collaboration

To offer a snapshot of conventional collaboration, here are a few observations that depict the fractured nature of how we relate in our world. While an entire book could detail the conventional collaboration story in granular detail, these lists offer six points of consideration at each level of society.

Note that many of these examples reflect *attempts* to collaborate. Yet the process and/or outcome does not square up with the mutual gain quality of collaboration. Beyond our current challenges, there have been countless historical occasions that preclude positive communication. And this was prior to interacting remotely via our digital devices, which adds a whole other dimension. The reasons why this story arc features so prominently in our world will be explored in greater detail in Chapter 7. But, for now, reflect on how you see conventional collaboration missing the mark. From your life experience, what contributes to its failure and success?

As you review the lists on the following pages, contemplate how a different way of relating can produce a different response to these and other complex challenges.

- How does the conventional way of collaborating affect you?

- What would it take to disrupt this current state of affairs?

- How can we evolve the practice of collaboration?

> **Examples of Conventional Collaboration Dysfunction**
>
> **At home…**
>
> - A space where we yearn to feel safe and cared for, yet, in many households, relationships are riddled with anguish such as crazy-making, relentless arguments, silent treatments, manipulation and blame games.
>
> - Splintered families are not uncommon. In a US survey, sociologist Karl Pillemer found that more than 25 percent of people live with family estrangement. In all cultures, people suffer when family ties are broken.
>
> - While family members are typically concerned with each other's welfare, codependency is widespread. This may be characterized by unhealthy rescuing, over-reliance or over-accommodation to feel loved.
>
> - Subconsciously, a family system can perpetuate addictive behaviors, poor boundaries and multigenerational abuse. This occurs in families across all cultures and social strata.
>
> - The World Health Organization estimates that one in three women worldwide have been subjected to either physical and/or sexual intimate partner violence.
>
> - According to the UN Office on Drugs and Crime, a 2018 report on the killing of women and girls indicated that 58 percent of victims resulted from domestic or family violence.

At work…

- Top-down delegation of work discourages cross-departmental collaboration. This practice communicates a one-way reporting line and tends to produce misaligned goals and priorities.

- Silo barriers create separation and even opposition, thus curtailing cross-boundary collaboration. This prevents leaders and teams from leveraging talent and unleashing creative discretionary energy.

- The unquestioned use of the carrot-stick approach continues in the workplace. This forceful, demoralizing energy, in the form of incentives and threats, is used to motivate and discipline people.

- Organizational decision-making orients power to those at the top of the hierarchy, disempowering staff and impeding progress. Jumping through management hoops is counter to collaboration.

- Organizations may have diverse personnel, but often there's little inclusion in the culture. An example is a work environment that does not support people who are deaf, have a vision impairment or use a wheelchair.

- Exclusive decision-making practices have work teams missing the bigger picture. The richness of vision, diverse perspectives and shared responsibility is lost.

In community…

- Racial and social injustice pervade the fabric of many societies. Policing continues to showcase systemic racial disparities. Implicit bias is an undiscussable topic in many circles.

- The justice system perpetuates the archetypes of victim-oppressor. As such, the system encourages people to step into these roles with judgment, fault-finding, blaming and shaming.

- In schools, power imbalances deter the student voice. Decision-making processes tend to sideline students. By and large, youth perspectives are seen as less important than the opinions of teachers and administrators.

- In hospitals, many patients do not access a holistic cross-disciplinary healthcare team to explore exercise, nutrition, lifestyle and alternative treatments. Symptom relief is the focus, rather than integrated healing.

- Grassroots social profit groups and nongovernmental organizations (NGOs) compete for fundraising dollars. Often, there is in-fighting for scarce resources and talent.

- Marginalized groups continue to be excluded from community solution-finding forums. The voices of elders, youth, indigenous tribes and people with physical and mental challenges are frequently absent.

At the national political level...

- The structural design of government sets up an adversarial relationship between political parties. As such, *collaboration* is a politically correct buzzword that often means competing for power.

- As a government authority, national healthcare regulators are financed by pharmaceutical companies. Patient safety ranks second to corporate profits. This collaboration points to a serious conflict of interest.

- Rather than speak to vision and platform ideas, the public hears political campaigns filled with opponent-bashing. Winning elections has become more important than serving the public.

- Negotiating agreements is about stacking the deck in one's own favor. In politics, self-credit, blaming and scapegoating are predictable patterns of behavior. A lack of political transparency fosters lower civic participation.

- When politicians exhibit authoritative behaviors, the real purpose of government, to collaboratively work in service to all, is sacrificed. Human rights violations are the fallout.

- Too often bureaucrats see public consultation as a check-the-box exercise, devoid of real meaning. The unspoken intention seems to be placating the dissatisfied or validating current policy.

In global affairs…

- The starting point to reconcile conflicting interests tends to be aggressive dispute mechanisms such as arbitration, lawsuits, trade tariffs, import restrictions and strings-attached aid.

- At times, geopolitical or economic factors have leaders rely on coercive negotiation tactics. Flat-out hostile interference in other country's politics is also practiced.

- When conflict erupts, leaders threaten or instigate a civil or cross-border war. Politicians face pressure to adopt an eye-for-an-eye stance. Collaborative diplomacy has become a lost art.

- Because governments are sovereign in their territory, collaborating on international agreements is a dubious proposition. Many are cynical about follow-through on multilateral commitments.

- The Credit Suisse Global Wealth Report notes that the world's richest 10 percent own 82 percent of global wealth. The top 1 percent owns nearly half of all household assets. Pervasive inequality leads to injustice.

- There are 47 Least Developed Countries that hold 880 million people. The LDCs, however, account for less than 2 percent of global GDP and 1 percent of world trade. This is a grievous power imbalance.

With Earth…

- Based on a study published in *Current Biology*, *The Guardian* reports that humans have destroyed a tenth of Earth's wilderness since 1995. Within this century, there may be no unspoilt places left in the world.

- Routinely, we forgo sustainability by polluting waterways, cutting down old-growth intact forests, stripping the soil of its minerals and infusing Earth's body with toxic chemicals.

- The UN Intergovernmental Panel on Climate Change reports that severe heat waves, fires, floods and droughts will increase in the years ahead with dire impacts for many countries.

- Climate scientists are forecasting a tipping point in the Amazon that will produce an unstable rainforest biome. This condition can lead to dangerous, large-scale damage.

- According to the International Union for Conservation of Nature, over 14 million tons of plastic end up in our oceans every year, injuring or killing marine life and harming humans.

- Too often, problem-solving processes in government and corporations do not include the question, "How will our decisions today impact Earth and future generations?"

The impact of trauma on how we relate

If reading these examples of dysfunctional collaboration has you feeling disheartened, take a deep breath. There is another path available. But, first, let's explore why this reality exists. One of the reasons why we struggle in our relationships is because of our universal experience of trauma. Trauma can be described as a response to any disturbing or distressing event that we *perceive* to be overwhelming—so much so that our nervous system cannot respond appropriately. Literally, our primitive brain stem stores our suppressed emotion as a coping strategy.

The word *perceive* needs to be underscored because trauma lies in the eye of the beholder. Regardless of how severe or minor others assess the originating source experience, our perception of what happened is what matters. Our narrative about the situation is where the energy sits. On this level, it's our story and the meaning we attach to what happened that leaves us feeling disconnected from ourselves, each other and Earth. This is not to discount the very real experience we had but to understand it from another angle.

> *"Trauma is not what happens to you but the story you make up about what happened."*
> Dr. Gabor Maté

Since we are born into a traumatized world, we inherit collective trauma. Violence, famine, genocide, crime, rejection and oppression are but a few traumas in our collective field. To some degree, we also carry the pain of our ancestors. Trapped energy is passed on from one generation to the next until it's resolved. Beyond the collective and ancestral levels, most of us undergo individual trauma experiences in our childhood or adult life. With suppressed emotion and inner fragmentation, we become strangers to our own heart. We separate from the whole. The us versus them psychology is, in part, rooted in trauma.

The universal phenomenon of trauma infiltrates the practice of collaboration, in ways known and unknown. Our capacity to authentically connect is also compromised. Symptomatically, some people feel disassociated or paralyzed to act. They lose the ability to focus, fully breathe or access feelings. Others have difficulty forming healthy attachments. One friend told me that, after experiencing a traumatizing event, she felt shut down and hopeless. The color of Life became gray. Her effervescence was muffled. Even though the nervous system has different ways of filtering unresolved trauma, at its core is a freezing effect. This can result in numbness, as a way of hiding. It's like wearing a spacesuit every day instead of regular clothes. Some people move through their whole life without realizing that their inner light has dimmed.

Persistent reactivity is another trauma-induced symptom. Reaction is action without feeling. Indeed, trauma may inhibit us from clearly understanding, speaking confidently or deeply listening. For some, anger becomes a constant mate. Instead of being centered and grounded while collaborating, we end up projecting, attacking, defending and blaming. Sometimes, we are not aware of the harm we unwittingly generate. We can only be as authentic as we are self-aware and self-connected.

With my own trauma story, I used to live as though I was running on autopilot. My habit of overcommitting was a coping strategy. My busy addiction was a distraction in covering up stuck energy. Underneath the stuckness was a feeling of hollow emptiness. It was challenging to be fully present with other people, let alone myself or with nature. My body felt like it was on high alert in anticipating a threat. Over time, I worked with many healing practitioners to release this stuck energy. I am forever grateful for the therapies of shamanic journeying, craniosacral and watsu massage, Rubenfeld synergy, body talk, eye movement desensitization and reprocessing (EMDR), somatic bodywork, all types of yoga, music therapy and deep brain reorientation. Each modality was beneficial in revitalizing my relationships and my approach to collaboration.

Even though trauma, addiction and other maladjusted behaviors can be detrimental to collaboration, we can heal and minimize the effect. The key is to attend to the inner pain rather than externalize it onto others. Like animals who shake to release trauma from their bodies, we too can release angst. With somatic awareness, we can let go of the memories stored in our body. In these tough moments of inner reckoning, know that it is possible to integrate the past, digest the sorrow and transform pain. Allow the trauma experience to be compassionately witnessed. In doing so, we open the door to healthier

> "At any given moment, we have the power to say, 'This is not how the story is going to end.'"
> Christine Mason Miller

interactions. This is the genesis of authentic collaboration, a new story of relating.

Duelling it out with dualistic thinking

In addition to trauma, people also share a proclivity for dualistic thinking. This is an insidious filter in our collective consciousness, contributing to our highly polarized society. A dualistic mindset assumes that there are only two contrasting, mutually exclusive viewpoints. It plays out as a pair of opposites with poles that attract and repel. Examples of dualistic thinking include bad-good, wrong-right, either-or and negative-positive. As a fall-out of conditioning, dualistic thought patterns contribute to our sense of feeling separate from others.

A right-wrong framework can be a source of safety for some people. It conjures up rigid absolutes and clear lines of what's acceptable. It may give us license to duel out differences. In believing we are "good," we may feel a sense of righteousness to take down the "bad." There's little room for subtlety, let alone deeper understanding. Dualistic thinking can easily lead to an I'm right/you're wrong mindset, argumentative language and belligerent behavior. This backdrop subverts the world of collaboration.

> *"Nobody is superior. Nobody is inferior. But nobody is equal either. People are simply unique, incomparable. You are you. I am I."* Osho

Another common duality found in relationships is better-than, less-than thinking. When we compare ourselves to others, we believe that we are superior or inferior. This process intensifies in school when children are put into competitive rankings against each other. When children are excluded from group activities, the sting of hurt and judgment can be long-lasting. As we grow up, we compare ourselves with others, cover up our shortcomings by boasting, exaggerate for attention or shrink when praised. Face-saving, in many cultures, takes precedence over authentic connection. By extension, this superior-inferior mindset underpins the commodification of Earth. It also weakens our experience of interdependence.

To rebalance, call upon the energy of eagle-condor to heal and bolster inner strength. Then, we no longer need to act superior to compensate for feeling inferior. We can see beyond black and white to notice relational implications and exceptions. We can open to creative contributions of all stripes and allow for perspective-taking. We can notice how we relate to and from our roles.

On a deeper level, when the mind becomes still, we may even touch the part of Self that is beyond form, concepts, time and space. Here, separation is an illusion. We begin to understand that information is fleeting, knowledge is temporary, yet wisdom has staying power. Wisdom comes forth when our eagle-mind is in service to our condor-heart. In these moments, we can ponder the nature of non-dualistic thinking and find peace in the mystery. We can approach the art of collaboration with a whole new attitude.

Comparing conventional and authentic collaboration

Given the universality of trauma and dualistic thinking, and this overall picture of conventional collaboration, how do we move forward? A place to start is to acknowledge our lived experience and name what's so.

To support this effort, consider the following bridge illustration which compares conventional and authentic collaboration. It carries four intentions: to re-imagine what's possible, offer shared language, spark self-reflection and stimulate meaningful dialogue.

> *"The limits of my language mean the limits of my world."*
> Ludwig Wittgenstein

Like the three-lane "self, others, Earth" bridge metaphor described in Chapter 1 and illustrated in Chapter 4, this bridge also has three lanes. Yet these lanes contain two behavior lists for various aspects or features of collaboration. These descriptors are based on my observations and study. It's an attempt to set apart two ways of relating that arise from different channels of consciousness.

Rather than view the behaviors as good-bad or right-wrong, see these behaviors as reference points in a highly nuanced spectrum. Each offers a contrasting experience in how we relate. There is great power in contrast in helping us distinguish between what we experience and what we wish for. See this info graphic as holding two stories: one that depicts the story of separation and one that sits in the field of connection. Given these descriptors, reflect on how you relate. What are your typical behavioral patterns?

AUTHENTIC COLLABORATION

As we know, there are countless behavioral choices available, depending on the relationship, context and our awareness in the moment. Since our interactions vary from person to person and day to day, each collaboration lane is separated by a dash. Given our perceptual lens, skill and resiliency, our behavior will shift from lane to lane. Every choice can help us see aspects of self. Both lanes are important in our learning journey.

Perhaps you hold a different story from the one detailed in this comparison chart. Whatever collaboration experience you've had, envision something new. Spark your imagination as it holds boundless ingenuity. We never know how our ideas begin the creative process. As Joseph Joubert noted, "Imagination is the eye of the soul." Visualize the aspects of heart-centered collaboration that you desire. Name those qualities to see how similar or different they are from what is offered in the bridge graphic. Feel into how you want to up-level your approach to collaboration.

TRY THIS: To personalize this chart, reflect on your own relationship practices. For ease, you may want to focus on a few important relationships to see if any themes arise.

Contemplation questions include:

- Using this list of words, what do you see as your strengths and growth areas?
- Overall, describe the way you relate with self, others and Earth?

- What words would you use to convey how you typically collaborate?
- What are the benefits and consequences of these behaviors?

- To develop the practice, how would you distinguish authentic collaboration?
- What do you want to start, stop and continue?

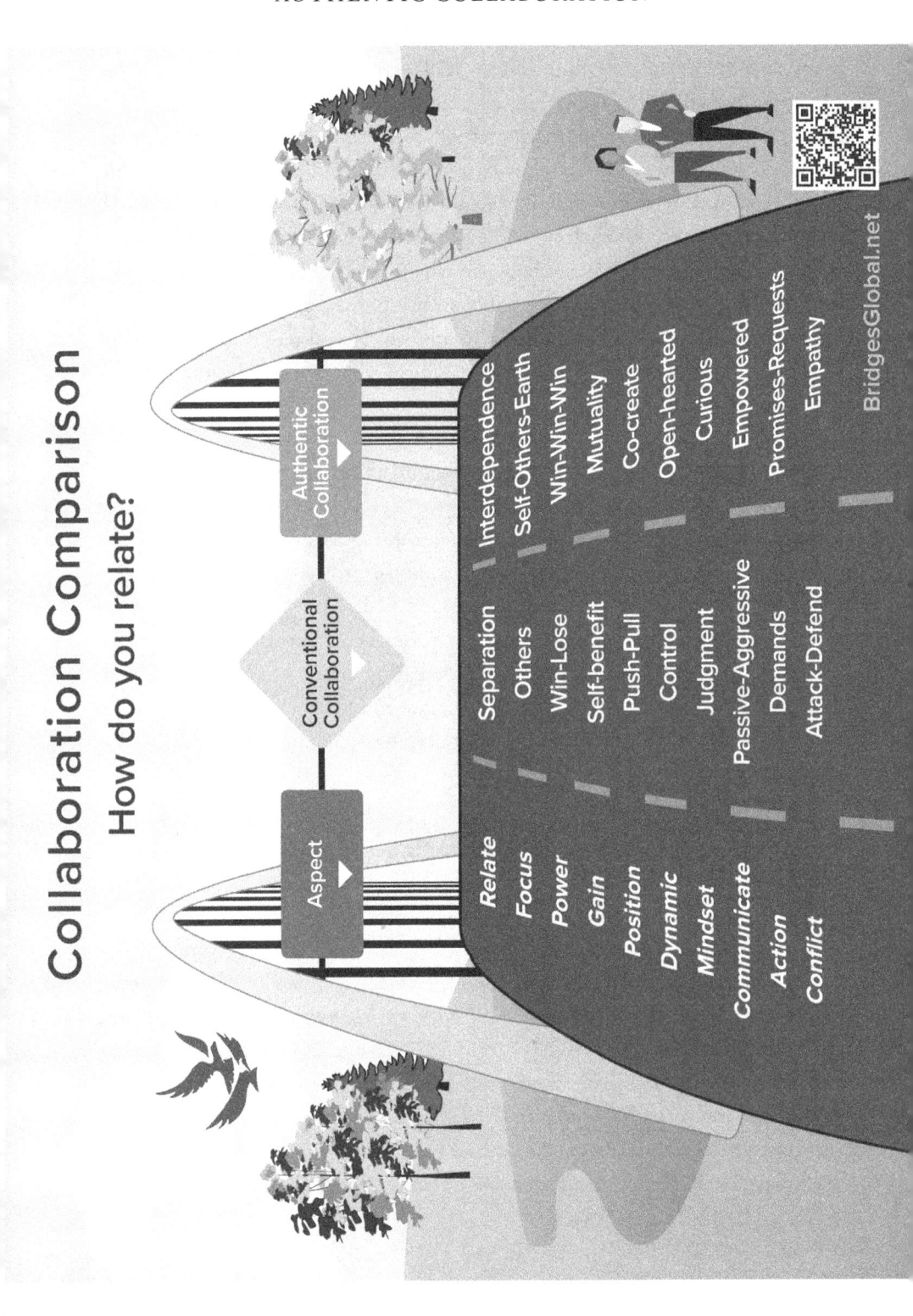

AUTHENTIC COLLABORATION

Collaboration Comparison
How do you relate?

Aspect	Conventional Collaboration	Authentic Collaboration
Relate	Separation	Interdependence
Focus	Others	Self-Others-Earth
Power	Win-Lose	Win-Win-Win
Gain	Self-benefit	Mutuality
Position	Push-Pull	Co-create
Dynamic	Control	Open-hearted
Mindset	Judgment	Curious
Communicate	Passive-Aggressive	Empowered
Action	Demands	Promises-Requests
Conflict	Attack-Defend	Empathy

BridgesGlobal.net

To move your reflection into action, kick-start a new conversation about collaboration with the people you care about. Scan this comparison chart's **QR code** to find the colored image on the website. Download, print and share. Or, if you're old-school, you have my permission to photocopy this info graphic. Post it on your refrigerator and pin it to a workplace bulletin board. Ask people how they would describe their way of relating. Notice what questions arise when people review the chart. Discuss how and when these behaviors show up in your life. For fun, cover up the road signs of conventional and authentic collaboration and see how another reader labels each column. If you feel discomfort when contrarian viewpoints are shared, pay attention to your body's signals. Listen with an ear to learn.

In whatever way you assess your behavior and experience of collaboration, I hope you celebrate your achievements and comfort yourself with tender understanding. At birth, human beings sign up for a full range of experience, from heart-expanding bliss to bone-crushing shame. Know that I commend you for your successes and your ability to withstand difficult moments. Co-creating is not for the faint of heart. Most of all, I salute you for your resiliency in riding the waves of relationship.

> *"We become resilient by learning how to embrace the beautifully broad spectrum of the human experience."*
> *Jaeda DeWalt*

We're at a choice point to evolve

When I ruminate on these collaboration distinctions, this Cherokee legend comes to mind.

An old Cherokee taught his grandson about life. "A fight is going on inside me," he said to the boy. "It is a terrible fight and it's between two wolves. One has anger, envy, sorrow, regret, greed, arrogance, self-pity, guilt, resentment, inferiority, lies, false pride, superiority, and ego." He continued, "The other is filled with joy, peace, love, hope, serenity, humility, kindness, benevolence, empathy, generosity, truth, compassion, and faith. The same fight is going on inside you—and inside every other person too." The grandson thought about it and then asked his grandfather, "Which wolf will win?" The old Cherokee replied, "The one you feed."

AUTHENTIC COLLABORATION

I believe that the wolf we feed in our culture is conventional collaboration. While there are many current collaboration successes, overall the field holds a great deal of suffering. That's why there's an "I" in *illness* and a "we" in *wellness*.

- What would it take to envision a bold new way of relating?
- How can we evolve so gain for one means gain for all?
- How can we balance personal interests *and* the common good?

Given our track record, I contend that the conventional collaboration approach is insufficient in addressing our complex challenges. The old playbook is insufficient. The Great Turning requires a trajectory turn and a different approach. It all boils down to choice.

Embracing choice starts with intentional decision-making such as who we invite to a meeting or how we interact at the dinner table or what we communicate to a stressed friend. Every choice makes a difference. At the community and global level, choices about policy, peacekeeping, laws and treaties influence our collective destiny. In some cultures, it's a daring choice to even *acknowledge* the importance of choice.

> *"It is not because things are difficult that we do not dare, it is because we do not dare that they are difficult."*
> Seneca

In the realm of collaborative relationships, choice does not mean we discard the old to make way for the new. Rather, it's about learning the lessons of conventional collaboration. Our evolutionary journey ought to preserve, encode and build on our current knowledge base. Conventional collaboration represents a certain value stream of relating so the paradigm provides crucial feedback about what works and doesn't work. Our relationship intelligence learning curve relies on this insight. Playing on the teeter-totter between old and new habits requires fortitude. Without question, it's a daunting challenge to step beyond a system while still operating within it.

Humanity is at a crossroad. Just as prehistoric humans experienced a leap in consciousness to collaborate, we now sit at another evolutionary juncture. With the rise of indigenous wisdom traditions and practices of mindfulness, appreciative inquiry, meditation, ceremony, U-theory, social sensing, yoga, restorative earth science, sustainability, empowered leadership and relationship intelligence, more people are awakening from the trance of conventional collaboration. Slowly, momentum is growing to regenerate the art of collaboration. People are expressing a desire to shift from fear-based separation to heart-centered unity.

Now is the time to develop ourselves as extraordinary bridge-builders. The future of humanity depends on how we *feed* the habit of authentic collaboration.

CHAPTER 4

ENVISIONING AUTHENTIC COLLABORATION AS A NEW PARADIGM

"Vision without action is merely a dream.
Action without vision just passes the time.
Vision with action can change the world."
Joel A. Barker

Creating a new future with a new vision

Imagine a world where authentic collaboration is commonly known and practiced. In many households, workplaces and communities, the act of relationship-building is attended to with care. The process is a galvanizing invitation to discover, accept and appreciate ourselves and others. Love is embraced as the purpose of relating. People view every form of Life as precious and, as such, the core needs of all are duly considered. Interdependence is understood not only as a concept but embodied in our essence. Just as a gentle spring rain brings Life to nature, meaningful connection enlivens our heart. The wound of separation begins to heal, along with dualitistic thinking and polarizing behaviors. Secure attachment and mindful communication allow us to fulfill our need for autonomy *and* belonging. Contradictory viewpoints are welcomed.

As we transform, we become more aligned with the truth of who we are. We feel the grace of integrated living, trusting that Life is unfolding in support of our highest good. With emotional safety, our body relaxes. Courageous, gentle truth-telling inspires us to see with new eyes and listen with new ears. The human voice compassionately uplifts those who are hurting. Personal mastery is adopted as an ease-filled, humble, virtuous pursuit. Together, we rise on the united wings of eagle and condor into the most empowered version of ourselves.

We reclaim our power to bridge-build into ayni and joyfully co-create the future we want.

> *"A vision is not just a picture of what could be; it's an appeal to our better selves, a call to become something more."*
> Rosabeth Ross Kanter

Believe it or not, this can be your reality. Bringing this vision to Life is possible. As Napoleon Hill reminded us, "Whatever the mind can conceive and believe, it can achieve."

Some people may read these words with longing, yet peppered with cynicism. Others may label this vision as lofty and far-fetched. For those, I offer a warm blanket of empathy. Judgment is a reaction to an unmet need. Cynicism is the cousin of lost hope. Both may be a mask for fear, anger or despair. I understand.

On occasion, I too slip into these moments. When difficult times occur and this vision seems unattainable, I fill the dark corner of my heart with the light of self-love and reassurance. In my mind's eye, I recall what it feels like to fully show up in relationship; to be accepted and celebrated for all of who I am, as I am. I'm grateful to have experienced this vision of authentic collaboration on a visceral level. It's become an in-the-belly knowing: a harbor in a storm and a soothing balm. It takes effort, at times, to remember that I can live from the inside-out. My external circumstances do not have to determine the texture of my relationships. Bottom line: my axis of power resides within.

The power of visioning

This entire chapter is dedicated to the vision of authentic collaboration because vision is what transforms the world. How so? Well, it's our perception that creates the world of our experience. Generating a new reality starts with our mind and heart as we envision what we desire. As conceptual beings, we do not have to stay stuck in thinking about what

> *What relationship vision captivates your mind and heart?*

we don't want. We have our mind power to conjure up the world we do want to create. Every day, whether we're aware of this or not, we reverberate energy waves and send out messages to Life. Individually and collectively, we attract what is resonant and congruent.

AUTHENTIC COLLABORATION

In the shamanic world, each person is seen as a dream-walker. With vision, we dream a new world into being. We transform reality by changing our perception and widening our understanding of what's possible. By altering our focus, we shift our energy and thereby the circumstances around us. This entails bridging our personal dream with the larger purpose of communal service. As responsible, creative beings, we all play a role in how Life develops.

A vision lures us into the future. It calls forth who we are becoming. People with vision are magnetic; they offer a tonic that stirs the soul. A vision empowers us to drop limiting beliefs and behaviors, creating space for new affirming ways of thinking to burrow into our neural network. By believing that our vision is already manifesting, we boost our optimism and change our energy field. We notice more opportunities and take more risks. Doors open and synchronicities abound. Our vision serves as a navigational system directing our focus toward goals that matter. We begin to attract more of what we want into our life.

> *"We become what we pay attention to."*
> Sue Monk Kidd

A compelling vision is rooted in the past, speaks to the future, yet has power to respond to today's reality. Many luminaries understood this power. Martin Luther King Jr. shared his dream of racial equality. Nelson Mandela began a South African national unity crusade with a vision of reconciliation, inclusivity and equality. Kenya's Wangari Muta Maathai, a 2004 Nobel Peace Prize winner and environmentalist, founded the Green Belt Movement with a vision to plant millions of trees and alleviate poverty. Mother Theresa institutionalized a global dying-with-dignity movement with a visionary call to caretaking. Mahatma Gandhi launched a nonviolent campaign to free India from British rule with a vision of self-sovereignty. Now, in the twenty-first century, our time has come to dream again and reimagine our story arc of collaboration.

Embracing a vision whole-heartedly is a leap of faith. No crystal ball tells us what's ahead. It is an audacious act to take on what our soul longs for, even when the horizon offers no certainty. When fear rises up, incorporating ritual and ceremony into the visioning process can help transcend the limitations of the mind. We can enter unchartered territory and

> *"There is pleasure in the pathless woods."*
> Lord Byron

fuel our journey with the power of nature. It's exciting for the soul yet fear-inducing for the ego. As the Spanish poet Antonio Machado wrote, "Wanderer, there is no road, the road is made by walking."

The artistry of authentic collaboration

> **The Art of Authentic Collaboration =**
>
> A respectful interaction with self, others and Earth.
> A shift from self-reliance to interdependence.
> A dialogue that blends mind creativity and gut savvy with heart wisdom.
> A mutual exploration of feelings, needs, values and ideas.
> A process to connect and co-create something new together.

In this vision for authentic collaboration, we call on the artist within. We're inspired to access all aspects of our mind, body and spirit. In fact, our whole body becomes engaged in this creative exercise. Our relationships become a blank canvas on which to paint our stories. Even with a painful history, we remind ourselves that every interaction offers a new beginning. As organic beings, we are ever-changing. Every day, we awaken as someone new. In turn, the pigment of our relationships also adjusts. Collaboration becomes a continual work of art.

Envisioning authentic collaboration depends on open-minded learning and heart-centered listening. In this space, we feel and know that each being on this planet can never be separated from the whole of community. Even in moments of despair and isolation, we are held in the embrace of Mother Earth. With the support of community, we release the exhaustion of over-self-reliance. In this field of love for self, others and Earth, we let go of our subconscious need for opponents. In sensing interconnection, we dissolve the habit of othering. The dark shadow of enemy images fade. Different perspectives are not seen as threats. The phrase *mutual gain* is used as everyday language. We begin to perceive relating as an art. The soft color wheel of empathy is generously offered. Daubs of laughter are

> *"If there is no enemy within, the enemy without cannot harm you."*
> African Proverb

stenciled in. Gratitude becomes the primer. These are the conditions of meaningful connection and complementary interaction.

If relationship-building reflects this palette of principles, authentic collaboration sits at the pinnacle of human interaction. This is the world I want to live in and co-create.

Unpacking the nuances of authenticity

With this vision, *authentic* is the key descriptor. The word *authenticity* comes from the Greek word *authentes*, which means acting on one's own authority. The term implies being grounded in our values, emotions and ethics. It speaks to the precondition of self-awareness. Each day, moment to moment, cultivating self-knowledge is an ongoing investment in becoming who we truly are. In doing so, our confidence and conviction grows. We give ourselves permission to own our uniqueness. As an act of liberation, we go against the grain of conformity and take a stand to be genuine. In some circles, it's a profound choice to be loyal to self.

> *"The privilege of a lifetime is to become who you truly are."*
> Carl Jung

Inherent in authenticity is the pursuit of inner coherence. The process of inner coherence is about aligning our mind, gut intelligence and emotions with our heart. When we attune within and sync into ayni, we move into the joy of right relationship. With greater ease, our words, thoughts and action meld in harmony. Intention and mindful breathing help to facilitate this process. For support, I ask Earth to be my authenticity partner. When I walk in nature, I instinctually feel Earth's coherence. She reminds me what it's like to live in a state of flow and unity. I've come to understand that becoming intimate with myself enables me to enjoy intimacy with others.

Authenticity is also a call to deepen integrity and experience the integral sense of being "whole and complete." Authentic wholeness arises when there's congruency between what we say, mean and do. When we relate from our inner center of love and wholeness, we reclaim our belonging to Life. With Life at our back, our integrity ramps up our authentic power. We express in a clear and compelling manner. We stop hiding our fears and compromising our values. We bravely reveal who we are. We are true to ourselves while remaining open and receptive to what matters to others. Collaborating with mutual respect becomes natural.

That said, authenticity is often a challenge. Our culture unwittingly fosters inauthentic expression. Society gives us rules and benchmarks to follow, promotes people pleasing, encourages workaholism and feeds perfectionism. These social tensions can override our desire for authenticity. Furthermore, some family cultures discourage people from developing a healthy sense of self. Relationships become enmeshed if a strong other focus was consistently modelled from an early age. It's not uncommon to hear people say they "lose themselves" in an intimate relationship. In addition, there are people who define themselves by their roles. When roles change or cease, the unquestioned assumptions come to light, revealing the dark crevice of the unknown. The question, "Who are you, really?" can leave behind a dusty trail of confusion.

In some circumstances, it's risky to authentically express. If a strong power imbalance is at play, relating authentically can be destabilizing. There may be negative consequences. Relationships may end. One time, I lost a job because I spoke my truth without carefully considering the implications. I also witnessed a friend who suffered in a toxic relationship. She believed that to be loved, she had to be different from who she was. This belief shut-down her authentic voice. Ultimately, wise discernment is needed to decide who and when to speak to about what and how much to disclose. Only we know how to weigh authentic expression with self-protection.

Balancing being open with the appropriateness of the context is tricky. When I'm unsure, I carve out silence and ask my body's wisdom to guide me. In a body centric dialogue, I listen deeply to the sensations within. I bring laser focus to what has me feel expanded and contracted, what opens me into authenticity and what closes me down. Unlike the mind, the body never lies.

Authenticity is not like turning a light fixture on or off. Rather, it has a dimmer switch. We continually choose the degree to which we honestly share. How we authentically express fluctuates depending on our childhood template, our relationship history, our degree of self-awareness and our perception of safety. When we experience rapport and caring, communicating authentically may be relatively easy. Yet, when conflict erupts and an attack-defend posture takes over, authenticity is often the first victim.

But here's the upside: We already are authentic human beings. We've simply covered it up with the conditioning, defenses and protective coping strategies that we learned in our childhood. So, for most of us, living and collaborating authentically is a life-long journey of discovery. The process starts with radical self-honesty. When authenticity deepens, self-connection amplifies. The trust bucket swells. This is the journey of becoming our own best friend.

Authenticity is a choice toward greater freedom and empowerment. In this field of resonance, we begin attracting people who also value this quality of relating. When we touch, feel and listen to our desires, needs and values, our authentic expression and consciousness expands. We access concealed wisdom. When we connect with our truth, we know better, and we do better. From this perspective, self-awareness is a never-ending flight of steps to the authentic sage within. When we're authentic with ourselves, we're able to authentically collaborate with others.

TRY THIS: As you reflect on and respond to these questions in a journal, challenge yourself to deepen your authenticity.

- What helps and hinders my ability to authentically relate?
- How do I alter my behavior based on what others think?
- What masks am I ready to let go of?
- In relating honestly with _____, what do I stand to gain and lose?
- How do I describe my uniqueness?
- What is one micro-truth that would change my relationship with ___?
- When did I not speak up when I wanted to?
- What do I really care about?

Illustrating Authentic Collaboration with a Bridge Metaphor

Since authenticity is a bridge to meaningful connection, let's further inspect the metaphor of a bridge. As noted, a bridge is a robust symbol for collaboration. It spans a physical divide, linking two fixed points that may otherwise never meet. We too can learn how to affirm each other despite relational divides.

> *"Reciprocity is a deep instinct; it is the basic currency of social life."*
> Jonathan Haidt

A bridge is also the perfect symbol for reciprocity. From this space of give-and-take, the spirit of ayni can take root with its magical blend of mutual gain. We can learn to sit alongside each other in an attempt to understand rather than confront with oppositional energy. On this passageway, we unite even when we are separated by the ground of our differences.

Bridges remind us that we can join the far right and far left while finding a midpoint of balance. In so doing, an and-both conversation can unfold. We can step beyond our isolating positions and find a middle ground. With curiosity, a bridge signifies that new insights and learning are always on the horizon. Even though we've been educated to separate through things like body comparison, different learning styles, gender stereotypes and reward and punishment, a bridge can span this divide. What's needed is courage to cross-over with an open heart. When we find ourselves in the crevasse of disagreements, mindful communication can still support connection. A bridge reminds us that unity is possible.

To visualize authentic collaboration within the bridge framework, consider the illustration on the next page.

Scan the **QR code** found on the bottom of this bridge image to download, print, post and share a colored graphic. As a conversation starter, ask people which words resonate with them. Discuss how this bridge model supports your own relationship vision and what other's desire. Every conversation brings this metaphor to Life.

Authentic Collaboration:
A Bridge To Meaningful Connection

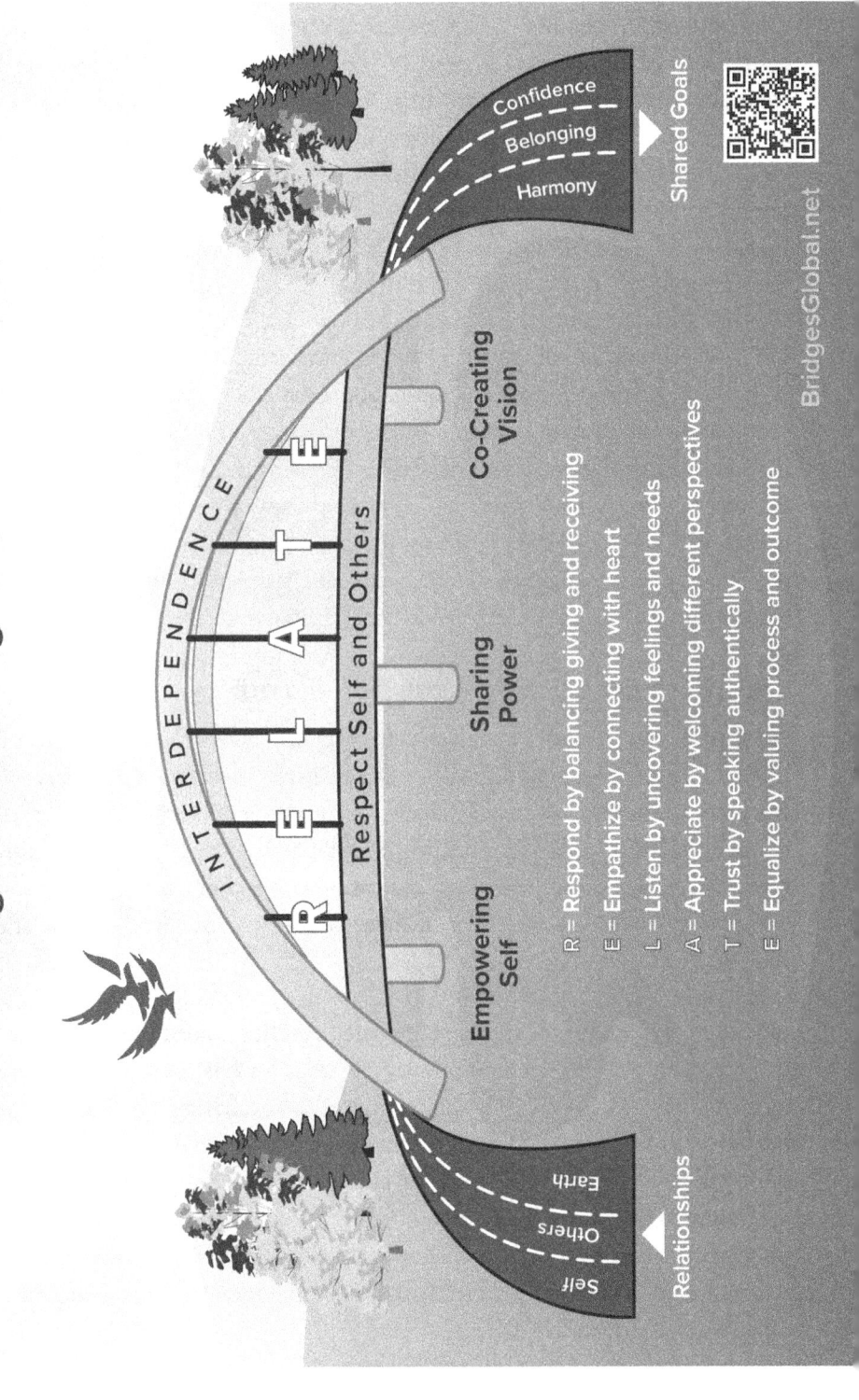

INTERDEPENDENCE

RELATE

Respect Self and Others

Empowering Self · Sharing Power · Co-Creating Vision

Shared Goals: Confidence, Belonging, Harmony

Relationships: Self, Others, Earth

R = Respond by balancing giving and receiving
E = Empathize by connecting with heart
L = Listen by uncovering feelings and needs
A = Appreciate by welcoming different perspectives
T = Trust by speaking authentically
E = Equalize by valuing process and outcome

BridgesGlobal.net

AUTHENTIC COLLABORATION

As described in Chapter 1, this tied-arch bridge is a metaphor for authentic collaboration. The design is resilient and durable. Arch bridges date back thousands of years in withstanding the test of time. Representing change and flexibility, these bridges can be built on either a solid pier or in unstable areas. Similarly, the practice of authentic collaboration taps into our own resourcefulness to withstand relational friction. The skills can be applied in high or low trust relationships. The architecture is structurally sound in dealing with varying levels of tension and traffic.

Likewise, authentic collaboration holds gravitas as it's based on relationship intelligence research and communication best practices. It's an empowering practice that supports our ability to connect with and influence others, resolve conflict and develop trust. The RELATE principles, described in detail in Chapters 8 through 13, are designed to help us weather all types of relational storms and squalls. We are more apt to have sensitive conversations that result in shared understanding, mutual respect and alignment. Embodying the values of authentic collaboration offers a lifelong bridge of discovery.

The bridge deck of respect for self *and* others

To unpack this bridge vision, let's start with the deck as it upholds relational traffic. This deck is about respecting all, regardless of different opinions, values, worldviews and personalities. That said, balancing self-respect with other respect is a delicate proposition. Connecting with what's personally meaningful while being open to another person's stand can test our character. Even if we don't like certain behaviors, we can still listen to and respect people while staying rooted in our own values.

Holding a respect-for-all approach involves mindful communication. It invites us to slow down and become present. At its most basic level, mindfulness is focusing our awareness on the moment and the exchange happening between ourselves and another person. The more we can open to both realities, the more we can hold space to consider alternative viewpoints. As a foundation, practicing mindful communication includes a clear intention, self-acceptance, the use of "I" statements when sharing our observations, speaking with care and being open to other perspectives. Conscious interaction is a commitment toward shared understanding.

AUTHENTIC COLLABORATION

Holding a "we" mindset is *the* great relationship challenge. Fundamentally, it entails welcoming discord as a natural, normal part of dialogue. Otherwise, dialogue means we must agree. We then run the risk of negating thoughts and feelings or agreeing to do what other's want to keep the peace. As points to ponder, consider these two questions: "How do I respond to opposition within and around me?" and "How do I negotiate to best support myself and others? When we consider all needs with care, we step beyond reactivity and into conscious interaction. A respect-for-all stance grows the conditions for healthy coexistence.

Respect is a paradox. It's a unanimous need yet what it looks or sounds like is different to each person. Depending on your culture, family conditioning, gender or generation, respect has many connotations. This may be why the Platinum Rule is supplanting the Golden Rule. Rather than assume others want to be treated the way we want, it's worth asking how they prefer to be treated. Greeting someone with a kiss on the cheek, for example, is respectful to some while inappropriate to others. Similarly, a lot of eye contact is considered rude in some cultures, while in others, eye contact is a sign of caring attentiveness. While respect can translate into a variety of behaviors, it's essentially about having positive regard for the feelings, needs, rights and customs of all Life forms. Respectful behaviors include self-responsibility, consideration, generosity, deep listening, honest communication and kindness.

A respect-for-all approach is the bridge foundation because people need a certain amount of esteem to effectively collaborate. As a universal value, respect implies all beings have inherent worth and significance. There is no proviso nor stipulation. Regardless of culture, age, religion, or race, our shared humanity affords us respect. This is not something to be earned, as culture may prescribe. Rather, respect is a basic human right, carved into the woodwork of democracy. We can disagree with someone's behavioral choices yet respect their personhood. This stance contributes to self-regard, psychological safety and authentic engagement.

> *Respect for all signals a progressive society. It's rooted in the mindset that we all matter.*

In reflecting on the respect-for-all interplay and the intrinsic affect we have on people, this insightful quote from Thomas Lewis comes to mind:

"All of us, when we engage in relatedness, fall under the gravitational influence of another's emotional world, at the same time that we are bending his emotional mind with ours. Each relationship is a binary star, a burning flux of exchanged force fields, the deep and ancient influences emanating and felt, felt and emanating."

Widening the bridge's three-lane roadway

The bridge's three lanes of self, others and Earth are distinctly unique yet interlaced cords in our human experience. They each contribute to how we collaborate. Since these three lanes are intricately intertwined, they are separated by a dash. We pass in and out of each lane routinely—sometimes concurrently—connecting and fortifying all three relationships.

On this bridge, there are no detours nor fast lane. We are attuned to the rhythm of Life and our own rhythm. We pay attention to Life's feedback to navigate our way forward. Developing all three laneway relationships gives us greater facility in moving from where we are now to where we want to be. Human health, quality living and survival depend on a well-maintained three-prong relationship. We're greater and stronger together.

Developing the self lane for greater confidence

Since we have touched on the value of a holistic collaborative approach, let's look at *how to develop* all three relationships. Starting with the foundational lane of self, self-respect also encapsulates self-worth, self-image, self-confidence and self-care—all wedges of the same pie.

How we respect ourselves revolves around our intrapersonal relationship. It begins by acknowledging the power of our mind. As creative beings, developing a relationship with our thoughts is key. Our thoughts reflect how we love ourselves, which in turn, influence our emotional landscape. This includes nurturing our self-image, pursuing our dreams, owning our desires and surrounding ourselves with supportive people. It's about choosing to unabashedly love ourselves as a radical act. In doing so, we dignify ourselves as an aspect of Life and thus build self-confidence. This is authentic self-collaboration at its finest.

The self-collaboration lane also includes caring for our body. For this is our sacred vessel that enables us to experience pleasure, fulfill our desires and accomplish our collaboration goals. Too often, we separate our mind and body as though they do not communicate. When we see a doctor with physical symptoms, rarely are we asked about our thought patterns, emotions, relationships, stress level or childhood story. Yet our bodily health is deeply intertwined with our psychological and emotional world. Case in point, our nervous system wires together all our bodily organs with our brain. As such, our stress level is intimately connected with our physiology. Our wellness practice needs to incorporate bridge-building between our mind and body.

Holistic self-care can include meditation, journaling, rituals, a daily movement practice, improving nutrition, sufficient rest and sleep, hydrating regularly, enjoying walks in nature, balancing work and play and taking long, slow breaths. While none of these suggestions are new, there's always room to improve self-care. This week, challenge yourself to start one new healthy habit that's meaningful to you. Remind yourself that how you care for your body correlates to how you attend to your relationships. Our outer confidence flows from inner well-being.

As our constant partner in life, our body is always communicating with us, carrying vital messages. It's a sign of self-respect to listen to our body's sensations, even if fear or pain arises. Embodied learning is digesting knowledge for a felt bodily experience. Developing our somatic intelligence is understanding how our body acts and reacts, how it copes with tension and alleviates discomfort.

A simple somatic exercise is to consciously move, dance or walk while focusing on what's happening within. Become self-attentive. Focus on the tempo of your breath and observe bodily sensations. Zoom in on your "sixth sense" called proprioception to track how your body parts move in space. Listen deeply. The more we attune to our body, notice our feelings and engage our senses, the more we are aware of our inner experience. We can then be at choice in aligning our physiology and psychology.

> "As an offshoot of colonialism, our culture venerates cognitive and linguistic knowing while marginalizing somatic intelligence. It's time to listen to our bodies."
> Dr. Twyla Kowalenko

Reflect on how to co-join the mind and body as allies. The mind may be able to grasp many concepts but it is our embodied truth that reveals how enlightened we truly are. This bridge-building practice is but one exercise of many that can build confidence: a desirable outcome that beckons us from the other side.

Longing to belong in the others lane

At a basic level, crossing the bridge lane of "others" means acknowledging that people hold opinions that are different from ours. Authentic collaboration does not restrict contradictory viewpoints for the sake of homogenized thinking. Rather, we learn how to bring into focus all angles and opinions to synthesize them productively. This involves expanding beyond tolerance to acceptance, come what may.

A way to practice acceptance is to reflect on what beliefs you see as unreasonable. Beliefs that were at one time considered "unreasonable" were, in hindsight, the cantilevers to growing a culture. For instance, anti-slavery was commonly perceived as unreasonable two hundred years ago. It was unreasonable to give women the right to vote one hundred years ago. As George Bernard Shaw noted, "All progress is made by unreasonable people." What is your comfort zone for expressing and considering nontraditional viewpoints?

One of my teachers in this regard was a person who used wheels to get around. As a quadriplegic, that's how he spoke of his different abilities. He wanted to be treated with basic dignity, as an equal, despite his mode of transportation. Motivated by a desire for belonging and social justice, he advocated for people with physical challenges his entire adult life. He spoke about how people talked down to him, both literally and figuratively. His preference was to focus on abilities rather than disabilities. With this awareness, I developed heightened sensitivity about how I communicated. For everyone has ability differences. This gentleman helped me understand the nuances of respect and how energy boomerangs in relationship.

Becoming aware of how we accept or judge others can help us grow our sense of belonging. Awareness breeds mindful choice. To what extent do we hold racist thoughts? How do we generalize people based on their skin color or ethnicity? Do we place people in categories because of their religion, gender or

> *"Mutual caring relationships require kindness and patience, tolerance, optimism… confidence in oneself, and the ability to give without undue thought of gain."*
> Mr. Rogers

sexual preferences? How do we rank order groups in society? We may be savvy enough to not express prejudice, yet people can still sense judgment. It's a background conversation that affects belonging.

When you feel judged, do you try to "fit in"? If so, notice how this decision has you deny aspects of who you are to be accepted. As a distinction, belonging enables us to feel embraced regardless of differences.

If we notice patterns of labeling, condemnation or punishment in our speech, we may want to cross back over to the self lane to reflect on how we're projecting. This process of inquiry not only builds self-understanding but also entices us to collaborate differently. With greater agency, we can turn down the volume of internal noise and allow kindness to radiate. We can choose words that are windows instead of walls. Ironically, when we accept and welcome others as they are, our *own* affinity and security in a group is strengthened. Life satisfaction depends on how we experience and cultivate belonging.

Developing relational harmony with the Earth lane

One way to begin deepening our relational harmony with Earth is to listen to her heartbeat and rhythm. This can only occur when we spend time in nature. Research shows that exposing ourselves to the natural world has direct benefits for our health. People who spend at least two hours a week outdoors are "substantially more likely to report good health and psychological well-being than those who do not." With greater well-being, we then feel more connected, nourished and inclined to reciprocate with environmental care for wildlife and habitat.

When we feel more connected with Earth, we also become mindful of our language. If we call Earth "it," we downgrade Life to be an object—implying we are separate from Life. Instead, consider using the pronoun *she*. Earth has been denoted as a feminine energy for thousands of years. Interestingly, feminine qualities are what's needed for effective collaboration: nurturing, receiving, listening, holding and caring. If we perceive Earth as holding the feminine principle that exists within everyone, this ricochets into how we relate with others.

AUTHENTIC COLLABORATION

As a sign of caring for Earth, consider how you balance your taking from her with your giving. How are you practicing ayni or harmonious living with your daily choices? Imagine a world where people equalize the scales of *receiving* daily Earth nourishment via food, clothing and shelter with *giving* back via environmental stewardship and restoration projects. Whether it be with money or human labor, there are many creative ways to support year-round, hands-on eco protection. Our role as Earth custodians is never-ending. Coming into right relationship with our source is a commitment that reaps untold rewards. It's a path that stimulates harmonious relations with all.

> *As Earth custodians, human beings have the privilege of balancing taking with giving back.*

Ideas to Bridge-Build with Earth

- Clean up neighborhood pollution and learn about your local watershed.
- Volunteer at a green-focused community organization.
- Educate yourself on eco-friendly funds to align your investments with your values.

- Plant native trees or offer funds to restore a damaged ecosystem.
- Take slow, daily walks in nature and learn about native wildlife.
- Write an eco-advocacy letter to a political representative.

- Ask about eco-responsibility initiatives or the externalized cost of doing business.
- Discuss eco-friendly changes to make at home with your family.
- Organize a community conversation to advance climate mitigation and adaptation.

The bridge arch of interdependence

The elegant arch of the authentic collaboration bridge celebrates interdependence. In reflecting on this concept, the Sanskrit tale of Indra's necklace comes to mind. This ageless metaphor is about looking into a necklace made of fine gems to see a net of jewels. Each jewel, simultaneously, carries the whole net. Because of the clarity of the jewels, each is seen in the other. If you gaze long enough, the interconnection sparkles. This is where the expression *caught in Indra's net* originated.

AUTHENTIC COLLABORATION

This metaphor reminds us that in each Life form, all others are reflected, not separate from the universe. We mirror each other in astonishing ways. At its deepest level, authentic collaboration recognizes that how someone shows up for me *is* me.

Like a necklace, there is no idea more ancient than a circle of collaborative relationships. In this respect-based circle, we each sit on the rim as a statement of equality. We discover that the one giving is actually receiving. The dialogue shifts from me versus you to the collective good. We discover, play and experiment with the intricacies of interdependence. As we disclose our hopes and fears, a feeling of aliveness pervades our being.

While a circle implies equality, relational power dyanamics are rarely equal. Consider the distinction between codependence and interdependence. While codependence and interdependence both mean dependence on others, the former arises from childhood trauma while the latter grows from an empowered relationship. Codependency is rooted in family of origin dysfunction whereupon members repressed emotions and neglected needs. Consequently, people rely on others to make decisions, resolve a situation or meet needs for them. Excessive caretaking can be the outcome. This tendency can also result in enmeshment whereupon people lose their sense-of-self when in relationship. Interdependence, however, unfolds when people balance self-sovereignty and belonging, being independent yet connected. This requires not only strong self-worth but also a willingness to be mutually responsible. Because interdependence describes a healthy partnership of equals, being dependent on others is taken in stride. The fear of being a burden, entangled or trapped ceases because we know our inner strength.

Generally, western cultures tend to be more individualistic whereas Asian cultures are more collectivist. For those whose identity revolves around self-sufficiency, interdependence is a common collaboration growing edge. If being self-sufficient is a strong value for you, consider the following questions:

- How will I be perceived if I let down my guard?
- If giving is my source of power, will receiving have me feel weak?

- If I open up and become vulnerable, will I be exploited?
- Can I negotiate healthy boundaries?

Explore what it means to need someone. Feel into your body's truth to sense the degree to which your relationships are healthy. If you perceive dependence on others as a sign of weakness, reframe this to be a non-negotiable part of the inter*dependent* topography.

While it's easy to retreat when a relationship moves through bumps on the bridge road, remember that exposing our soft heart entails a strong belly. Anyone who has fallen in love knows that true interdependency is a bold, brave stance. Understanding interconnection has profound implications for collaboration and beyond.

My own grappling with interdependence

At one time, the concept of interdependency conjured up a deep layer of resistance within me. My mind said, *If I need support from others, I'll be at risk. I can't count on people.* Even though I longed for deeper love, abundance and support, I was afraid of opening myself fully to more heartache, sorrow and disappointment. My subconscious belief was *needing others equals pain*. I struggled with the paradox that self-protection can be co-joined with an open heart. Eventually, my yearning for a new quality of relationship prevailed and I courageously allowed light to filter into the cracks.

> *"There is a crack in everything. That's how the light gets in."*
> Leonard Cohen

Through grace, I was able to lean into the tension of distrust. I began listening to my gut intelligence to help me with decision-making. I no longer allowed the fear of conflict and rejection to eclipse my desire to speak up. I let go of the misperception that my safety rested in aloneness. Because I belong to Earth, I am never alone. By tethering myself to the natural world, I developed the strength to remain empowered *and* rely on others.

Interdependence is an invitation to let go, let Life. It's about merging my will with Life's will. This action invokes the universal fear of losing myself in relationship—be it with others or with the flow of Life. It calls into question how separate I perceive myself to be. I dance with one part of me that desires connection while another part fears intimacy. Life beckons me to let go of control: to sit in the flames that burn away ego attachments while trusting Life to provide me with oxygen to breathe. In this alchemy lies the space between personhood and soul.

If you also experience a flash of fear, be reminded that we are wired for interdependence and whole-system equilibrium. Because we are a part of nature, we have balance, homeostasis and equanimity built into our system. The jewel of interdependence is our normal state.

When you slip into the seduction of separateness, recall a memory that brings you back into harmony with all that is. To a moment of heart surrender. For me, it's a sweet memory of scuba diving in the Red Sea. In this underwater paradise, I recall being awestruck in observing a vast field of interconnection. I was transported into a new reality with all living beings in collaborative flow. A celebration of diversity. Perfection in coexistence. As I swam, a peaceful sensation pervaded my body. It felt like oneness. This memory has now become my anchor to embody unity and belonging. It reminds me of Rumi's words, "You are not a drop in the ocean; you are the entire ocean in a drop."

Power pillars to uphold the bridge with a focus on sharing power

There are three mighty power pillars to uphold the respect-for-all bridge deck. These pillars can withstand tremendous force and pressure. Likewise, in our relationships, a great deal of power is required to support authentic collaboration. In this model, power is distinguished in three ways.

Bridge Power Pillars

1. Level of Self	>	Empowerment
2. Level of Others	>	Sharing Power
3. Level of Earth	>	Co-creating Vision

While Chapter 7 elaborates on all three power pillars, suffice to say that authentic collaboration entails understanding the nature of power and how to use this energy for the benefit of all.

Exploring the meaning of power as an external force

Given the role of power in this bridge architecture, let's explore the concept itself. Depending on who you ask, different definitions of power will come to light. Some posit that power is the ability to influence and get things done. They speak about sheer force of will, hence the term *willpower*. Others contend that it revolves around choice and having the capacity to support your own and other's needs. From another perspective, a moral lens is used to see power as connected to strength of mind or character. Social psychologists John R.P. French and Bertram Raven identify power as having six distinct bases: coercive, expert, legitimate, referent, reward and informational. In some cultures, power connotes social standing, caste or clan affiliation. There is also authority power, which is often tied to a role or title.

In many of these descriptors, power is seen to be *externally derived*. This is because our collective conditioning frames power as a socially conferred status. In this context, power comes from rank, authority, money or even physical might over others. Given that the experience of power imbalance, injustice and domination is very real in our world, many people perceive this to be "true" power. Countless policies, laws and cultures reflect and reinforce this dynamic. That said, it's important to note that oppressive structures are typically accompanied by interpersonal and internalized oppression. Either way, the subject of power is complex and often emotionally charged.

While role-based power does exist, it is superficial, transient and often force-oriented. If the title or decision-making authority is taken away, the person's corresponding power can, and often does, diminish. As such, secular or temporal power is temporary; it may provide a surge of ego yet it's not sustainable. Someone who exhibits bully or hostile behavior, for example, may appear to be powerful yet this fear-based behavior is often driven by personal insecurity. People who abuse power typically have their own childhood trauma story. From my perspective, abuse of power often comes from a disconnection from the heart, a projection from a sense of inner weakness or a compensation for repressed pain. As

> "Power is of two kinds. One is obtained by the fear of punishment and the other by acts of love. Power based on love is a thousand times more effective and permanent than the one derived from fear of punishment."
> Mahatma Gandhi

our own stories will attest, power stemming from love is far more inspiring and impactful.

Authentic power as a noun, verb and adjective

While external power is one side of the coin, the flip side reveals *internally derived power*. I refer to internal power as *authentic power*. Vital to authentic collaboration, this concept is a noun, verb and adjective.

As a noun, authentic power is the essence of our being. It emanates from Life as a universal energy, accessed with every breath. Like our essence of love, we carry this energy as our birthright. It comes from Self versus self. We are a conduit that streams this energy in service to Life. In her eloquence, Marianne Williamson described human beings as lamps, with a cord that connects to an electricity Source. Our authentic power comes from this Source, however you define it. We are born with the capacity to "light up." The question is, how often do we choose to plug in?

By virtue of being human, we all have the same potential to carry and express authentic power. Our hearts beat the same. So, if power is a universal, delta, Life-force pursuit, why do we experience varying degrees of power? Put another way, if authentic power originates from an inner fountain that never runs dry, how do we block the flow? While it seems that people naturally want to harness their authentic power to fulfill on their purpose, many obstructions impede the current of energy. This can include trauma, low self-esteem, avoidance of self-responsibility, lack of clarity on values, procrastination, conflicting commitments, holding on to grievances, poor boundaries and victim consciousness. When we unblock our flow, and move into right relationship with self, our power once again surges. Great wisdom, love, passion and understanding streams forth.

Looking at power in this way challenges the notion that power is evil. In actuality, power is not virtuous nor evil but rather a neutral energy that we infuse with our values. This implies how our willpower is used. Every day, we choose to use our power as a source of corruption or a force for good. While accessing our power is an archetypal journey

> *"Power is neither good nor evil, but its user makes it so."*
> Erin Hunter

that knocks on everyone's door, our choice is what determines our experience of power...and collaboration.

As a verb, the expression of authentic power is the exercise of will in supporting self *and* others. It follows the energy of desire. With self-awareness, we are more apt to notice our desires and from where they come. We are well-served in questioning whether our desire comes from our ego personality or the guidance of our soul, the aspect within that is eternal. If the desire we feel is aligned with our heart yearning and our soul's destiny path, we become powerful co-creators with Life. When we exercise the will of our heart, we keep the big picture in mind while noticing the generosity of Life. If desire is rooted in our personality, it may be wise to loosen the clench of reactivity and attachment to outcome. Over attachment to desire is another way we block the flow. We can suffocate relationships, narrow our focus, react impulsively, constrict our joy and sabotage collaboration. If we become zealous to make things happen with our will, our actions may seem powerful to others but it's blinding (and often limiting) to the doer. Non-attachment offers power, freedom, autonomy and greater choice.

As an adjective, authentic power is rooted in alignment. This alignment is felt and broadcasted when our thoughts, words and actions are in sync. On a deeper level, power alignment is experienced when our personality merges with our soul, our mind harmonizes with our heart, our masculine is in service to our feminine and our body is grounded in Earth. A feeling of unity, vitality and inner coherence ensues. Charisma springs forth as this quality of power produces a magnetic energy. When we are in this inner space of alignment, we are centered. We can sense it in our bones.

> *Inner coherence is the by-product of owning our authentic power.*

Without a doubt, it's an empowered feeling to experience alignment in having our inner parts operate in harmony. As Dr. Joe Dispenza states, "We know that it takes a clear intention (a coherent brain) and an elevated emotion (a coherent heart) to begin to change a person's biology from living in the past to living in the future. That combination of mind and body—of thoughts and feelings—also seems to influence matter. And that's how you create reality." When we cultivate this quality of aligned power from the inside out, collaboration takes on a whole new vibration.

To align with power, calm the mind to better understand what's happening within and around us. Pause, notice and validate our interior experience before discerning how power is being used or misused. If we lose inner power, notice where the leak is and how it shows up in our behavior. It's essential to not "collect" power per say but rather to continually let go and allow the energy to move through us. In strengthening our connection with our heart, we augment our power. We relate with greater honesty and self-trust. Others are given permission to follow suit. Essentially, the vision of authentic collaboration encourages us to come into right relationship with power.

TRY THIS: Review some of the ways these bridge power pillars are weakened and strengthened. Journal about how you reduce and expand your power.

Power pillars weaken due to:	**Power pillars strengthen with:**
• inner dissonance	• daily self-reflection
• chronic stress, overthinking	• honesty about opening to power
• judging feelings	• radical self-acceptance
• effort, struggle, resistance	• know that what's needed is within
• conflict, confusion, hesitancy	• avoid "could/should" words
• believing that Life is unfair	• expressing gratitude for what's so

Relating with the bridge's six vertical ties

The last key element of this tied-arch bridge metaphor is the six vertical ties that are attached to the deck. The purpose of these ties is to push the deck tension outward into the abutments to stabilize the bridge. They also help distribute the weight of the traffic, holding and balancing the deck load.

Comparably, each tie represents an authentic collaboration guiding principle, forming the acronym **RELATE.** The RELATE principles support the ever-changing load of collaborative relationships. Each provides an important and unique aspect of the art of bridge-building. As the vision backbone, Chapters 8 through 13 are exclusively dedicated to these RELATE principles.

Consider which principle most resonates with you now and why.

RELATE Principles of Authentic Collaboration

R = *Respond by balancing giving and receiving*
Mindful response enables people to reciprocate for mutual gain.

E = *Empathize by connecting with heart*
Genuine empathy, given by the heart, nurtures and transforms relationships.

L = *Listen by uncovering feelings and needs*
Practicing the seven levels of listening empowers whole-hearted presence.

A = *Appreciate by welcoming different perspectives*
Affirming viewpoints celebrates diversity and expands our vista of reality.

T = *Trust by speaking authentically*
Trust is the by-product of open, honest, direct, gentle communication.

E = *Equalize by valuing process and outcome*
When we balance the *how* with the *what*, we respect relationships *and* results.

Each of these RELATE principles support meaningful connection, the basis of effective collaboration. This, I believe, is at the source of success, however its defined. When people respectfully work together, and honor Earth in the process, the interdependent flow is remarkable. Authentic power is visible. The creativity that arises is like music from a grand orchestra. Individual instruments are essential yet secondary to the powerful concord of sound. In a concert, musicians do not overpower the other: it's the melody between them that counts.

Imagine these RELATE principles becoming a common way to interact between work colleagues, countries, disciplines, religions, political parties, neighbors and family members. This takes commitment and practice. If we decide to adopt this vision and become conscious bridge-builders, we open our heart to mutual respect for all. We stand on deck, take the helm and cast out the meshwork of diversity. With every mindful interaction, we attract more early adopters and grow toward a tipping point. As the ripple effect expands, we generate positive change in our cultures and systems.

A bridge-building vision to activate the growth of humanity

With this bridge vision in mind, the practice of authentic collaboration may be humanity's most significant growing edge. Future generations are counting on us to presence this edge and uplevel our way of collaborating—for our sake and to co-create a more liveable world. The medicine wheel of Life is beckoning us to step up, step out and step together. It's an idea whose time has come.

The first step to embracing this vision is to shift our response from "Yes, but" to "Why not?" and "What if?" Allow yourself to be still and feel into your desire. Become the dreamer. Co-create a story of what's possible in your important relationships. Notice what is seeking resolution. What relationship obstacle inspires you to become your own hero or heroine? Dialogue about how to live in your heart to activate authentic collaboration. As dream-walkers, we write the script for our own book of Life. Everyone can create a beautiful, purpose-filled impact in our world.

> *"Be still and know that you are that which you desire to be. The end of longing should be Being. Translate your dream into Being."*
> Neville Goddard

As a change-maker in your own circle of influence, explore what mindful collaboration looks like for you. What vision is calling out to you? Feel into your personal growing edge and test the waters of deeper connection. Sense the boundary of your comfort zone. Adopt a new behavior that's a stretch in moving you toward your version of wholeness.

To move this bridge vision—or your vision—into action, experiment with the only four things we can control—how we think, speak, listen and behave. Look for and acknowledge what unites people rather than what separates. Allow the clashing of perspectives to reveal something new. Courageously express and notice the swell of vulnerability in your body. Risk everything by exposing your dreams. Explore what sustainable living means for you and your community. Suspend the need to know and deeply listen. Try on the idea that people behave in a way that makes sense to them, given their history and circumstances. In every moment, we're all doing the best we can.

A visionary beacon of hope

Consider this bridge model to be a beacon of hope during this time of great change. Society's complex challenges require a different quality of relating. Leaders are awakening to realize that individual, cultural and system changes are rooted in collaboration. We are slowly understanding that not one of us is as smart as all of us. The whole is truly greater than the sum of its parts. Collaborative leadership and teamwork are needed to jump-start a new level of solution-finding—at home, at work and in community. Relationship-building is no longer seen as a "nice to do" sideline activity—it *is* the work.

> *"Yesterday, I was clever, so I wanted to change the world. Today, I am wise, so I am changing myself."*
> Rumi

How we relate is our ultimate legacy. In this expression, we exercise our passion, purpose and persistence in service to what matters. We explore what our deepest gift is to others and what love really means. For the bridge must be made with love to withstand the inevitable winds of conflict.

When we crisscross the three-lane bridge, we inch toward interdependence and the beauty of ayni. We respond to the messages of our own soul while furthering the evolution of the world soul. As Neil Gaiman encourages us to consider, "The one thing that you have that nobody else has is you. Your voice, your mind, your story, your vision. So write, draw, build, play, dance and live as only you can."

In activating the vision of authentic collaboration, we develop our humanity. This is how we fulfill our potential and shift the trajectory of our future. With every interaction, we build the bridge of authentic collaboration as we walk across it. Side by side, we march this dream into reality. Every conscious act of respectful communication is a courageous step toward a desirable future.

CHAPTER 5

EXPLORING THE NATURE OF RELATIONSHIPS

*"All beings, including each one of us, enemy and
friend alike, exist in [dance] patterns of
mutuality, interconnectedness, co-responsibility and ultimately in unity."*
Joan Halifax

The dance of relationship

Understanding the nature of relationships allows us to cross the bridge of authentic collaboration with greater ease, harmony and joy. Since relationships are multilayered, it's helpful to become aware of its many aspects and intricacies. Countless visible and invisible dynamics are threaded into this fabric. In relationship, we face insecurity, flirtation and passion—and yes, even contradiction. Every day, we experience attraction and repulsion. We yearn for connection yet fear abandonment. We desire intimacy yet worry about being smothered. We want to be seen yet dodge vulnerability. Relationships validate our self-identity yet also evoke defensiveness. We link anger with blame and love with reward. We seek out relationships that support our needs and discard those that do not measure up. Undeniably, collaboration holds the totality of all relational dynamics.

As Albert Einstein remarked, if he had an hour to save the world, he would spend the first fifty-five minutes understanding the issue, and the last five minutes solving it. If we take the time to reflect on the multifaceted nature of relationships, we'll develop greater insight about the art of collaboration. Sense-making how and why we behave the way we do is a part of skill-building. With greater understanding and discernment, we can amplify our ability to negotiate, deal with differences, achieve more goals and blossom the potential for authentic collaboration.

AUTHENTIC COLLABORATION

Using the metaphor of dance, every relationship has a unique rhythm with unknowable choreography. Indeed, the sequence of steps is messy, unpredictable and forever changing. Even so, it's worthwhile to note some of the common patterns that underlie the ebb and flow of relating. Many themes emanate such as confidence, motivation, maturity, accountability, authority, control, sovereignty, hiding and speaking up.

> *Life is the dancer and relationships are the dance.*

While some issues are specific to individuals and cultural milieu, many dance tunes are universal. In the ballroom of relationship, we all carry the fear of rejection, the need for safety, the search for meaning, the anger of being shut out, the spark of inspiration, the pursuit of shared understanding, the upset of an unkind word and the wish for greater influence. How we communicate is bound up in our memories of the past and our desires of the future. In every region of the world, the music of our heart is revealed by how we swirl and twirl in relationship. Our strengths and dysfunctional habits are showcased in how we pivot and turn with others. Sometimes, dynamics feel like a brazen four-step hustle. Other times, we need to jazz up our interactions with laughter. As a "performance art," authentic collaboration flows from how we dance with self, others and Earth.

The skip and sway of childhood development

It is, of course, in our early years that our interpersonal patterns foster individuation—the journey of becoming who we are. The nature-nurture blend of childhood influences how we skip and sway. The prototype of our future habits and practices takes shape. In ways we can't begin to fathom, we recreate behavioral blueprints as adults that replicate how we received love and appreciation as a youngster. Unwittingly, we bring our unresolved childhood issues into our adult relationships. Our siblings help us deal with repressed mother and father issues. Our friendships enable us to heal memories of schoolyard exclusion hurts. Our work colleagues draw out power dynamics so our younger self can relearn how to play in the sandbox. Our romantic partners present opportunities to resolve long-held triggers. Even our early relationship with nature reveals how grounded we are as a grown up. Our younger year stories are tucked away in the recesses of our mind, implanted in the beauty and ugliness of our adult relationships.

AUTHENTIC COLLABORATION

How we collaborate stems from the conditioning of our childhood. The first six years of our life are critical to shaping the narrative we carry about self, humankind and the natural world. This is when we begin to understand the world and our role in it. From our family of origin, we learn about trust, esteem, love and grief. Depending on whether we feel cherished and connected or alone and shut down, our self-esteem flowers or withers.

Psychologists confirm that, as babies and toddlers, we attach to our caregivers by how we are responded to and nurtured. This shapes our identity, sense of value and even behavioral patterns. If, for example, we develop an insecure attachment with our parents, this may generate a pattern of bolting from intimacy, silencing ourselves or acting out. If we are given the message that it's not acceptable to speak up, this may result in people-pleasing to seek approval. If we are repeatedly told that we are beautiful from the inside, self-confidence is more apt to flourish. The positive upside is that no matter how connected or disconnected we felt as children, we all have the capacity to experience secure attachment. This potential is built into our DNA.

During our early foundational years, most of us develop an inner schism as a coping strategy. This protective mechanism is the result of experiencing tension between expressing our truth and receiving the love we need. In many families, it's challenging to reconcile these two aspects. Depending on how we were celebrated and disciplined, we grow up believing that certain behaviors elicit a love response while other behaviors result in punishment. In the mind of a child, the path to love necessitates a certain degree of conformity to our caregiver's wishes. Love and survival are subconsciously held as one and the same. We thereby develop a conflict between living our authentic truth and wanting to be loved. This either-or duality becomes infused into our relationships. It also influences the degree to which we connect with, trust and live in our body.

> "The way we talk to our children becomes their inner voice."
> Peggy O'Mara

In our teenage years, this inner conflict may create facades. We show one thing to others while feeling something different. For the sake of belonging and needing to "fit in," we sacrifice authentic communication. We may fear that we'll betray those we love by speaking our truth. By donning a persona mask, we exaggerate aspects of ourselves that are admired and bury other parts deemed unacceptable. When we don't receive the attention or praise we need, we grow up with the belief that "I'm not good enough." This commonly-held belief, in turn, permeates our relationships. For many people, the light-hearted playful skip and sway of childhood fades. Scarcity or not enoughness trickles into our being: a sense of "lack" competes with attempts to bolster self-esteem. All these fibers from youth are stitched into the cloth of collaboration. Indeed, the tentacles of our childhood memoir are deeply embedded in our relationship woes and triumphs.

The swirl and twirl of separation and unity

All relationships hold the paradox of autonomy or connection. The extent to which we feel "separate from" or "unified with" influences how we walk in this world.

Human beings are conditioned by the paradigm of separation. The backdrop of separation is so omnipresent that it's like a fish not seeing the water in which it swims. The notion of "otherness" has become an unquestioned facet of life. While the roots of this paradigm extend far back in history, seventeenth-century scientists further entrenched the notion of separation by promoting Cartesian mind-body dualism and a Newtonian mechanistic worldview. Reductionism is still taught today. We have learned to analyze, dissect, label and understand all living systems from the perspective of parts, rather than the whole. With this limited lens, we notice disparities, rather than commonalities. We see Life as linear rather than as a complex reality with many points of logic. As such, we diminish the intelligence of the heart, intuition, belly and our sixth sense. The ground of collaboration is soaked with the swirl of separation.

> *"Man knows himself only to the extent that he knows the world; he becomes aware of himself only within the world, and aware of the world only through himself."*
> Johann Wolfgang von Goethe

Perhaps, the feeling of separation is first experienced when our umbilical cord is severed at birth. In the flash of a scissor cut, the felt sense of womb unanimity is gone. With it goes the feeling that all our needs are effortlessly and continuously supported. For some, this feeling of disconnection may trace back to in utero, particularly if the mother was exposed to domestic violence, substance abuse or lack of care. A pregnant woman who feels distress releases stress hormones that impacts the development of the baby's brain. Research shows that in utero babies sense the psychological and emotional stress of the mother.

Furthermore, the very act of birth can hold traumatic memory in our cellular tissue. While difficult to prove, babies can have an internal bodily awareness of abandonment. During maturation, this sensorial experience of "being left" can ooze into our being and, by extension, our relationships. As our ego personality develops, a host of separation-oriented beliefs can seep into the mind. These abandonment-related beliefs include, "I'm not deserving of love. I'm not worthy of care. I'm alone." Many iterations cascade from this wound.

In spite of these beliefs, it's important to realize that we have never been separated from Earth or Life. For the nature of Life is *unity*: the cosmic ecosystem is our source. All sentient beings derive from the same field of energy. Nothing is solid. Each of us is a "shimmer of motes," vibrating in a celestial sea of particles. Many ancient wisdom traditions attest to this notion of non-dualism or interconnection, including Jungian psychology, Taoism, Sikhism, Monism, Buddhism, Zen, Hinduism and contemporary physics. I wonder, *If we held unity consciousness as a tent pole in our worldview, how would our experience of collaboration be different?*

> *"One day you will ask me which is more important? My life or yours? I will say mine and you will walk away not knowing that you are my life."*
> Kahlil Gibran

Consider this dichotomy: Each person is a fractal in the holographic universe. We are differentiated beings yet part of the composite. People perceive themselves as autonomous, yet we are inter-reliant beyond imagination. We want self-sovereignty, yet we also need to belong. Unity is a desired state, yet we need the contrast of separation to understand the nuances of relationship. Relationships offer a dance to find our groove— swirling out for distance and twirling in for connection. Our collaboration efforts reflect this rhythm.

The rhumba of contrast and choice

Unquestionably, contrast is a necessary aspect of our human experience. Binary thinking is commonplace. We cannot see the dark without light, feel warmth without cold, experience love without fear, or tranquility without conflict. Too much sameness dulls the spirit. Contrasting experiences offer the gift of disruption to support our growth and evolution.

As in a photograph, the sharper the contrast, the sharper the image. Disparities help us learn and make distinctions. In doing so, we expand our ability to understand and derive meaning from our relationships. Conflict, for instance, can teach us about boundaries. Scarcity gives us lessons about sufficiency. Grieving loss has us value what's important. Sickness helps us appreciate well-being. Separation gives us insight into connection. The rhumba of contrast and contradiction is an everyday relationship dance.

> "Sometimes opposites attract; sometimes like attracts like. The harmony and dissonance of relationship is the music of life—and a path to self-realization."
> Linda Kohanov

In an intimate relationship, contrast brings us ecstatic love and defenceless vulnerability. When I reflect on my own past relationship pain, I clearly see that contrast was needed, on some level, for my soul to heal. My heart had to close to experience the freedom of opening. My disappointment was an entryway to healing. When I heard criticism and reacted with hurt, I realized that I had not yet integrated this aspect of myself. Relationship feedback shines a spotlight on our strengths and areas of growth. Without contraction, we can't expand.

In lockstep with contrast comes choice. Our choices reveal our desires and aversions. Like a spinning pinwheel, our mind circles with labels for people and things. We sense-make our contrasts. If we magnetize what we don't want, it's an indication of what we subconsciously need but dislike. We may attract partners who are self-centered to help us prioritize our own needs. Or, if we don't know what we want, we may attract an experience that gives us clarity about our desires. If we have people in our life who do not validate us, this may be Life's reminder to self-validate.

As an act of co-creation, self-responsibility is a compelling choice. Because we each contribute to our stories, there's always a piece to own. Even if we find ourselves feeling hatred, jealousy or greed, it's freeing to give ourselves permission to feel and own the experience. Rather than judge, become curious about these thoughts. Keeping silent about our judgment doesn't mean the energy is not transmitted. People can sense this energy and boomerang it back. Emotions, actions *and* thoughts can give rise to relational resistance. Whether we're aware of it or not, we are always in the process of co-creating our relationships. It's a question of how. Every interactive rhumba is a choice in how we vibrationally respond. As Jean Nidetch pointed out, "It's choice, not chance, that determines your destiny."

The ballet of self-growth: accepting self while being open to change

On the heels of contrast, I invite you to ponder this paradoxical notion: in our soul essence, we seek to evolve yet we are whole, complete and beautiful. We do not need to self-improve but rather *discover who we really are*. So if we want to change something about ourselves, make it an exercise in self-love. Do it *for* self-care, not in spite of ourselves. Hold the paradox that we are noble beings and we are continually growing. If we want to fix or get rid of some aspect of ourselves that we don't like, notice how we end up generating resistance. When we resist the resistance, we keep in place that which we don't want. This habit is a form of self-abandonment.

Contrary to popular opinion, fighting with reality is counter to our well-being. It serves us to reflect on the ramifications. Typically, fighting with what's so ends up producing angst and dis-ease. Because our personhood is fragmented due to trauma and conditioning, different personalities coexist within each of us. Meeting these various personalities to support healing is a delicate ballet dance in self-acceptance. This means learning to be okay with who we are regardless of past choices, flaws and mistakes. It means uncorking our suppressed emotions to notice, accept and release the energy. It also entails calming our inner critic by tuning into the message underneath the voice. For example, if we judge ourselves as negative and pessimistic, respect the underlying need for hope. Pessimism may be hiding an unfulfilled longing. It is possible to simultaneously *embrace all* of who we are, while still *being open* to change.

This same principle applies to others. If we attempt to change other people because we judge them as wrong, bad or inappropriate, we engage in manipulation. Force is exercised—be it with energy, words or actions. Even under the guise of "doing

> *People respond to us according to how we relate to them.*

good," any type of force energy that's used to change people is a form of violence. It's an act of dishonoring. On a subtle level, this can include convincing and persuading, which tends to evoke resistance. When people are pushed to do what they do not want to do, this may be perceived as aggression.

If force is used to catalyze change, the change cannot be sustained. This is because fear underpins force, judgment and control; it's built on a deck of cards. To the extent to which I act out of fear is the extent to which I generate fear in the relationship. Pushing and pulling people toward the desired future doesn't work. People only change when *they* want, not when you want. As such, become aware of intention and motivation when collaborating. Give them a sampling of what's possible and people will get on board as they wish. People need to be who they are and to become who they want to be. These are not only fundamental human rights but prerequisites for healthy relationships.

The waltz between the masculine and feminine

Speaking of contrast, another significant relationship feature to unpack is the duality of feminine and masculine. This yin-yang polarity exists within all genders, no matter where we sit on the spectrum. The feminine and masculine interplay points to an artificial yet helpful dynamic. By artificial, note that our true nature is integrated wholeness. We are one unified being even though the felt human experience is fragmented. Earth, along with the human system, is an energetic whole *and* a set of parts.

The feminine aspect is said to be that part of self that creates, listens, allows, receives, connects, nurtures and moves with flow. The masculine aspect takes responsibility, focuses, reasons, acts, protects and supports. Some refer to the feminine as intuitive while the masculine is logical. Others describe the yin aspect as compassionate and the yang as courageous. However you define and hold these energies, both have light and shadow. We need both yin-yang energies to work together to collaborate and move our purpose into the world.

Dancing with our own unique rhythm of masculine-feminine is what I call a tantra waltz. The Sanskrit word *tantra* means "woven together." The feminine and masculine energies are forever weaving together the fabric of how we relate. When our yin-yang energies are harmonized, we are in balance. When they are at battle, we experience inner conflict or resistance. Astonishing authentic power arises when the higher aspects of these two drums beat in sync. The tantra waltz of mutual yin-yang respect brings forth inner calm and peace. Some might say this is our first inner collaboration dance.

Depending on our culture, context and conditioning, it's easy to tilt heavily toward one aspect rather than the other. Often, the tilt is toward the masculine, a split coming from the influence of patriarchy. Etymology-wise, the word *patriarchy* comes from *padre,* or father priests. Patriarchy literally means "the rule of the father." Some scholars state that the spread of patriarchy, as a social system of domination, started about six thousand years ago (4000 BCE). Now, patriarchy is widespread in the world, suffused into almost every culture. It's become a universal code of conduct that carries a set of values and rituals. As sociologist Dr. Carol Gilligan explains, while patriarchy is a "harm-inducing hierarchy that elevates some men over other men and all men over women," this separation is inherently destabilizing for everyone.

Due to patriarchal bias, people in the west tend to favor masculine doing over feminine being. Productivity is seen as a higher value than relaxation. At one time, this imbalance was evident in my life. For all intents and purposes, my masculine-feminine energies were divorced. In discovering this tantra angst, I began to have an inner healing dialogue with my yin-yang aspects. As it turns out, my masculine need to contribute and achieve outranked my feminine need to slow down and tune into my intuitive wisdom. In reaction, my feminine felt rage in being dismissed and silenced. Both sides suffered. My masculine was exhausted and frustrated while my feminine voice felt utterly closed down. These polarizing energies glared at each other from either side of the boxing ring. This lack of inner coherence soiled my outer relationships with passive-aggressive tendencies. For instance, I would agree to do something yet secretly resent feeling obligated. It took a great deal of compassionate arbitration to bridge-build within.

Responding to this yin-yang brawl involved facing the power struggle that comes with the dragon of patriarchy. As Gary Zukav noted, "A power struggle collapses when you withdraw your energy from it. Power struggles become uninteresting when you change your intention from winning to learning about yourself." To support these dueling energies, I created space for my masculine and feminine to be heard. I embraced, validated and honored each part. Over time, my fatigue lifted, my breathing deepened, my speech slowed and my movement decelerated. As it turns out, my masculine-feminine reconciliation waltz was a field test to discover the real meaning of authentic self-collaboration. This dialogue continues today.

> *"If any human being is to reach full maturity, both the masculine and feminine sides of the personality must be brought up into consciousness."*
> Mary Esther Harding

Our tango with control

During our infant and toddler stage, we experience our first taste of what we can and can't control. Without words, we sense into our relational power by assessing our caregiver's reactions and trying to get our needs met. We learn the tango of control to avoid being "out of control." Even though control offers a false sense of security, somehow it becomes an essential coping strategy. As we grow, we seek a degree of predictability and certainty.

During this early conditioning, many people collapse the concepts of control and power as though they are one and the same. Yet, control comes from fear while authentic power comes from our essence. The former is a coping strategy rooted in insecurity while the latter is an uplifting energy sourced from our soul. When we harness our authentic power, we may feel a sense of control, yet our deeper wisdom will remind us that there is very little in our control. It's worth noting that the more empowered we become, the less need we have for control.

When we move into adulthood, we learn even more about the tango of control in relationship. Although we try to control others, we discover, often the hard way, that we can only control ourselves. As previously noted, we can only control the way we think, speak, listen and behave. Everything else we influence. As such, focusing on these four parts of self is a true investment in our empowerment. Even if we seem to be successful in controlling others through demands, aggression, guilt or manipulation, this desired behavior change does not have sticking power. Fear-based force

> *"Incredible change happens in your life when you decide to take control of what you do have power over instead of craving control over what you don't."*
> Steve Maraboli

energy is, by definition, unsustainable. Attempts to control compromises the integrity of our relationships.

On a spectrum, controlling behaviors can be as subtle as convincing, persuading, cajoling on the one side or blatant with demands, intimidation and aggression. On the surface, it may seem as though control works as a strategy to support our needs. But control comes with a price. As psychologist Dr. Marshall Rosenberg astutely wrote, "When the other person hears a demand, they see two options: to submit or to rebel. Neither is effective in healthy relationship-building." If we believe that controlling people leads to the change we want, notice how the change has been artificially propped up with fear. The tango of control erodes the cement on the bridge of authentic collaboration.

The disco of trust

Besides control, trust is another universal choice point in the orbit of relationships. Some suggest that it's the first decision we make in our early years. While the elusive quality of trust is widely believed to be the bedrock of every relationship, it plays out paradoxically. It's in our nature to desire trust but still want the option to shield against potential harm. Depending on the disco vibe, the door of trust continually swings to open and close.

Albert Einstein stated, "The most important decision we make is whether we believe we live in a friendly or hostile universe." This decision either builds or depletes trust. When things go our way, we tend to relax into trust. However, when unpleasant circumstances inevitably pay a visit, it's easy to form negative belief loops. Common limiting beliefs that influence our ability to trust include: Life is unfair. Earth (or Life) is cruel. Life is punishing.

> *Do you perceive Life as friendly or hostile?*

If you have thought or spoken these or similar words, how does this inner conflict affect you? Moreover, how does this distrust impact your ability to relate with others? Perceiving Life as hostile can perpetuate the notion that others and our bodies are enemies, and that Life is problematic. It ends up becoming a battle with self that generates a vicious cycle. What we resist persists in attracting more of the same patterns. Inadvertently, we end up repeating again and again what we don't want in our lives. The disco of distrust can prevent us in giving and receiving what we want.

With the privilege of travel, I have a heightened appreciation for the role of trust. On one risky escapade, I remember leaving home with words of caution ringing in my ears. Yet, I held on to the belief that "Life is friendly." I intended to travel with ease, not with a fear knot in my stomach. Then, one day, I was attacked by a group of five men in a dark alley in South America. In their attempt to steal my money belt and backpack, I was robbed and beaten. Shaken to the core, I was at a choice point. I could continue my journey with an open mind and trust in the flow and friendliness of Life, or believe that Life was hostile. If I chose hostility, I would become an anxious traveler. I would likely end up flying home prematurely with an unrealized dream. This was not an option.

So, I continued to travel…and heal. I consciously adopted a new set of beliefs to renew my trust. Self-talk took on a whole new meaning. I noticed how my body contracted with fear-based beliefs and expanded with heart-centered thoughts. With the former, I became a prisoner in my own hotel room, handcuffed to my perception of danger. With the latter, I opened to the mystery, yielding to the magic, awe and beauty of Life. I dug deep to reconnect with and trust my intuition, and to the goodness in others. The more I did so, the more I attracted amazing people and experiences. I soon discovered that adventure was not about seeking new landscapes but having new eyes. This same truth applies to the adventure of relationship.

The hip-hop of projection and expectation

Projection. Here's how it works. We all have assumptions, needs, feelings, desires and values that influence how we show up and connect with others. What we do not observe and lovingly own becomes projected outward. Most of the time, this process is unconscious. If we have an unpleasant emotion such as guilt or anger, this can take the form of judgment. If we are afraid of vulnerability, this can result in attacking those we dislike or perceive as weak. Psychologists label this externalization as projecting shadows: those personality parts we perceive as unacceptable. It's a way to protect the ego from uncomfortable

> *"What happens in the world is real, what one thinks should happen is projection."*
> Jacques Fresco

thoughts and impulses. Instead of owning this, we attribute them onto others. As psychologist Carl Jung observed, "Projection is an unconscious factor which spins the illusions that veil his world. And what is being spun is a cocoon, which in the end will completely envelop him."

In addition, Jung noted that "All projections provoke counter-projection." What we are unaware of will be projected back onto the projector, giving rise to a mutual acting-out. An example is a spouse who has an affair yet claims that her partner is unfaithful. Or someone who has not dealt with his childhood abuse flings his pain onto his pets with excessive control and punishment. Or, when a climate activist who has repressed grief over global warming angrily judges those with a large carbon lifestyle. Human exploitation and damage to the natural world is often a reflection of buried wounds that play out in commerce. On the flip side, we also project positive opinions onto people such as only perceiving a new lover in a glowing light. We see what we *want to see*.

Since all relationships have a degree of projection, doing our own shadow work alleviates this pattern. This involves a practice of self-responsibility in withdrawing the projection and, instead, tracing back to the origins. It takes a heightened degree of self-awareness and radical honesty to acknowledge, digest and integrate what has been disowned.

> *Relationship expectations can be a way of dealing with lack—an attempt to fill up the emptiness within.*

Expectations are also projected into the hip-hop of relationships as a way for people to disconnect from the present moment and forecast what they want to happen. Unmet expectations from the past may create regret, grief, sadness and shame. Projected unmet expectations about the future may create depression, anxiety, feelings of inadequacy, impatience and hopelessness. Too many expectations can create a sense of entitlement for the giver and obligation in the receiver. It's a delicate tight-rope. This aspect of relationship requires ongoing recalibration.

While not good nor bad per se, expectations can set the stage for disappointment and stress. This is because expectations can be a muted form of control: communicating our desire so that others conform to our wishes. In the workplace, it's a tricky proposition to communicate expectations because what one person may perceive to be realistic, another person may see as unrealistic. If the relationship is not strong enough to honestly dialogue about expectations over time, then people can and do resort to maladaptive choices such as calling in sick, disengaging, doing the bare minimum or even quitting. If an agreement was not honored, it's helpful to unpack the expectations. Were they spoken and doable? Was there shared understanding? The power imbalance of work roles can make expectations a thorny issue. These issues constitute a portion of the collaboration contemporary dance mix.

The foxtrot of the human-Earth relationship

In modern history, the human-Earth relationship seems to be based on one key tenet: the environment belongs to humans and is thus a component of the human economy. Given this, it seems logical that people use as much "natural capital" as possible to operate and grow the economy. This is a false belief since humans share the planet with millions of species *and* ever-increasing growth is scientifically impossible on a finite planet. Earth is waking humans up to this reality by way of extreme weather events, a 60 percent average population decline of vertebrate species, the loss of half the world's coral reefs and a third of all wetlands. I often wonder, *What would it look like if this one assumption was reversed to support the commonwealth of Life?*

Years ago, I took this question into a four-day solo vision quest to develop a stronger relationship with Earth. This nature immersion practice is ancient, as indigenous peoples have used this contemplative rite of passage since the dawn of humanity. My intention was to commune with spirit, plant and animal guides and use ceremony to step into the unknown. I fasted so a feeling of emptiness could allow for new insights. I began by calling in a vision not only for my own well-being but to elevate others as well.

During this vision quest, I was shown two things in my dreams. The first was how every being benefits from the protective ozone layer, air and water of the planet as well as the medicine, food and energy sources that come from the land. Yet, we have not established a shared sacred responsibility to steward Earth and all our relations. A second revelation pertained to bridge-building between humans and

> "What you do not know you will fear. What one fears one destroys."
> Chief Dan George

Earth. We need to rewild our spirit by adjusting to her rhythm, listening to her whispers, walking barefoot on her soil, feeling our hair rustled by her wind and having our cheeks sun-kissed. We need to let go of our fear, appreciate her wisdom and surrender into her care. On the heels of this quest came a question: "How can people find ecologically sound solutions when their soul is not attuned to the soul of Earth?"

Now, I see the human-Earth foxtrot as essential to transforming our destiny and how we relate overall.

The rock and roll of self-transformation

At a yoga retreat I attended, I heard a story about a group of monks in Thailand. In 1957, these monks decided to relocate a monastery, which included moving a huge clay Buddha statue. One day, a monk noticed a crack in the statue. A golden light beamed out from the crack. Becoming curious, he took a hammer and started chiseling away. Lo and behold, he uncovered a statue made of solid pure gold that had likely been covered with clay to protect it from an invading Burmese army. An incredible treasure was waiting to be unveiled.

Similarly, people also have beautiful golden rays of heart love, light and beauty within their essence. This is our true nature, waiting to be expressed in our relationships with self, others and Earth. Nonetheless, layers of clay have been packed into our persona by family and societal conditioning. Over time, we take on habits to protect our vulnerable hearts. The protective clay slowly hardens until we forget who we really are. Some common limiting beliefs include:

I'm not safe. * I can't trust. * I can't forgive. *
I can't rely on others. * I'm inadequate.

The great news is that none of this conditioning is permanent. We can chip away at the clay of our coping strategies and replace old relationship habits that no longer serve. When we become aware of our mental models, we have the choice to transfigure our relationships and collaborate from a space of greater ease. The key is understanding that our subconscious beliefs override our conscious beliefs and, in turn, form our habits. In becoming aware of our behavior, we can change those beliefs and responses at will.

Neuroplasticity research shows that we have the power to create new neural pathways and rewire our brains with affirming beliefs. Our electromagnetic field is never fixed. New circuitry can amend our brain structure, function, memory and learning. With a daily mindfulness practice, we can develop the discipline to think, say and feel into a new set of beliefs. With love, grace and forgiveness, new brain synapse connections can form. Our heart of gold becomes the great integrator, healing our nervous system and melting the protein bonds of repressed emotion. We can adopt and embody empowering beliefs such as:

> *"Nothing ever goes away until it has taught us what we need to know."*
> *Pema Chödrön*

*I'm capable. * I am worthy of respect. * I am valued. *
I am love and abundance. * I create peace.*

It's an act of self-emancipation to unwind belief threads, noticing how they shape our bodies and behavior. Even if our childhood was filled with negativity, we can create fulfilling, enriching relationships at any point in our lives.

To rock and roll your self-transformation journey, consider the following questions with gentle curiosity. Feel into the clay that wants to crack open. With new eyes, see the gold within you.

Reflecting on the Nature of Relationships with Self, Others and Earth

1. How does your childhood story influence your relationships?
2. How do you dance between separation (distance) and unity (belonging)?
3. How does your self-talk affect how you relate with others?
4. What is your relationship with power and control?
5. What brings you pain and happiness in your relationships?
6. If your feminine spoke to your masculine, what would she say? Vice-versa?
7. How would you describe the degree to which you trust Earth or Life?
8. What projections and expectations are you noticing today?
9. What is the dance of drama in your life?
10. What self-transformation choice do you want to make today?

The polka between relationships and collaboration

While all these aspects offer only a glimpse of the relationship terrain, they all point to its ultimate purpose. Relationships offer a portal to discover that we are love, loved, loving and loveable.

> *"One does not become enlightened by imagining figures of light but by making the darkness conscious."*
> Carl Jung

With this in mind, may we feel inspired to dive more deeply into our personality and soul. May we remember who we really are, and who we want to become. May we better understand the contours of collaboration. May we bring greater awareness to our interpersonal dark shadows. May we bring fresh eyes to our long-term relationships. May we reclaim our power as initiators of both cause and effect. Side by side, let's lean into and on each other to see people without labels, pre-judgment and fixed conclusions. From the inside out, let's rewrite our narrative, realign with our heart and choose uplifting behaviors. Let's live inside the expression of our gifts.

It's time for the scoop and sway of our relationships to recalibrate with love. A happier home life, organizational impact, community vitality and global peacebuilding are all at stake.

CHAPTER 6

REFLECTING ON WHY AUTHENTIC COLLABORATION MATTERS

"Ultimately, the only thing that matters in life is the quality of our relationships."
Margaret Mead

The bullseye of *why*

The compelling question of *why* lies at the center of the Golden Circle. Simon Sinek, an American leadership coach, popularized this Golden Circle to help leaders differentiate their value proposition. This Circle holds three concentric rings: the inner *why*, middle *how* and outer *what*. After examining patterns about how great leaders and organizations think, act and communicate, Sinek expounds on the idea that "people do not buy what you do, they buy why you do it." He notes that many people can explain what they do and even detail how they deliver on their what. Yet, many are challenged to articulate succinctly and powerfully their why.

On a deeper level, our why story reveals the bridge arc of who we really are. How we tell our story is what moves others to believe in, champion and invest in our dreams. This is as true for individuals as it is for organizations and communities. On a larger scale, our stories even mold the rise and fall of movements. Our stories are the teapot from which we pour out our creativity, sorrow, hopes and fears.

> *"Meet me in the middle of your story when the soul is worn but wise."*
> Angie Weiland-Crosby

So this begs the questions, "Why does authentic collaboration matter to you? What is your motivating story to develop healthier relationships with self, others and Earth?"

My *why* story

While the chronicle of my life is multi-faceted, here is a slice that frames my *why* story. It revolves around the closing and reopening of my heart, a process that I am deeply invested in and will continue until my last breath.

As a newborn, I entered this world with an open, pure, innocent heart. Yet, with chronic, complex trauma experiences throughout my childhood, my heart began to close. The details don't matter but the effect did. I felt numb inside. I found it difficult to authentically express at home and at school. My heart lost its luster as I became hyper-vigilant. I either had a hard time trusting or I over-trusted. The deep connection that I craved as soul food eluded me. It was like reaching for a snowflake only to have it melt in my hand. My desire for authentic connection, and the feeling of safety and belonging that I imagined it would bring me, seemed to be forever a stone's throw away. To borrow a phrase from Shakespeare, my focus was not "to be or not to be" but rather "to connect or not to connect." That was the question that stirred me.

In my younger years, I struggled with being guarded and defensive yet also wanting to be open-hearted. This inner conflict had me feeling distant from people. Detached. Invisible. I stood on the periphery of Life, looking in from the outside. I recall holding on to fight energy, anticipating attack or rejection. My overactive nervous system was tenaciously "battle-ready." In my relationships with family, and eventually with colleagues and romantic partners, I carried an energetic sword of protection, just in case the dagger of judgment appeared. When people came knocking, very few could penetrate the facade. I saw loneliness in the eyes of people around me because I too felt the pang of separation. My important relationships had a chronic push-pull dynamic, with my heart aching for yet avoiding intimacy. In my relationship blueprint, I sought out connection yet felt misunderstood. Self-criticism became my side companion. If someone had scratched below the surface, the wound of isolation would begin to bleed. I remember wanting to be gently held.

> *"To heal is to touch with love that which we previously touched with fear."*
> Stephen Levine

In adulthood, I enjoyed many caring relationships, but my heart felt somewhat anesthetized. My outer self took on travel, adventure and public service. I lived in New York and throughout Africa while working globally. I loved this lifestyle, yet a persistent low-grade tremor of fear haunted me. I discovered two parts of myself walking side by side: one that felt comfortable everywhere I went in the world and another part that did not feel safe. I presented with confidence even though parts of me were frozen from the inside out. Friends noticed patterns of over-accommodation and over-responsibility. An undercurrent of relationship power struggles, conflict aggression and betrayal had left an indelible mark.

At one point, a convergence of events led to a personal crisis; my father was dying, my workaholism became relentless, a significant work relationship deteriorated and another romantic partnership ended. I began to experience deep exhaustion. Soul fatigue. Self-neglect had taken its toll and my inner fire waned. Even though I slept for more than twelve hours a night, I woke up tired. Daily functioning became strenuous. For the first time in my life, I was concerned about my health.

As a thoughtful gesture, a friend gifted me with a card that sparked a choice-point. The card held a quote by Anais Nin: "And the day came when the risk to remain tight in a bud was more painful than the risk it took to blossom." In reading these words, I knew I had to melt my heavy heart armor. I took the risk.

When did you last take the risk to heal your heart?

I decided to plunge down a whispering well. It had steep sides and felt like a bottomless pit. I sought out wise teachers who led me to the light of my truth. They helped me realize that my ice-laden parts, and all the emotions buried under the groundwater, were crying out for loving attention. I brought my outward scattered energy inward to crawl into the quiet recesses of my mind. With courage and curiosity, I began to climb out of this dark well by reconfiguring my relationship with self. I tenderly inched toward my feelings of shame, frustration and hopelessness. Every time I embraced my vulnerability, I gained a new foothold. Slowly, my raw, tender, quivering heart found its voice. By honoring the empty ache inside, I swung over the edge to transcend the well of pain. My inner freeze gradually started to thaw.

AUTHENTIC COLLABORATION

With support from loved ones and a kind-hearted coach, my younger, disenfranchised parts received devoted care. I slowly digested the ache while tasting the bitter-sweetness of radical honesty. I listened to my heart and rebuilt my self-worth. As I grieved, I noticed incremental growth spurts in my relationships. I boldly owned my perspectives, even when I felt vulnerable. I set healthier boundaries and asked for what I wanted. In my daily yoga practice and by journaling, I reflected on my reactive impulses, developed my emotional literacy and tuned into my intuitive guidance. The yoga of relationship enticed me. My journey of healing revolved around compassionate space-holding for myself—space to be heard, space to discover. I experienced love as spacious presence—a state of being that allows me to be me and you to be you. From this relaxed space of acceptance comes the flowering of genuine connection.

> *"Compassion to oneself and all that lives is the most powerful transformational energy in the world."*
> Dalai Lama

In one defining moment, a teacher took the time to notice me, the real me. An invitation soon followed to step onto the path of shamanism. I immediately received a revitalizing booster shot. As a nature-based healing wisdom tradition, shamanism involves connecting with Earth, animals, plants, stones, the elements and spirit guides. This source of energy medicine offered a series of mystical experiences that transformed my life. My connection with my heart and with Mother Earth expanded. I clearly saw how these threads dovetail. Through soul retrieval, rituals, fire ceremonies, nature walks, drum journeys, kirtan chanting and dream work, my wounds became wonders. With the *power of nature* and the grace of authentic *self*-collaboration, I integrated more fragmented aspects of myself.

As I made peace out of the pieces, I felt a greater sense of wholeness. The muscle weight of relationship intelligence strengthened within me. Authentic collaboration became something real versus imagined. I was able to navigate multicultural experiences and complex organizational dynamics with greater ease. I grew my bravery in having hard conversations. Developing a healthier, honest self-relationship became my priority. With nourishing connections, I felt a new-found optimism.

AUTHENTIC COLLABORATION

My desire for meaningful connection has been instrumental in shaping who I am and who I've become. Now, my relationships blossom with a different fragrance. With the softening of my heart, I can attune to and express the gentleness of my spirit even more so. Challenges, of course, still arise and I continue to live imperfectly. Yet my mantra has become the practice of detached love: accepting and nurturing myself and others without control. Just as I want people to respect the role I play in their lives, I also respect how people want to connect (or not) with me. I've learned that the hooks, attachments and promises we rely on offer no guarantees. I'm growing to understand that in an authentic collaborative relationship, there is space to fully show up as who I am and for others to do so as well. In each moment, we choose how we want to relate.

> *"There are two great days in a person's life—the day we are born and the day we discover why."*
> William Barclay

With this as one aspect of my story, the *why* of my life is to unleash empowerment, foster meaningful connection and inspire greater heart expression. My story evolves as I do. Authentic collaboration has become the vessel to hold the potential for ayni or respectful relating with self, others and Earth. This is my Golden Circle bullseye.

The micro story is in the macro

I believe that the kernel of my story also lives in the collective psyche. The micro is in the macro. How do you balance self-respect with respect for others and Earth? When your heart is bruised, how do you heal? How do you reopen the part of you that is closed? These story lines are universal.

I liken these common human threads to Joseph Campbell's archetypal hero's journey. The odyssey starts with a call to adventure. At some point, the path leads us into the abyss, where we experience the clichéd "'dark night of the soul." A process of atonement brings forth an inner-outer reckoning. As we let go, we let come. In growing and transforming, we return "home" to our hearts. We discover that our relationships are a gift to be embraced, even if it comes wrapped in a ribbon of pain. We realize that the ultimate gift is our presence, pun intended.

However you describe your *why* story, I bow to your shadow and light. I pay tribute to the shape, curves and lines of your relationship stream. Undoubtedly, each being on your path has contributed to your own unique brand of radiance.

Nine other reasons why authentic collaboration matters

In considering your personal *why* story and the wider community of our world, I invite you to reflect on why authentic collaboration matters from nine other angles.

Key Reasons Why Authentic Collaboration Matters

Collaboration is in our nature.
1. Interdependently, we survive by connecting with self, others and Earth.
2. We are clan-oriented social creatures.
3. Humans are biologically and socially predisposed to cooperate.

Collaboration supports core human needs.
4. Authentic collaboration fosters connection, belonging and well-being.
5. People learn and grow through collaboration.
6. Collaborative work cultures deepen engagement, performance and trust.

Collaboration is a crucial path to address complex issues.
7. Complex systems change necessitates collaboration across sectors and disciplines.
8. Collaboration unleashes creativity and innovative solutions.
9. Sustainable outcomes arise from authentic communication and shared ownership.

Collaboration is in our nature.

1. Interdependently, we survive by connecting with self, others and Earth.

On this tiny blue dot spinning in space, human survival depends on our ability to respect and care for Earth. If we ignore the subtle ripples of Earth consciousness, we diminish our own Life force. Like trees, we cannot remain standing without our relational root system. Many are seduced into thinking that we are independent, autonomous, self-governing people on this planet, yet our cord to Earth can never be sheared…until our last breath. Even if we hold allegiance to our country, every human being is ultimately an Earth citizen.

AUTHENTIC COLLABORATION

As the adage goes: "No person is an island." This maxim alone provides impetus to grow our collaboration skills. On the most self-centered level, we need to cooperate with others to achieve basic goals such as obtaining housing, clothes and food. We cannot maintain any lifestyle without the contribution of a village. It is a grand misperception to believe that what we do does not affect other Life forms. Whether we're aware or not, our thoughts, words and actions cascade out to the world every day.

This African proverb underscores the nature of interdependency: "When a small toe is hurting, the whole body swoops down to attend to it." When one part of the Earth body suffers, all residents suffer as well. On the flip side, when one being expands into greater peace, others rejoice. The pageantry of soil, trees, plants, animals, wind, clouds and sun is a testament to the joy of Life. This is authentic collaboration at its best.

> "We need joy as we need air. We need love as we need water. We need each other as we need the earth we share."
> Maya Angelou

When I visited the Sahara Desert, I was amazed to see camel-mounted nomads living in harmony on inhospitable land. The desert, at first glance, seemed uninhabitable. Yet, I learned that countless animals, insects, plants and shrubs have adapted well to the harsh environment. The plants help the soil retain water, prevent erosion and provide life-giving shade to insects. In the food web, hawks prey on a desert lizard or snake, which in turn feeds upon rats or insects, which feed upon cacti or grasses. Be it in deserts, forests, oceans, meadows or mountains, the interplay of nature holds mystery, medicine, magnetism and mythology.

When I worked in Tanzania, I witnessed the interdependence of Life on proud display again in the Serengeti Plains. There, the great zebra and wildebeest migration unfolded in grandeur. I was amazed to see millions of animals traveling across the landscape, co-journeying with mutual support. While the wildebeest has a good sense of hearing and smell, the zebra has excellent eyesight. One's strength is the other's weakness. Together, both animals receive extra protection from predators. With swarm-like synergetic intelligence, the zebras feed on the long tough plain grasses while the wildebeests feed on the shorter grasses. They complement and support each other as lifelong traveling partners.

Recent discoveries in physics also shed light on the astounding interconnection held within Life. As it turns out, the fundamental building blocks of matter are *not* particles. Rather, a quantum field is what underpins our universe. This field is a continuous fluid-like substance that holds and moves particles in a constant interchange. David Tong, a quantum physicist, explains that these electric and magnetic fields are what gives rise to the different interactions between particles. Both the particles in our body and those in the ecosystem of nature produce a tiny ripple in the underlying quantum field.

On this level, authentic collaboration matters because the practice recognizes that every interaction affects the quantum field: each energy-filled body plays a role in the cosmic web. Thanks to science, we now know definitively that Self, others and Earth are three strands in the same relational field.

2. We are clan-oriented social beings.

As clan-oriented beings, humans lead healthier lives with strong collaborative social ties. The five "blue zones" in the world underscore this fact. These zones, located in Greece, Italy, California, Costa Rica and Japan, have the largest concentration of centenarians in the world.

At the turn of this century, journalist and explorer Dan Buettner began to research this Blue Zone longevity phenomenon. He included scientists such as medical researchers, anthropologists, demographers, and epidemiologists. They searched for evidence-based common denominators. Their research showed that there are five characteristics shared by "blue zone people" who live beyond 100 years of age:

1. exercise daily with low-intensity physical movement,
2. eat a mainly plant-based diet,
3. have a sense of purpose,
4. derive meaning in a faith-based tradition, and
5. enjoy caring relationships in a strong social network.

This last point accentuates the value of authentic collaborative relationships in which respect and caring are cultivated and savored. For example, in one of the blue zones, Okinawan, Japan, *moais* are created. These moais are groups of five friends, a small social pod, who are committed to one another for life. Authentic collaboration draws from this tone of social connection in offering the benefits of mutual support, belonging and well-being.

Some may argue that *self-interest* is more apparent in the world than a collaborative clan-oriented social reality. As proof, they reference the many ways people are oppressed and disenfranchised. They characterize the global economy as a dog-eat-dog system whereupon the rich get richer at the expense of others. They point to the Darwinian mantra, survival of the fittest, and how that mindset reveals itself in many cultures. Selfish gain, savage conflict and violence penetrate our media and entertainment channels. Punishing prisoners with isolation continues to be a form of torture in jails. War rages on. Human rights violations persist. In government, party advantage overrules political cooperation to move legislation forward. Lobby groups endure. With deep pockets, these interest groups sway the vote, regardless of what's in the best interest of the greater whole. Suffice to say there is ample reason to conclude that self-interest is alive and well.

While self-interest does exist, we are nonetheless biologically wired to cooperate. The truth remains—we need each other as social beings. Instinctually, we understand that the welfare of others impacts us on some level. At a primal level, when we look out for the well-being of others, we're actually supporting our own protection. Our inner resiliency is linked to the health of our outer relationships. As an adaptive necessity, people benefit from communal collaboration. Ethically, our conscience prompts us to consider how our actions affect others. We suffer in the absence of connection and belonging.

> *"Human beings are social animals. We were social before we were human."*
> Peter Singer

In our global economy, individuals, communities and nations depend on one another more than ever. The rise of a capitalist free market is based on the exchange of goods and services. With free trade, imports and exports allow our store shelves to be filled with an assortment of items. The barter of goods depends on give and take. When gas prices rise and fall based on cross-national supply and demand, we all feel the pinch in our wallets. Even our social systems are impacted by the division of labor. As clan-oriented beings who need each other, we coexist with the intertwining thread of commerce. Authentic collaboration is a campaign for healthy interdependence and prosperity for all.

3. Humans are predisposed to cooperate.

Our human evolutionary heritage is cooperation, a cousin of collaboration. As social animals, humans not only need to cooperate to survive but want to do so as well. We naturally desire community. When we receive love, support and resources, we look for ways to reciprocate. As such, reciprocity accounts for a large part of cooperation. Our friendships bear this out. If someone offers a random act of kindness, we want to follow suit—and even pay it forward. Healthy reciprocation is a doorway to aliveness and an invitation for caring outreach.

Authentic collaboration is all of this and more. It's an opportunity to support each other, co-create something new and negotiate needs for the sake of mutual gain. Working together with respect offers goodwill and an all-around positive karmic boomerang. It's a goal enabler by blending the inspired action of masculine energy with the creative flow of feminine energy. Cooperating and collaborating as a team fosters peer learning, creativity, task sharing and inclusive decison-making.

In the book entitled *Origins of Altruism and Cooperation* by Robert Sussman and Robert Cloninger, the authors posit that humans are naturally cooperative, altruistic and social. People only revert to violence when stressed, abused, neglected or mentally ill. Their findings come with interdisciplinary evidence from anthropology, psychiatry, biology, sociology, religion and medicine. "Cooperation isn't just a by-product of competition, or something done only because both parties receive some benefit from the partnership," writes Sussman. "Rather, altruism and cooperation are inherent in all primates, including humans."

While working in the Middle East, I had the good fortune of witnessing altruism and cooperation when I coached a community group. This group was focused on the depletion of trees in their region since the village depended on trees as their fuel source for cooking. Improper forest management, over time, resulted in clear-cutting and poor regrowth. When people came together to discuss this issue, there was an instinctual need to combine forces for the benefit of all, including the forest. Choosing not to would lead to serious repercussions for every living being in that territory. So they embarked on a collaboration journey with each other and the forest to map the causal factors of local deforestation. Together, they paid attention to Earth's patterns and identified ecologically sound solutions. One of the action steps was to write and submit a proposal to secure 75,000 fuel-efficient cooking stoves. This group was successful in not only acquiring the donated stoves, but also in developing a community-wide environmental education program. They listened deeply, asserted with care and respected diverse viewpoints. Earth stewardship was held as their primary consideration. With a united effort, the community group designed a regenerative program to restore the remaining forest by planting over 100,000 native trees. This remarkable story speaks to our predisposition to cooperate for the greater good.

> "Interdependent people combine their own efforts with the efforts of other to achieve their greatest success."
> Stephen Covey

Collaboration supports core human needs.

4. Authentic collaboration fosters connection, belonging and well-being.

The need to belong is universal. In the practice of authentic collaboration, we grow the conditions for emotional safety to cultivate genuine connection and belonging. With emotional bravery, we make conscious choices about who we are, who we want to become and how to co-create the results we want. Quality dialogue supports the tendons and ligaments of relational connection. With a slower pace of speaking, empathetic listening and meaningful sharing, the heart opens to receive the gift of togetherness.

Belonging improves people's well-being. With social bonding cues and behaviors, the brain produces neuropeptides such as oxytocin. These so-called happy hormones have a positive effect on our emotions, contributing to relaxation, trust and psychological stability. Stress subsides. Loneliness abates. Group affinity helps build resiliency to cope with hardship. Belonging gives us a sense of security, purpose and even shapes our identity. Given that the bridge of authentic collaboration supports social connectivity, inclusion and open-hearted dialogue, this way of relating is directly tied to mind-body-spirit well-being. The experience of mutual respect nutrifies the soul.

5. People learn and grow through collaboration.

The path of learning is central to authentic collaboration. Conscious relationship-building is a field saturated with rich compost to grow our potential. The opportunity for individual learning and group co-learning is built-into every interaction.

From my own collaboration experience, here's a snippet of what I've learned and continue to learn.

After a sensitive family interaction, I saw the double bind of a "problem" mindset. These two beliefs kept me stuck: I am the problem, and the problem is outside of me. The former evoked shame and guilt while the latter left me powerless. With this insight, I began to de-colonize my mind with a new understanding of self-responsibility. I unshackled accountability from the toxicity of blame.

With a work team, I saw our pattern of being inward-focused. To counter this habit, I suggested we change course and speak to our clients about how *they experienced* our service delivery. Their feedback helped us feedforward in focusing on future-oriented solutions. As we reconfigured our department, the dialogue caused fear and resistance. We made a deliberate choice to not only be goal-focused and data-driven, but also to respect our experience of change. With a process of open, honest communication, we overhauled our operations *and* our ability to function as a team.

I once completed a 25-foot firewalk by briskly walking on red, hot coals with bare feet. While the experience was set-up to demonstrate mind over matter and emotional prowess, I realized that my trust in Earth had deepened to a whole new level. Because I trusted Life, I anticipated ease and foresaw no blisters, no burn, no harm. The firewalk was effortless. My state created my story. I learned that the thoughts and words I attach to my experience becomes my experience.

A friend and I were collaborating on a project when she felt triggered. Conflict erupted. Instead of trying to change her behavior, I changed *my* behavior. Rather than react with upset, I dropped into my heart and gave her an unexpected loving response. She was startled into silence, giving us time to pause and reconnect. I learned that it takes two to tango but only one to change the dance.

Community volunteering has long been a part of my life. My collaboration with one group was particularly effective. Looking back, I noted three distinctions. First, we dignified the unique learning and contribution styles of each person. Secondly, we welcomed real-world, relevant knowledge and ongoing feedback from those we served. Based on our refined understanding, we adapted accordingly. Third, we asked tough questions because we saw our work together as an altruistic learning experiment. Failure was reframed as a chance to co-learn and adapt again. A respect-for-all learning dialogue was a mainstay in our culture. It gave me a memorable experience of peaceful relations.

> *"The means is dialogue, the end is learning, the purpose is peace."*
> Dr. Jane Vella

From these interactions and many others, I've come to understand that there is a circular relationship between authentic collaboration, learning and growth. This interplay is designed to support our pursuit towards personal mastery and healthy community-building. When we learn, the organizations we are a part of learn. Our growth emits feel-good emotions which, in turn, nurtures meaningful connection. And so, the virtuous wheel turns.

6. Collaborative cultures deepen engagement, performance and trust.

A relational field shapes every organization's culture, be it in business, government, media, arts, healthcare, agriculture, social services or education. This is the cultural undercurrent of how we solve problems, make decisions and get things done. How we collaborate affects our ability to perform, tackle issues, make progress and feel fulfilled. In a Forbes article, writer Adi Gaskell references a joint study between the Institute for Corporate Productivity (i4cp) and Rob Cross, Edward A. Madden Professor of Global Business at Babson College. This study found that companies which promoted collaboration were five times more likely to be high-performing.

AUTHENTIC COLLABORATION

The sports arena also reflects the positive effects of collaboration. When a basketball team develops strong collaborative relationships, each player demonstrates court vision. This is the skill of attuning to fellow players while executing to block, dribble, charge forward or shoot. It's also about looking for a teammate who is open and able to take a pass. In addition, team collaboration ramps up accountability. It's less threatening to take responsibility for mistakes if the team responds with respect. When care is shown, people are more inclined to become and stay engaged.

> "Talent wins games, but teamwork and intelligence wins championships."
> Michael Jordan

In municipalities, actively engaging residents spawns a citizen-centric culture. Sharing power with citizen-led committees, for example, can support and advance issues such as housing, transportation, educational outreach and environmental stewardship. The benefits of collaboration include an effective use of resources, a shared work burden, enriched community life and greater social cohesion. The days of City Hall "going it alone" are over, given the complex issues we face.

How to engage people is often a workplace preoccupation. I recently read this line in a newspaper: "We live and work with a screen saver attitude." The article described how many of us are on yet off at the same time. We show up but are not fully present. The term *engaged* is defined as those who are involved in, enthusiastic about and committed to their work and workplace. Engagement is highly correlated to performance and positive organizational outcomes. Gallup research shows that the annual percentage of engaged US workers has averaged only 30 percent during the past eighteen years. On a global level in 2022, engagement sat at 21 percent. Only 33 percent of employees are thriving in their well-being. This staggering level of disengagement correlates with the lost art of collaboration.

Authentic collaboration offers a powerful antidote to disengagement. When people work with respect and trust, transformation can (and does) occur. I saw this unfold in an organization that experienced fast and deep-cutting changes. This reorganization plummeted morale while staff turnover skyrocketed. As a consultant, I

> "Great things in business are never done by one person. They are done by a team of people."
> Steve Jobs

conducted a needs assessment to discern ways to reverse this downward spiral. The findings were clear and consistent: authentic collaboration was a recommended leverage opportunity.

To catalyze transformation, the management team started by adopting a solutions-oriented, no-blame approach. When complaints surfaced by employees, empathetic listening and inquiry were offered. Questions were designed to elicit creative thinking so that the team would shift away from fault-finding and into brainstorming. Many employee ideas were green lit to support and encourage decision-making responsibility. New task teams were formed so those impacted by the decisions were engaged. Cross-departmental collaboration was incentivized and applauded so task teams began thinking beyond the confines of normal practice. The top-down accountability system was dismantled as teams invested in trust-based relationships. Small group decision-making was given leeway as managers realized that their attempts to build full team consensus created complacency, coercion and compliance.

Over and above these changes, a company-wide learning program was rolled out to develop the skill of making clear, positive, doable requests. This program supported people in transforming their complaints and ideas into support requests. The more people ask for what they want, the more likely it is they get their needs met. Lastly, managers agreed to ongoing mutually supportive feedback conversations. With a promise of zero negative repercussions, people were invited to offer appreciations *and* constructive comments. Divergent thinking and dissent were reframed as an innovation enabler. Gradually, inclusive communication opened across functions and levels. As collaborative behaviors seeped into the culture, trust was slowly rebuilt.

> *Tomorrow's management systems will need to value diversity, dissent and divergence as highly as conformance, consensus and cohesion."*
> Gary Hamel

Respectful collaboration is the breeze that turns the windmill of trust and team performance. An enterprise call Cloverpop conducted research that bears this out. When high-performing teams work in a collaborative environment with inclusive decision-making, people thrive. In a compelling study, Cloverpop found that companies who practice inclusive decision-making:

- make better business decisions 87 percent of the time,
- drive decision-making two times faster with half the meetings, and
- improve decision team results by 60 percent.

Skillful collaboration helps widen and deepen conversations while eliciting greater creativity and productivity. Encouraging fresh perspectives is a potent way to problem-solve, enhance performance and achieve market differentiation. The collaborative power of a diverse workforce is a competitive advantage for any organization.

Collaboration is a crucial path to address complex issues.
7. Complex systems change necessitates collaboration across sectors.

Complex systems change is about shifting a structure or process for greater functionality, capacity and/or collective impact. A complex issue has, by definition, many piece parts. Understanding these parts and how they interrelate *necessitates collaboration* across sectors, disciplines and departments. When collaborating to respond to complex issues, rules and logic are insufficient.

It's a daunting undertaking to mobilize and align diverse actors around a shared purpose. With the upturn of information technology, the upsurge of globalization and the upswing of our environment crisis, the complex issues we face require collaboration upskilling. The relational ecosystem needs to become stronger and more resilient. Out of this need comes the burgeoning field of systems thinking, adaptive systems, complexity science, living systems and agile systems design. These practices and tools are intended to help us effectively respond to our so-called wicked challenges.

With the mindset of authentic collaboration, it's easier to see the interweave of complex issues. We can more readily transcend the simplistic mechanistic paradigm. Expanding beyond a linear mindset of "this causes that" is also easier—for reality is not a series of chain-like reactions. There are many invisible factors to consider such as beliefs, emotions, cultural factors and systemic variables—all of which affect people and influence the texture of complex issues. For instance, believing that societal poverty is due to a shortage of jobs is incomplete. Deducing that ocean pollution

> *"We do not live single issue lives."*
> Audre Lorde

is caused by plastic alone is false. Growing more food so people don't starve is naive. Providing shelter for the homeless addresses only one piece of the puzzle. There are many seen and unseen variables that contribute to these issues. Systems change requires collaboration to understand the fuller picture. As we co-learn, we come to see that Life is multidimensional, non-linear, infrequently rational and rarely black and white.

To spotlight a story about authentic collaboration and complexity, consider a unique leadership-in-action program designed to produce climate results in Africa. In this six-month learning-by-doing program, I served as a co-facilitator in gathering change-makers from across sectors in several countries. We enrolled groups of leaders from civil society, the private sector, government ministries, media, youth leaders, indigenous leaders and non-governmental organizations (NGOs) to collaborate and innovate on sustainable solution-finding. The goal was to produce a large-scale "greening" change at the level of organization and community. Leaders were invited to develop an innovation project to apply their new skills *and* generate real results on the ground. In other words, we strategically engaged change-makers to break silos, build bridges and shift systems related to climate mitigation and adaptation.

In this program, a group of bankers decided to transform their bank's corporate social responsibility (CSR) practice with an eco-initiative. Due to their passionate commitment to Earth care, this team of six visionaries adopted a polluted river to rehabilitate. They started their innovation project by partnering with community eco-champions to co-create a shared vision. Their objective was to clean-up the river so that the village could access clean drinking water within one year. By collaboratively engaging people across community strata, they carved out an action plan. On weekends, they labored at the river's edge to clean up garbage, restore the shoreline, dredge the river, control erosion and conduct pre- and post-water testing. They also went upstream to discuss water quality issues and pollution controls with corporate owners. The bankers even collaborated with teachers and youth in the school system to craft an eco-education curriculum program.

> *"If you have come here to help me you are wasting your time, but if you have come because your liberation is bound up with mine, then let us work together."*
> Lilla Watson

At the end of six months, the bankers announced that the river's water quality had improved dramatically. Their commitment to action impacted the well-being of thousands of villagers. Many were inspired to continue the effort long-term. To celebrate, the bankers showcased the outcomes with sister banks, and soon all branches in the country instituted a new CSR policy: to extend support beyond check-writing and institutionalize active community engagement. In effect, this small group of individuals used the power of multi-stakeholder collaboration to not only address a complex eco-societal issue but also transform how business was done.

8. Collaboration unleashes creativity and innovative solutions.

In addition to complexity, collaboration is also tightly entwined with innovative solution-finding. When we veer from self-sufficiency to mutual support, we're more likely to achieve greater results and impact. Accomplishing something bigger than self necessitates bridge-building. United, we can spark creative group intelligence, along with enhancing intrapreneurship and entrepreneurialism. Collaboration sets the stage to greet unconventional ideas, vet and refine strategies. It's the engine that drives low engagement into high-speed creativity. When minds align with heart intention, the panorama of possibility exponentially grows. Authentic collaboration can lead to innovation and goal achievement because the passion and power of the collective is upheld.

> *Innovation comes from an environment where people can dare to authentically connect, challenge the status quo and share new ideas.*

Many years ago, I gathered twenty-five women to spend a full weekend planning a teen esteem program for pre-adolescent girls in our community. We were motivated by research that showed tween girls experience a 30 percent drop in self-confidence between the ages of eight and fourteen years. Impacted by these findings, we set out to co-create a program to inspire, educate and empower girls during this stage of their lives. These women generously gave their time, creative energy and love to co-design an uplifting program. This process was so heartening that we decided to co-facilitate its delivery in our elementary schools. The program was deemed to be an innovative solution to mentoring girls in a meaningful, nurturing way.

> *"Team collaboration is the secret that makes common people achieve uncommon results."*
> Ifeanyi Onuoha

More than two decades later, the program continues to be offered. In hindsight, authentic collaboration was the unsung protagonist in this story. The strength of our respect-filled relationships, in service to others, moved the needle from ordinary to extraordinary success.

9. Sustainability arises from authentic communication and co-ownership.

In serving the United Nations, I subscribe to the mission of sustainable development. Collaborating in an integrated manner is imperative to advancing the UN Sustainable Development Goals (SDG), part of the 2030 Agenda for Sustainable Development. As a global compact, the SDG blueprint consists of seventeen universal yet nationally owned goals.

SDG #17 is all about partnerships—the only goal dedicated to process rather than outcome. Specifically, it's about strengthening partnerships as the means of implementation. Yet, remarkably, none of the nineteen targets and twenty-five indicators for SDG #17 speaks to the skill of collaboration. In fact, the word is not mentioned. While the UN acknowledges that North-South, South-South and triangular cooperation and partnerships are crucial to achieving results, the *how* of collaboration is noticeably absent. It's a missed opportunity. Since the other sixteen SDGs depend on productive collaboration and shared ownership for sustainable results, further investment in developing this competency would be a game-changer in creating "the future we want."

That said, let's look at the broader definition of sustainability. This concept is about human beings aligning with the natural world and her set of bio-instructions.

> *"Sustainability, ensuring the future of life on Earth, is an infinite game, the endless expression of generosity on behalf of all."*
> Paul Hawken

Economically, this means ensuring that whatever we take from our environment to sustain our lifestyle does not harm future generations. This not only requires a spirit of generosity but mindful production and consumption. Put another way, sustainability involves developing the means for a process or state to be maintained for as long as is wanted. In every context, this necessitates collaboration. Relationship-building cannot be divorced from the sustainability conversation. Designing tenable systems or an institutional change depends on how we interact and problem-solve. Empowered decision-making vis-à-vis collaboration is what sustains any effort.

In the realm of relationships, authentic communication is the jet fuel for sustainability. Why? Lasting impact depends on people working in good faith to co-create results. When diverse voices are sincerely engaged across a system or organization, decisions have greater legitimacy. More resources, wisdom and talents are involved. There's value in sharing risks and rewards. Besides, it is only through genuine connection that we feel safe enough to honestly talk about sustainability. Otherwise, it's a nice-to-use word with no substance. Describing the relationship between authentic communication and sustainability is like understanding that a garden blossoms with the help of sunshine. It's an obvious connection.

Embedded in the concept of sustainability is shared ownership. What precedes ownership is the true engagement of stakeholders. When people are fully engaged in owning a process, they bring more of who they are to the table and, therefore, have more vested interest in sustaining the work in the long run. With shared ownership, trust and accountability develop. Agreement follow-through becomes more likely. People are inclined to clean up a broken agreement by renegotiating or deciding on another course. Sustainable action thrives with these preconditions.

In coaching another group of environmental champions in Africa, I witnessed how collaboration, shared ownership and sustainability overlap. These eco-champions worked together on a community project to crowd-source monies in support of rural climate adaptation initiatives. To accomplish this goal, they initiated a voluntary 1 percent green payroll levy. The effort quickly grew to include many organizational teams. Soon, hundreds of people signed off on donating 1 percent of their paycheck. The money pot multiplied.

Eventually, some donors were invited to support the project fund's governing process. When donors began sharing ownership, a sustainability light switch turned on. They naturally wanted this money well spent so they were happy to assume fiduciary responsibility. As stewards of public trust, they acted in good faith with open, transparent governance. Donor accountability ramped up

> *"People want to have ownership over decision-making as this brings autonomy."*
> Stan Shih

credibility, which, in turn, motivated even more people to contribute. These eco-champions experienced success, in large part, because the process was collaboratively co-owned.

The overarching reason why authentic collaboration matters

Beyond these nine reasons as to why authentic collaboration matters, consider another significant rationale. It has to do with our shared *why* story and purpose. One might say that our Mother Ship is the journey toward ayni. Coming into right relationship with self, others and Life is our collective soul call. In doing so, we discover the truth of who we are.

In the pursuit of ayni or sacred reciprocity, the means merges with the end. When we relate with respect and love, the love we seek is found within. If we bring heart presence to collaboration, we live more vibrantly. If we connect to the inner gold of our shared humanity, the veil of separation lifts. If we step into the stream of belonging, we can sense the flow of interdependence. If we honor the voice of Earth, we discover that all who carry breath are gathered under the Sacred Tree of Life. Ultimately, the hidden treasure of authentic collaboration is greater peace: the inherent and latent relationship potential that is ours to behold.

As the African proverb states: "If we want to go fast, go alone. If we want to go far, go together." In this challenging time of the Great Turning, let's learn how to go far and fast together. With ayni as our source of inspiration, let's allow the vision of the authentic collaboration bridge to be our guiding force.

CHAPTER 7

EXAMINING COLLABORATION BLOCKS AND ENABLERS

"We are all afloat in the Great River.
All are carried along.
Some swim against the flow.
They, too, are carried along."
Wu Hsin

Blocks and enablers

Even if we understand the value proposition that entices us to journey across the authentic collaboration bridge, the throughfare can be full of stop-and-go conditions. The best-laid plans can be derailed by the gravel of communication and the bumpy edges of conflict. Common interactive traps include groupthink, cynicism, half-truths, reproach and refusal to discuss what truly matters. A sincere attempt to collaborate can be sidelined when people wear the robe of aggression, when non-conformist ideas are silenced, when crucial feedback is swept under the rug and when a *yes* really means a *no*.

A great deal of awareness is needed to notice the ripple effect of our interpersonal patterns and to course correct. Recognizing the blocks and enablers can help ensure a smoother ride. At the very least, we can learn to center and ground ourselves to mindfully respond and facilitate a new path forward.

Think back to a recent collaborative process. Was there deliberation about the risk factors and enablers? If there was an emergency or crisis, preparation may not have been possible. Yet, if pre-planning was feasible, note the extent to which the following enablers were taken into account.

AUTHENTIC COLLABORATION

> **Enabling Factors that Support Authentic Collaboration**
>
> - People care about the issue at hand, and those at the table.
> - There's sufficient trust and goodwill.
> - Each person is open to learning.
>
> - People perceive shared purpose and potential benefit in partnering.
> - There is value placed on respect, authenticity and emotional safety.
> - People feel empowered to explore uncharted territory.
>
> - Effective communication, interpersonal and negotiation skills are evident.
> - There's a willingness to co-create a vision with a win-win-win outcome.
> - People believe there's enough time to co-develop a plan of action.

Even if these factors are considered, no amount of pre-planning can determine how a collaboration unfolds. Relationships are unpredictable, and interacting is organic. Participating with a generous spirit and a willing attitude can set the stage for success yet trips and hazards can still block results. The real test is meeting people where they are and being willing to change gears. The art of bridge-building involves the opportunity to self-connect while flexing to what's needed in the moment.

While a complete list of authentic collaboration blocks and enablers could be a book unto itself, consider the partial list on the next page. This categorization is also inspired by Ken Wilber's integral meta-theory. Four domains of reality provide a robust frame to explore this topic. The intention here is to kick-start reflection and dialogue.

As you review, select those blocks and enablers that most speak to you.

What has been your lived experience?

Authentic Collaboration Blocks and Enablers

Individual Beliefs	Behaviors
Blocks ○ Limiting beliefs and a bruised heart ○ Inner values conflict ○ Self-esteem and reputation insecurity ○ Need to control, to know, to be right ○ Strong attachments and cynicism	**Blocks** ○ Victim-thinking and blaming ○ Fear-based behavior (judgment) ○ Integrity gaps—say one thing, do another ○ Addictions ○ Criticize and dismiss people
Enablers ○ Observe self-talk ○ Lean into emotional discomfort ○ Listen to intuition ○ See pain as a message ○ Reflect on right relationship	**Enablers** ○ Empowered agency and conscious living ○ Communicate with soft power (carefront) ○ Discern and act on commitments ○ Be open to different perspectives ○ Attune to nonverbal messages
Culture	**System**
Blocks ○ Lack of conflict intelligence ○ Collaborative behaviors not recognized ○ Unquestioned assumptions ○ Punishment if norms are challenged ○ Competition, avoidance, rigid rules	**Blocks** ○ Hierarchy that fosters dominance ○ Organizational silos ○ Bottleneck decision-making procedures ○ Exclusionary process, info withheld ○ Unclear goals, roles, rules
Enablers ○ Share power in considering all needs ○ Focus on strengths, not deficits ○ Assert views, respect boundaries ○ Celebrate inclusivity and achievements ○ Practice empathy and daily gratitude	**Enablers** ○ Co-create vision in a participatory manner ○ Agree on clear responsibilities ○ Offer collaboration job aids ○ Develop an accountability structure ○ Welcome all with circle conversations

There are as many factors that influence collaboration as there are relationships. For the sake of brevity, let's extract and explore three common blocks and corresponding enablers from this list. Each set aligns with the three collaboration bridge power pillars at the levels of self, others and Earth.

Level	Blocks	Enablers
Self (Beliefs/Behavior)	Victim-thinking	Empowering Self
Others (Culture)	Conflict	Sharing Power
Earth (System)	Hierarchy	Co-creating Vision

I) Victim-Thinking Block: Enabler of Empowerment (Self)

Victim-thinking is a seductive mind trap laden with limiting beliefs. It can etch deep synapse grooves in the brain. When this trap is activated, it carries the belief that we're unable to support our needs in that moment. With this mentality, we may not have the wherewithal to tap into our inner resources or ask for support. We may be quick to self-sabotage, feel hurt or believe that happiness is beyond reach. At other times, we may feel defeated or even targeted. Victim-thinking is a changeable experience, given the mind's fleeting nature. Yet, if victim-thinking continually grips the psyche, it renders people incapable, non-resilient or unwilling to act. Victim-thinking affects all of us from time to time.

When I succumb to victim-thinking, I experience a sense of powerlessness. I observe a desire to control others, blame Life or focus on what's missing. I want to be rescued, or at the very least reassured. With this life-depleting energy, I come from a place of lack, which has me project scarcity onto the situation or relationship. Either I'm not enough or what Life offers me is insufficient.

I see this pattern in others as well. It may contribute to people who complain about the government, feel apathetic at work or upset when their partner doesn't meet expectations. Underlying beliefs may include: Life is against me, there's no point in trying, I can't get what I want, the system makes my life miserable, no one cares about me or I am/you are flawed. When we feel victimized by someone or something, the self-talk becomes "If you or it changes, then I'll feel better." Power is seen to be outside of self. Since we cannot control that which is beyond self, this mindset renders us helpless. Resignation can set in. If this belief system becomes infused into our habits and values, we walk a path of suffering. Persistent victim-thinking affects not only how we relate but ultimately our destiny.

> *"Your beliefs become your thoughts.*
> *Your thoughts become your words.*
> *Your words become your actions.*
> *Your actions become your habits.*
> *Your habits become your values.*
> *Your values become your destiny."*
> *Mahatma Gandhi*

An experience I had with community leaders in North America demonstrates how victim-thinking and limiting beliefs can halt collaboration in its tracks. Change-makers from ten leading organizations across different sectors gathered to dialogue about how to stimulate and diversify economic growth. This topic was of interest to everyone as it was routinely discussed in the community and in local media. My hope was to explore a program that could be customized to produce concrete, innovative economic results. I anticipated a rich exchange as this was a formidable, seasoned group of leaders.

After a lengthy conversation of the benefits and risks, the group came to a twofold conclusion. They did not have the authority to move this idea forward nor the ability to generate funding as a cost-share prospect. In short, they perceived themselves as having little power. I was surprised to hear one limiting belief after another. Like a contagious virus, the group mindset was infected with scarcity and lack. At one point, someone uttered, "Yes, we see the value of this proposal and need to take action, but it seems we don't have the influence to make this happen."

While I saw these leaders as the community's A-team, they saw themselves as victims to a larger system. They played the game by tossing the ball to others whom they believed had "real power and clout." At one point, I asked the question, "If not you, who will lead on this issue?" Yet visionary, confident, can-do thinking was not to be found. Fear and pessimism won the day. Because of this experience, I was prompted to look at how this group mirrored my own victim-thinking. With compassion, I realized, once again, that authentic power resides in the mind and heart, not in a title.

Given the undesirable ripple effect of victim-thinking, why do we choose this mindset? To what extent are we conscious of this pattern? In some cases, this behavior may have been modeled for us during childhood. Perhaps a multigenerational family pattern of learned helplessness was normal. Chronic feelings of frustration, apathy and sadness often accompany this state of lack. Excuse-making can be habitual. If we struggle with self-responsibility, trying on new attitudes can be foreign. For some, victim beliefs and words can be a call for help. A friend once admitted that it was an attention-seeking strategy. Her bouts of unlovability evoked the victim schema. It was her way of saying, "I need to be seen, heard and held with care." Like a moth to a flame, this woman's self-destructive pattern had her avoid responsibility by repeatedly "playing the victim"—taking the path of least resistance. One day, she gathered her courage and acknowledged that her victim-thinking was a form of self-betrayal.

> *"Most of us spend most of our time trying to fix and control the outer circumstances, instead of resolving the lacking feelings back into Being."*
> Patrick Connor

When we take on this acquired trait of victim-thinking, authentic collaboration also becomes a victim. Meaningful connection is diminished when behavior becomes co-dependent, self-critical, manipulative or narcissistic. Martyrdom renounces any attempt to collaborate. When we consistently disrespect ourselves, it's hard to offer respect to others. The pattern of low self-worth may be rooted in past trauma, pain, a history of abuse, persecution or unfair treatment. If this speaks to you, detect how victim-thinking sits in your body. Notice how this energy leaches your "joie de vivre," or enjoyment of Life. Become curious about how you lose and gain power. Reflect on how you can transform this tendency with a courageous new choice.

Empowering Self

Healing the habit of victim-thinking begins with the act of self-responsibility. As responsible adults, we are "able to respond" in feeling what needs to be felt. From this insight, new choices will become self-evident. Even if we experience a relationship or situation to be difficult and seemingly unchangeable, listening and responding to our feelings is the starting place of empowerment. This honest act of inner reckoning, when done with sincerity and honesty, can be a pivot point into a new way of being and relating. In this moment, we remember that we're in the pilot's seat,

> *"Between stimulus and response there is a space. In that space is the power to choose our response. In our response lies our growth and our freedom."*
> Stephen Covey

flying into the future as a co-creator *with* Life. We do not have to wait for others to decide our fate.

This mental state of empowerment is linked to the understanding that our perspective influences reality. Our perception defines who we believe we are, how people ought to behave, and how the world should operate. The external world shows up as a projection of our belief system, individually and collectively. Life reflects what we need to see, witness or experience to grow.

In 1942, Viktor Frankl was a recently married Jew living in Austria. On one horrifying day, the Nazi soldiers captured and deported him to the first of four concentration camps. He spent three years experiencing one ghastly atrocity after another. Many members of his family were killed during the Holocaust. After the war, Frankl could have understandably allowed victim-thinking to dominate his life. Instead, he took on radical self-responsibility in transforming his pain into service. He decided to become a psychologist and help others who were suffering with post-war trauma. With the spirit of self-determination, Frankl began to earnestly study the impact of attitude, the goodness of people and the meaning of Life. He realized that the outcome is not determined by what happens to us but *rather by our response.*

Frankl is known for the following quote: "The one thing you can't take away from me is the way I choose to respond to what you do to me. The last of one's freedoms is to choose one's attitude in any given circumstance." With these words, he reminds us that our life is primarily shaped not by events but by our mindset and stories. The power of choice is ever present. Yes, our culture has a huge influence on us, yet our perception lies at the root of every response. Therein lies empowerment—the antithesis of and a remedy for victimhood.

Diving into the *how* of empowering self

> *"The way we feel about everything comes down to two things: the pictures in our mind and the words we use."*
> Marissa Peer

The bridge pillar of empowering self is about discovering and living what's personally meaningful. Living congruently with our values is a life-long self-connection journey. Empowerment, in essence, is synonymous with integrity. As a universal soul calling, integrity is an invitation to embrace our most vulnerable parts while noticing the pictures in our mind and listening to the words we use. The more we observe and make choices from our heart, the more inner alignment we experience. This self-development process is a step-by-step journey into ayni.

The process of empowerment welcomes all aspects of self to be our collaboration partners, including our mind, heart and behavior. Let's linger with this idea using the iceberg metaphor. Consider that the above-water iceberg represents our behavior and the underwater iceberg denotes our mind. The ebb and flow of the ocean is our heart energy. While the tip of the iceberg reveals our behavior, these choices are interconnected with our mind and the swirling ocean energy of our heart. We may perceive behavior to be the focal point of attention when collaborating, yet this is only a part of the picture: a small gradient of a deeper inner narrative. Below the ocean surface is where the real action lies. Therein resides our beliefs, intermixed with the heart current of our lives. Beliefs are reoccurring thought patterns that are adopted as true and real. It's tempting to believe that our beliefs are fixed, yet the tides of Life routinely change our limited subjective thoughts. In the thick layers of the iceberg, our beliefs are embedded with emotions, values, preferences and needs. Our subconscious mind, submerged with what's real and imagined, shape and surface our behavior and reactions. They are the drivers that determine why we do what we do.

> *"The subconscious mind can not tell the difference between what's real and what's imagined."*
> Bob Proctor

All these forces under the waterline of awareness have a significant impact on how we empower ourselves. Our collaborative relationships are impacted by this stream of consciousness. Given that the average person thinks 60,000 to 70,000 thoughts per day, it is only by diving into our mind that we can understand how our thought patterns influence our behavior. As we deepen self-awareness, we can be at choice in how we evolve beyond the bardo of yesterday's thoughts. We can try on new uplifting beliefs, language and attitudes. As a practice, we see that Life is energy. We begin to create change by design, not default. We step out of fate and into a self-chosen destiny.

AUTHENTIC COLLABORATION

In the waters of self-empowerment, we plumb the depths of our consciousness to notice areas of suffering, joy, constriction and expansion. When feeling love, celebrate the flow. When feeling fear and resistance, consider the misperceptions churning about. It takes gentle curiosity to notice our growing edges and courage to loosen the clutch of fear and victim-thinking. How can you surface the ice blocks of your limiting beliefs? How can you chip away the malaise? How can you melt the frozen energy cubes with the fire of self-love?

> *Courage is the propelling force that shifts us out of victim-thinking and into authentic expression.*

Some of the most common growing edges in collaborative relationships include self-esteem, self-responsibility, trust, commitment, discipline, letting go, adapting to change, open-heartedness, balance and flow. Learning to self-connect and lean into an edge is how we transcend the tension and build the muscle of resiliency. Think about a healing massage. When too much pressure is applied on a tension spot, the ouch factor overrides the soothing effect. When too little pressure is applied, there's insufficient contact to meet the tension. A delicate, compassionate touch is needed to sink into and transmute the energy. With a laser focus, we can tune into that which wants to be expressed, release the contraction, and bring forth healing.

As an empowering first step, carve out time and space to quiet your mind and listen to your body's wisdom. Breathe into your gut intuition, your second brain, and trust the sensations, questions and images that arise. When you meet your body with gentle presence, you can sense a truth that lies beyond words. Whatever comes to light, sit with it as a toddler does with a new toy—mesmerized and fascinated. What new way of thinking becomes apparent beyond the old construct of your identity? What new meaning do you want to make about the past, to reshape your future? Ask your heart and ancestors for clarity and guidance. Visualize how these new thoughts look and feel. You can literally alter your electromagnetic field with the photons of new uplifting beliefs.

> *Self-empowerment involves asking the question "Who do I need to become to express my best self?"*

As Dr. Joe Dispenza wrote, "Teach your body emotionally what it would feel like to believe in this way…to be empowered…to be moved by your own greatness…to be invincible…to have courage…to be in love with life…to feel unlimited…to live as if your prayers are already answered." This is the *how* of self-empowerment— embracing a growing edge to shift out of victim-thinking and into higher consciousness. Ultimately, we alter the landscape of authentic collaboration one person at a time, one behavior at a time, one belief at a time.

A story of inner bridge-building: empowering self in action

If a self-empowerment practice is a new idea, know that Life has an uncanny way of supporting us when we set a sincere intention. The key is to bow to our growing edge and not fight with what's so. I learned this lesson when my life seemed to come to a stand-still, a grinding halt. For a period of two years, nothing I worked on or toward seemed to manifest, both professionally and personally. I felt frustrated and powerless to affect change. Even with tons of effort, work became futile. Relationships ended and stalled. Progress, as I defined it, eluded me. I felt betrayed by Life. In this state of confusion, I turned my attention inward. I sensed that I needed to let go of my need to know and the shame I felt about not knowing. So I took the term *standstill* literally as I deepened into stillness. My practice was to feel into the unknown, embrace uncertainty and accept what was.

The turnaround journey was incredibly fear-inducing. At every turn, I grasped on to my old comfort zone and tightly clung to my need to know. I asked Earth for the grace to surrender. It was a long road to capitulation. Letting go was, in a word, terrifying. It felt as though I was on a trapeze bar. I had to muster my courage to let go of the old bar while swinging to meet the new. In mid-flight, I realized that I held on to nothing but faith. I prayed for a net to catch me. Egoic notions of falling and failing swept through my body. My palms still sweat at the memory.

It was during this free-fall that I heard my inner voice murmur, "Whether known or unknown, everything is in service to my highest good. I am supported. As I say yes to Life, Life says yes to me." With that insight, I released the judgment I had toward Life and the anger that came with betrayal. I felt cradled in the arms of Life. On the other side of the abyss was deeper trust. My need to know and control subsided. As I realigned with joy, my work life recalibrated. I became more

(*The way out is the way in.*)

conscious of how I used my energy to assert needs and power boundaries. Projects that I struggled to push forward either fell away or I felt no inclination to continue. New opportunities came forth organically. Relationships strengthened as I deepened my authentic sharing. I experienced greater ease with collaboration because I began relying on my body's wisdom to guide me forward. For the first time, my mind and gut took direction from my heart.

Transforming collaboration with empowering beliefs

Contrary to popular belief, the door to empowerment only opens from the inside. No one can empower others. This bridge pillar is made from the steel and grit of personal choice. In changing our perspective about people and events, we create a different story about what was—and thus what will be.

As Dr. Wayne Dyer noted, "If you change the way you look at things, the things you look at change."

When we choose to build up our self-empowerment and take on new affirming beliefs, we become an ally to self. We become centered and grounded in our speaking and listening. With heart awareness, we offer greater intentionality, clarity, focus and presence. Our relationships take on a different tenor. With this practice, we discover there's an open, positive feedback loop between empowerment and collaboration.

TRY THIS: When reviewing this sample list of limiting and empowering beliefs, reflect on your own ways of thinking.

- To what extent do you notice victim thinking creep in?

- What empowering beliefs ring true for you?

- How can you transform your limiting beliefs to be in service to the vision of authentic collaboration?

AUTHENTIC COLLABORATION

The Block of Limiting Beliefs	The Enabler of Empowering Beliefs
My self-respect depends on others' approval.	My voice matters. I confidently speak my truth, come what may.
I will be punished if I make a mistake.	My life is about learning and growing, not perfection. I own my choices, regardless of others' reactions.
Success depends on fast solutions, not collaborative dialogue.	Our success is how we define it together. How we collaborate is as important as what we decide.
I do not trust others.	I use wise discernment in deciding who to trust. I am open to exploring new ways to build trust.
I cannot depend on people.	I build trust through meaningful connection. I belong to and rely on my Earth community.
I don't have authority to make decisions.	My authority comes from my mind, heart and "we" intelligence. I make decisions that are aligned with my values.
I'm afraid of my power.	I am enough. I inspire others with my authentic power.
It's safer to stay under the radar.	My safety ultimately comes from inner connection.
If I'm vulnerable, I will be taken advantage of.	I deeply listen to my intuitive guidance. I embrace my vulnerability as a power source.
I'm afraid of the tension of conflicting views.	When conflict arises, I pause to reflect. I engage with curiosity and courage.
I can't have an impact.	I am clear on my purpose and value. I celebrate my creative gifts.

II) Conflict Block: Enabler of Sharing Power (Culture)

Conflict can and does arise in every collaborative relationship. By conflict, I am referring to a state of disharmony and disconnection, resulting from seemingly incompatible ideas, values or interests. This is a normal, inevitable occurrence whenever people come together and interact over time. As such, conflict in and of itself is not negative but rather a part of Life. Disagreement is a part of the fabric of negotiating needs. If conflict is handled with mutual respect, this process can result in greater trust and growth. Conflict can be as beneficial to relationships as rainstorms are to Earth. If, however, the communication generates harm, then conflict becomes a block to collaboration.

> *"Conflict is natural and normal. It's a change in energy flow."*
> David Augsburger

According to psychotherapist Dr. Esther Perel, all relationships follow a cycle of harmony, disharmony and repair. She points out that conflict is not really the issue. Rather, it's a question of *how we repair* the disconnection that matters. This pertains to both initiating the repair and receiving the effort made by another. Both skills are held in this container. I've noticed this distinction when someone I care about initiates a repair conversation. Sometimes, if the hurt was significant, it takes a while for me to truly *receive* this person's caring outreach.

One way to begin relationship repair is to become aware of how we react. On the spectrum of conflict reactions, avoidance is on one side. This choice may offer quick relief to step out of the fire, but it doesn't allow for relational repair. Instead of exploring what's really happening, the conflict noise is hushed. The power imbalance underneath the issue continues. With avoidance and distancing, the ravine becomes deeper, wider and darker. There's no opportunity for bridging and learning. On the other side of the spectrum lies aggression. This can show up as criticism, an ultimatum, gossip, threats or even violence. Given this avoidance-aggression spectrum, where do you typically land?

> *"Once you label me, you negate me."*
> Soren Kierkegaard

A lack of conflict intelligence can jeopardize any relationship, no matter how strong the connection. When emotions run high, our limbic brain becomes triggered. We hook into dysfunctional patterns of relating. Before we realize what's happening, the attack-defend runaway train jumps the track. Judgment injures the ego. Emotional triage may be needed to stop the bleed-out of life energy. We may even need to crawl into a silent safe zone and tend to our wounds. With severe behaviors, we may implode with self-harm or explode to the detriment of others. These all-too-human tendencies result in the common 7-F coping strategies: flight, fight, freeze, freak, fawn, fix and foe. These life-alienating behaviors are intended to protect yet the sting of sorrow often remains.

With so much upset, it's not surprising that people associate conflict with pain. Many of us have never learned how to heal and repair conflict. Or, when hurt, we lose our ability to hold safe space for conflict dialogue. It's a delicate skill to peel back the layers of a misunderstanding. Conflict has an uncanny way of showing us our collaboration growing edges.

Sharing power as a conflict antidote

> *"Conflict issues typically distill down into one of three buckets: power and control, caring and closeness and respect and recognition."*
> Dr. Esther Perel

The practice of authentic collaboration reframes conflict as an opportunity to reconnect with the antidote of mutual respect and power-sharing. Since power and control issues are among the most common reasons why conflict unfolds, power-sharing is a viable remedy. At the very least, it's crucial to the condition for conflict repair.

Sharing power also happens to be the central pillar of the authentic collaboration bridge. It involves balancing how we use our will while supporting others to express their will. Sharing power is about finding the sweet spot between being true to self while being respectful to those around us. This necessitates stepping back and feeling for the whole and discerning how we're impacting others.

Related to a repair conversation, the process starts by requesting permission. Rather than assume, ask if the person is ready and willing to have a conversation. Check-in with yourself to assess how open you are in hearing another perspective. Relationship repair begins with accepting what's so, regardless of agreement. We can still accept and appreciate people even if they hold different viewpoints. When others feel accepted, they are more inclined to authentically share their desires and struggles. These minor ways of sharing power can have a major impact on a repair conversation.

Despite the act of sharing power being an invisible energy, it looms large in how we relate and collaborate. This foundational principle attempts to equalize power rather than perpetuate the habit of powering-over others or losing power. The former is about dominating and controlling people while the latter is about slipping into victim-thinking. We tend to swing back and forth in our everyday interactions looking for equilibrium.

Our ability to share power is tested when conflict arises. This is when our character, maturity and self-efficacy are revealed. Power-sharing presupposes that we all have power. So, in the realm of authentic self-collaboration, we might start with the question: "To what extent do I express my power?" We might also be inclined to reflect on power imbalances in our relationship and how we contribute to that dynamic. As Caitlin Killoren wrote, "When there is an imbalance of power, the dynamic typically evolves into three different negative types: demand-withdrawal, distancer-pursuer, and fear-shame." Reclaiming power is perceived by some to be a high-risk venture that can alter the relationship undercurrent. Speaking assertively can rejig the power balance and cause an unanticipated outcome or loss. When power is discussed, our boundaries come to light.

Learning how to share power can take many forms, such as:

- how we move our body when interacting,
- how much we listen versus talk,
- how we open or shut down dialogue,
- how we influence a system,
- how we set and maintain boundaries,
- the degree to which we choose to engage, and
- how we use our words and tone of voice.

Depending on the context, the topic of power can be uncomfortable to discuss. It becomes the proverbial elephant in the room. It can feel awkward talking about who gets heard or why some people have their needs supported while others are ignored. Even our identity can be challenged as power cuts to the core of who we are. Collaboration can easily derail if people feel threatened. Communicating about power-sharing takes confidence, gentle inquiry and tenacity.

Conflict recovery: sharing power within self

When I'm experiencing conflict and met with blame, I notice my tendency to feel confused, talk fast, take shallow breaths and shift into all-or-nothing thinking. My energy feels hurried. Amid the barrage of a word assault, I swiftly build a fortress as a defense shield. My instinct is to retreat into my citadel stronghold and hunker down. Not being understood is an old wound, so my mind can flood with information to explain or prove a point. This defensive posture expends a lot of energy and allows misperceptions to fester. Occasionally, I catastrophize, withdraw into turtle silence or become bear-like with self-protection. These are the moments when I need to focus on self-collaboration via a compassion-filled conflict recovery process.

> *When in conflict, how do you react when met with blame versus being met with compassion?*

Conflict recovery is initiated by asserting the need to pause. Quiet space, accompanied by long, deep breaths, helps us dial-down reactivity, calm our thoughts and regulate our emotions. As taught by Raphael Cushnir, a leading voice in personal and professional development, "the cause of harmful patterns in our lives is unfelt emotion." Through pausing to self-connect, we "find the flinch and ride the wave" of the feelings that surface. Rather than dismiss or push away, feel the emotions directly and consistently—even for only a few seconds. This typically feels uncomfortable as it's counter-intuitive. It's easier to speak about the feeling versus feel the feeling. Yet, with compassion, emotional regulation becomes invigorating and freeing. It's a beautiful expression of authentic self-collaboration.

To support emotional regulation, consider the RAIN practice developed by Tara Brach, a world-renowned mindfulness teacher. RAIN is a simple yet profound reflection process. The intention is to allow our suffering to just be there, without bypassing or wishing it away. It's an exercise that reminds us of the inner-outer interplay. The more chaotic we feel inside, the less we can attune to others. The more present we are with ourselves, the clearer and more centered we can be with others. In embracing all of who we are, we remind ourselves that we are not our emotions or thoughts. Our real identity is loving presence.

> **Tara Brach's RAIN Process: A Mindfulness Practice to Process Emotions**
>
> **R** = Recognize what is happening within.
> **A** = Allow the experience to be there, just as it is.
> **I** = Investigate with interest and care.
> **N** = Nurture with compassion.

With this RAIN practice, we recover from conflict by dedicating time and energy to self-sooth. It's like re-parenting our inner child who seeks reassurance and comfort. Consider doing this whenever the need arises, not just when it's convenient. If we develop the habit of compartmentalizing our emotions, yet never get around to processing them, these energies become repressed. When we cradle our uncomfortable emotions, we allow the sensations to be as they are so they can dissipate on their own accord. Hurrying the process is counter to self-acceptance.

Emotional self-regulation is authentic collaboration between one's body, mind and heart.

When it comes to self-regulation, notice the words used are *cradle, process, allow*—not *control*. Control implies managing with force. It can also infer "to get rid of." This conjures up self-judgment, which, in turn, generates resistance. Instead, emotional self-regulation involves skillful inner listening. We monitor self-talk, distinguish between thoughts and feelings and investigate what's happening within. We self-connect to discern the message of our emotions. With this insight, we are at choice to initiate, inhibit or modulate action. Put another way, emotional self-regulation means letting go of control and energetically adjusting to normalize.

Questions to ask may include:

- How am I feeling?
- Why am I hurting?

- What part of me needs to be heard?
- Emotion, if you could speak, what would you say right now?
- Whose voice is this really?

The key to emotional self-regulation is to not think about your feelings by figuring it out but to *actually feel*. It's a highly nuanced way of relating to lean back, become a patient space-holder, micro-focus on bodily sensation and wait for the emotion to speak. It takes fortitude of spirit to stay in the chaotic mystery until "it" is ready to be heard. Forgo the inclination to suppress, avoid or hide. Open your heart to the cosmic wisdom that wants to come through you. If the emotions are too intense, close your eyes and, with your mind's eye, see yourself a few feet in front of you. Psychic distance can help digest strong emotions. Either way, there are no shortcuts to releasing. A repressed emotion will only dissolve when it has been *fully owned* and embraced. *Acceptance is the precondition for transformation.* Even if we do not like nor agree with what we are experiencing, we can still accept our feelings. This is power-sharing with self, a primal practice of inner communication that reconnects, recenters and restores.

> "Do you cry about your experience or are you actually in it, feeling what needs to be felt?"
> Peter Levie

TRY THIS: At this moment, stop reading to reflect on a recent conflict you experienced. Bundle up with a cozy quilt, made from patches of self-nurturing and self-care and RAIN on yourself. Cradle those feelings with the tenderness of a loving mother or father.

Power-sharing via Nonviolent Communication (NVC)

When I lived in New York, I was introduced to a life-changing approach to bridge-building. One day, while browsing in a bookstore, a book suddenly fell off the shelf, hit my head and plunked itself into my awareness. The book was titled *Nonviolent Communication: A Language of Compassion*, written by Dr. Marshall Rosenberg. Ironically, a work colleague had recommended this same book to me the day prior. A week before that, I met a woman who was an NVC coach. Given this synchronicity, I bought the book and eagerly read the first chapter. The words spoke to me of depth and honesty. I decided to immerse myself into the world of NVC. I discovered that this brand of authentic collaboration can transform the most difficult conflict into a dialogue of shared understanding.

Psychologist Dr. Rosenberg, the founder of NVC, realized early in his career that the typical approach to handling conflict was inadequate. Too often, people adopt the pattern of attack-blame-defend, leaving people powerless to bridge-build with care. Since Marshall believed that people naturally want to support the needs of others when in choice, he developed a communication approach based on the Gandhian principle of nonviolence.

> **Guiding Principles of Nonviolent Communication**
>
> - Observe free of evaluation.
> - Express feelings free of judgment.
> - Identify needs free of strategy.
> - Make requests free of demands.

Fundamentally, these four principles are intended to foster a new way of speaking and listening. When skillfully used, NVC shifts us away from resisting, avoiding and fixing conflict to creating the conditions for shared understanding and healthy conflict resolution. We sense into our own and others' feelings and needs to genuinely connect. Rather than judge, we practice sharing our observations, communicating with empathy, asking for what we want and finding mutually agreeable solutions. We widen the "me" and "we" spaces by making clear, positive, doable requests based on the needs of each person. I see this collaborative process as power-sharing in action.

"Judgment is an alienated expression of an unmet need."
Marshall Rosenberg

In the NVC world, human needs are universal. This includes the need for belonging, love, esteem stability, growth and affection. When we communicate at the level of needs, connection can be restored. When focused on the level of strategy, conflict can erupt. For example, the need for respect does not evoke upset as we all desire this in our relationships. Yet, the strategy of *how* we respect others may or may not be what people want. Clinging too much to show we care can be off-putting. Giving too much space to respect independence may trigger a fear of abandonment. NVC offers a valuable dialogue practice to explore how to best support unmet needs. In and of itself, a needs discovery dialogue is an impressive first step toward respectful bridge-building.

As an NVC coach explained, needs sit behind every feeling. If pleasant feelings are experienced, such as love, joy, peace and contentment, then perhaps needs of connection, ease and flow are met. The fruit of these met needs might include understanding, intimacy, inspiration and gratitude. If unpleasant feelings arise, this points to unmet needs. For instance, the underside of fear is a need for safety or security. Beneath shame may be a need for self-worth. Associated with guilt is often a need for integrity. Connected to grief is the need to acknowledge loss. Anger may be coupled with the need for boundaries, fairness or justice.

> *People can evoke feelings, but others do not cause us to feel the way we do. We are responsible for our own emotional landscape.*

All feelings are valid and important as beacons of information. If we take the time to discern what's happening within and among us, this connection elicits creative conflict resolution. By exploring feelings and needs, NVC upholds the principle of mutual respect.

A story about sharing power in the face of authority

The workplace is ideal to practice rebalancing the scales of power with mutual respect. This can be challenging for many people given the power dynamics between management and employees. At one time, this was my story. I worked with a manager who seemed to identify with his authority role. Our relationship was strained at the best of times. I felt a low level of rapport, trust and amity between us. During one full team meeting, after I offered a project status update, my manager began screaming at me. In non-evaluative NVC language, I observed that he spoke to me using a volume, tone and pitch that I found difficult to hear. My body froze like a deer in the headlights. I felt shut down in embarrassment, humiliation, anger and hurt. When the meeting ended, I left the office and seriously thought about quitting my job.

AUTHENTIC COLLABORATION

That evening, I recalled the words from an NVC coach who stated that self-empathy is imperative if we want to offer sincere empathy to others. So I spent time in deep reflection, feeling what needed to be felt. It took many hours to arrive at the heart space of compassion. My typical coping strategy was to stuff my feelings under the veneer that all is fine. I defended against sadness with an "I don't care" attitude. It took everything in me to lean into the discomfort and acknowledge my vulnerable truth—I do care. With such turbulent emotions, my conflict recovery RAIN process was more like a downpour of hailstones.

> "How people treat you is their karma. How you react is yours."
> Wayne Dyer

When it came to observing what happened free of evaluation, I imagined that I was looking through the lens of a video camera. I replayed back what was said and done with as much neutrality as I could muster. When judgment surfaced, I brought my attention back to my heart. I explored my feelings and unmet needs in my body and then in a journal. Childhood memories came up for healing, revealing occasions when I felt similarly. Slowly, I filled up my reservoir of self-love and created space to sense into what this manager may have felt. I realized that we likely had similar unmet needs. I fell asleep that night knowing that I was given another experience, however unpleasant, to integrate the heart intelligence of NVC.

> "When we're upset in the moment, it's never about that moment."
> A Course in Miracles

The next morning at work, I remembered the words of Alice Walker: "The most common way people give up their power is thinking they don't have any." So I summoned my courage and knocked on my manager's door to request a conversation. My intention was to communicate authentically, clearly state my boundaries, stay in curiosity and bridge-build to restore connection. After expressing my need for respect and understanding, I asked if he would be willing to share what happened for him during the meeting. Surprisingly, he let me know what upset him. I asked how I could support him in alleviating his stress. We talked about what respect meant to each of us. It was an honest, sticky exchange. We eventually decided to co-own the damage in our relationship as every dynamic is a two-way street. Instead of fault-finding, we made a promise to repair the harm and communicate more frequently and with greater care.

Our dialogue was an attempt to reconnect and collaboratively share power to bring forth the spirit of NVC.

Sharing power as the by-product of heart alignment

During a conflict, talking about power usually involves confrontation. This behavior can be harsh and jolting, evoking fear and belly constriction. To experiment with authentic collaboration, consider "carefrontation" instead. Carefrontation is about maintaining a state of detached caring that flows out of being heart-centered. Conflict gives us the opportunity to practice detachment by being engaged yet disentangled. It's a subtle distinction in connecting with our heart versus our ego personality. This compassionate stance endows us with open-mindedness, curiosity and a willingness to discover. Carefrontation and conflict repair is not about relating flawlessly but about offering love.

> *"Our belonging cannot be lost, only forgotten. Develop a strong back, soft front and a wild heart."*
> Brené Brown

In referencing the heart, note that the Sanskrit word *anahata* points to the heart chakra to highlight the synergistic interplay of being engaged yet disentangled. Anahata means "unhurt, unstuck and unbeaten." It also translates to "sound produced without touching two parts." Interpersonally, this is about exchanging viewpoints with a peaceful heart. The rough energy of confrontation fades. Although this may seem like a paradox—to have an open heart yet still be detached—embodying anahata heart energy is liberating. It's anchored in belonging and acceptance: allowing the person and the situation to be exactly as it is.

TRY THIS: In seeing your heart chakra as the bridge between the spiritual and physical worlds, experiment with a simple activation gesture. Place your right hand on your heart center and your left hand over your right hand. Tune into the diamond of your wild heart. Absorb the color of green, representing love and transformation. Encircle green compassionate light around you and someone you feel conflicted with.

Reflect on what carefrontation might look like between you. Start a slow conversation, soul to soul. Tune into your body for guidance. When each has said what was needed, sink into the silence of just being together. Without words, see

> "We're fascinated by the words, but where we meet is in the silence behind them."
> Ram Dass

what unfolds. By harnessing your heart's ability to stay in detached caring, you can more readily bridge-build with soft power.

Saying good-bye while growing conflict intelligence

Even with sharing power, NVC and soft power interlaced into authentic collaboration, not every relationship will last. If a relationship is broken beyond repair, consider this not as a failure, but rather an opportunity to heal, grow, forgive or mend a past hurt. When letting go, we are reminded of the adage: "Relationships are meant for a reason, season or a lifetime."

When the purpose has been served and the end is at hand, say goodbye with love and gratitude. If possible, initiate a caring, closure conversation. Free your spirit with words that need to be said. Take the high road. While every relationship ending is contextual, a graceful completion involves mindful interaction. Opening the heart during the comings and goings of relationship *is the quantum shift* needed in the world. This is what sustains power-sharing as a new way of relating.

As one step forward, spend a few minutes to complete the following conflict intelligence assessment. Circle your strengths and areas of improvement. Reflect on how you can further develop your conflict intelligence. Commit to one new behavior that you feel inspired to practice.

If you find yourself blaming another, consider how this person is a mirror to you. Ask for feedback from a trusted friend. Allow for vulnerability in seeing yourself from a different set of eyes. Expanding self-knowledge ushers in greater choice. Remember that growth begins outside your comfort zone.

After completing this exercise, when you're resting in the quiet of your heart, write out all the reasons why you feel grateful for the gift of your significant relationships—even when conflict arises or the connection ends. Appreciate your willingness to practice, learn and authentically collaborate.

> **Developing Conflict Intelligence**
>
> Assess your conflict intelligence by considering the degree to which you demonstrate these authentic collaborative behaviors in one important relationship.
>
> 1—Not at all 2—Occasionally 3—Some of the time 4—Most of the time
>
> 1. _____ I separate the person from the behavior.
> 2. _____ I set an intention to mindfully collaborate.
> 3. _____ I pause to self-connect and respond, not react.
> 4. _____ I respect my own and other people's boundaries.
> 5. _____ Without interrupting, I listen attentively with empathy.
> 6. _____ I rephrase back what I heard to check for understanding.
> 7. _____ I deeply listen to uncover feelings and needs.
> 8. _____ I am self-responsible for my part of the dynamic.
> 9. _____ I observe what happened without judgment or blame.
> 10. _____ I get curious, rather than jump to conclusions.
> 11. _____ I am creative, flexible and open to sharing power.
> 12. _____ I practice carefrontation with detached caring.
> 13. _____ I forgive, noting the harm of keeping a grudge.
> 14. _____ I make clear requests for support.
> 15. _____ I see the value of conflict as a learning opportunity.

III) Hierarchy Block: Enabler of Co-creating Vision (Systems)

It's true. A hierarchical structure can help organize how work gets done. When groups are classified, roles are defined and decision-making parameters are laid out, the needs of consistency, reliability and stability can be supported. Even though systems can become bureaucratic, an efficient system can be built. As W. Edwards Deming noted, "Every system is perfectly designed to get the results it gets."

Yet, how does a hierarchical structure serve the process of collaboration? From my perspective, the negative effect of hierarchy outweighs the benefits. Whether we're referring to a family, organization or community system, hierarchy diminishes the conditions for authentic collaboration.

The term *hierarchy* comes from the Greek words *hieros* ("sacred") and *archein* ("rule or order"). It typically connotes a pyramid ranking of authority positions. According to Sergio Caredda's research, the first time the word *hierarchy* was used dates back to the 6th century AD, when theologians classified the different levels of angels. The concept then migrated into describing clergy. In contemporary society, hierarchy is an offshoot of our inherited patriarchal system. Patriarchy is a dominance hierarchy that stratifies and ranks people. Accordingly, the two concepts of hierarchy and patriarchy are closely interlinked. Both hold a dominator-dominated way of relating. Our humanity is eroded with this power imbalance, almost imperceptibly. Subconsciously and subtly, the attitudes of patriarchy and hierarchy separate people—both men and women. It's counter to both gylany, a partnership-based system, *and* democracy, a system based on full, active and equal citizenship.

> "A dominator-dominated way of relating is internalized from birth by every child brought up in a traditional, male-dominated family."
> Riane Eisler

Even though hierarchies play a functional role in all realms of Life, its nature promotes asymmetrical power. This type of power dynamic refers to a relationship whereupon one person has control over a subordinate, but not vice-versa. In organizations, hierarchies tend to encourage roles of authority that foster dominating behaviors, blind obedience and majority rule. As a result, loss of critical thinking, status quo stagnation and abuse of power are evident. When there's a strong chain of command, people lose their vested interest in both the process and outcome. Roles become inelastic, communication is impeded, people conform and simple procedures devolve into cumbersome tasks. A pyramid structure can also prevent staff, suppliers and clients from sharing design, product or service feedback. Sometimes, managers assume that people enjoy being told what to do and how to do it. Participatory methods to meaningfully engage people are sacrificed in the name of efficiency.

Hierarchical silos also stifle the spirit of collaboration. While silos exist for the sake of organizing work teams around goals, projects, skills or specific services, this structural barrier ends up creating many painful issues. Working in silos sequesters teams, bolsters exclusive decision-making, slows down workflow and festers ingrained thinking. The syndrome "we've always done it this way" is propagated. When decision-making rests in the hands of one or a few, the process bottlenecks and causes aggravation. Moreover, people develop system blindness when fixated on a departmental objective: the big picture is lost with its many interconnecting parts. Tunnel vision has us forget that everyone is on the same team. Each person is a contributor to the system. In some workplaces, silos allow people to hide, play safe and be small. Precious talent is lost. If the soil of collaboration dries up, the grapes of creativity die on the vine.

Another by-product of hierarchy is information-hoarding. When knowledge-sharing is limited to certain circles or becomes inaccessible, productivity is hampered. Hidden agendas proliferate. People tend to make up stories in a transparency vacuum. If information is withheld to compete or punish, an adversarial reflex taints the work culture. Fear and doubt spreads when there is a lack of socialization among the ranks. The power of relationships diminishes when people only relate from their roles. It's vital that colleagues connect as human beings rather than as human doings.

> *"In organizations, real power and energy is generated through relationships. The patterns of relationships and the capacities to form them are more important than tasks, functions, roles, and positions."*
> Margaret Wheatley

With hierarchical power imbalances, top-down control and bottom-up compliance becomes the norm. Middle management is sandwiched between the two in contending with demands from both groups. People become dependent on leaders to "fix it." When there's a role system of perceived importance, staff autonomy tapers, ideas are muffled and morale peters out. In effect, the divisive nature of a hierarchical structure splits a team. In the face of these challenges, authentic collaboration is a bridge to transformation. In crossing over, we begin to reorient power, question assumptions and co-create a more viable way of working.

Systems change bottom-up success story

Many people believe that shifting a system can only happen from the top-down. I beg to differ. Power can be expressed up and down the hierarchy chain, producing change that sticks. This next story showcases what's possible with courageous bottom-up collaborative action.

One organization I worked for held weekly mandatory full-team meetings. Week after week, I noticed the same pattern occurring—the manager spoke 80 percent of the time and everyone else listened passively. It seemed like a classic hierarchical power imbalance. After a couple of months, this manager came to my office and asked if I had any feedback to offer. I sensed he was genuinely open so I inquired about the lack of team participation in our meetings. I suggested that there may be other ways to better engage everyone's talents and collaborate toward our shared purpose. Possibilities included group problem-solving, co-creating new programs, brainstorming ideas, decision-making, team-building or roundtable project dialogue to improve quality and service. Although confounded, he was receptive to my feedback and willing to experiment.

To foster a collaborative culture, I proposed that we adjust the "rudder trim tab" of the team ship to transform the meeting process. We started by rotating the facilitator and note-taker roles. We also began circulating the agenda well in advance so everyone could populate the list of topics they wanted to discuss. I further suggested that we develop team guidelines to establish how we wanted to interact, problem-solve and make decisions together. To open this delicate conversation, we began to dialogue about psychological safety, trust-building and accountability. Together, as a team, we considered new ways to support each other. One colleague initiated the topic of rewarding team efforts, not only individual contribution. For the first time, co-creating goals and power-sharing became a discussable topic.

To change a system from within a system, a new consciousness is needed.

Slowly, our team process evolved. The hierarchal bridle of control loosened as team members became engaged and felt empowered. Performance up-leveled. Within a few months, other departmental teams caught wind of these changes and followed suit. Group facilitation skill-building became a popular in-house workshop. This experience convinced me that individuals at all levels of an organization can indeed influence policy and procedure. It begins with a new collaborative conversation. Since people create systems and structures, it's people who can change that which no longer serves.

The enabler of co-creation: facilitating a discovery process

An effective way to address hierarchy is to co-create vision. It's the third power pillar of the authentic collaboration bridge. While rarely discussed as a collaboration enabler, co-creating vision is vitally important for shared commitment and inspired action.

Let's start by analyzing the concept of *co-creation*. In simple terms, co-creation is about innovating together to produce something of value. It implies a mindful way of engaging people and Life in a discovery process. This is a step-change from imposing change using mandates, demands or pressure tactics. The discovery process is, by definition, participatory and inclusive. Co-creation means investing in meaningful dialogue that will surely elicit contradictory views and ideas.

Facilitating a discovery dialogue requires refined process skills since a variety of needs, values and desired outcomes will surface. It's helpful to prepare people to be open to what emerges in this uncharted territory: the journey may call into question certain norms and beliefs. Since the process speaks to change, what is known may no longer be relevant. I enjoy using Daniel Boorstin words: "The greatest obstacle to discovery is not ignorance—it is the illusion of knowledge." With healthy disruption, co-creation allows new, innovative ideas to come forth.

Because co-creation can be loaded with various layers, entanglements and ambiguities, it's a group process that can't be rushed. When divergent needs surface, the bridge road can be slick and hard to navigate. Time is needed to shift out of self-focus and into the group field. Allow for stories to be told. Warm up the room by exchanging hopes, fears, aspirations and commitments. Elicit people's wisdom. It takes patience to weave together the threads and look for common ground. Jumping into logistics and agreement-making prematurely is futile. If a co-created project or service is not formulated with true ownership, people find a way to exit through a back door. Short-changing the dialogue up front can produce back-end problems. If done well with true mutual agreement, follow-through is more apt to produce real results.

Reconfiguring the triangle into a co-created circle

As a container for a discovery dialogue or any type of co-creation, consider the revolutionary power of circle conversations. This is an excellent peer-based structure that engages everyone. The process counters the effect of hierarchical power imbalance. The hallmarks of circle communication are evocative dialogue, power-sharing, genuine connection, creative insights, inspiration and co-owned decisions—all elements of authentic collaboration. It cries out "We're in this together." When working in circles, we realize that the colonial mindset is antiquated. We also realize that people long to have conversations that matter.

> *Circle conversations are a stand for equality and inclusion. It's a revolutionary way to co-create community.*

In a circle, the premise is that wisdom exists in each person around the rim. We assume that everyone has golden nuggets of truth and a story to share. All voices are welcome yet each person is at choice in contributing. Passing around a talking piece helps gear down the conversation and avoid speaker interruption. No one speaks unless the talking piece is held. This ancient indigenous listening practice also holds periodic pauses. Offering an opportunity to pause supports people with self-connection and authentic communication. Whether at work, home or community, circle dialogue can unleash wisdom, unlock conflict and unchain the power of co-creation.

The next time you have an important group decision to make, reposition the chairs in a circle and see what unfolds. In some cultures, this may be a bold action, yet the payoffs will be striking.

Co-creating vision with the hand of Life

Blending the spirit of co-creation with the power of vision is a recipe for compelling action. When we access our own heart's vision to join with the aspirations of others, we tap into a powerhouse of possibility. Co-creating vision is a journey that explores the magic of merging people's values, passions and talents to describe a desired future state. An authentic inquiry leads us to the soft voice of our heart. When a common vision is co-created, we are

> *"Your vision will only become clear when you look into your heart. Whoever looks outside, dreams; who looks inside, awakens."*
> Carl Jung

motivated to take the conversation to the next level. It awakens us to our core values. This becomes the *driver for collaboration* in giving us energy and a sense of group direction.

Vision connects people to their shared purpose and the big picture. It becomes the reason behind the actions people take. Co-created vision and shared purpose answer the questions of what the group does, for whom and why. Whenever people are enabled to participate (versus directed) with values-led leadership, a sense of enthusiasm and aliveness resurges in the culture. The outgrowth is shared meaning and unified action.

The co-visioning process also creates space for the voice of Life to speak. By paying attention to the feedback of Life, we become the Creator's companion. The hand of Earth or Life is an invisible force that some people label as intuition, a sixth sense or an energy that comes from a higher organizing principle.

To play with this idea, host a co-creating vision conversation with a group of fellow collaborators. When two or more people gather with a shared intention, see what previously unimagined ideas spring up. Invite people to imagine a wide-open space of vast, exciting opportunity. Ask, "How can we drive into the future by looking at what's ahead rather than peering into the rear-view mirror?" Too often, our past dictates (and limits) our future. Instead, request that people courageously break open their heart desire. What wants to emerge? Let go of agendas, expectations and preconceived outcomes. Allow Life to direct the flow. When we pause and listen to the brilliance of Life, co-creation is a source of joy.

Whenever possible, I bring groups to the wild of nature to co-create vision. This change in space can open the floodgates of creativity. Boardrooms and windowless meeting rooms offer stale dialogue compared to what magnifies in the beauty of nature. When nature becomes our muse, she has an uncanny way of whispering in our ear and calling to our innermost chambers. It's moving to read about eco-activists who take direction from nature or musicians who lie under the stars with a new tune or scientists who invent while strolling along a shoreline. Leave space for the hand of the universe to orchestrate her music. Serendipity will surely arise. As social change activator Jean Houston suggests, "When the Quantum Field is drawn into your vision, it adds elements,

> *"There's no such thing as being alone in this universe, and so there's no such thing as creating alone. Every impulse, every creative gift of beauty, everything is a co-creation."*
> Gary Zukav

coincidences, and resources to the vision, as well as the people, ideas and opportunities to help you realize your new story. This is the interdependent co-arising of you and the Universe together."

Evidence of co-created vision is when people become inspired, aligned and committed to something larger than self. They become like a tuning fork: Life will respond. When inspired, we are "in spirit," living in alignment with our soul. We serve as an instrument for Earth to move through us. By fostering our heart connection in the interdependent flow, we move into the realm where anything and everything can happen. This sweet nectar is what feeds innovation, twists reality and produces the alchemy of energy moving in concert. When people join with expansive vision and shared purpose, collaborating becomes a diving board into a deep, spacious pool of new opportunities.

What questions inspire you to co-create vision?

- Who do we call to the co-creation table?
- In our co-creative process, what cause or idea brings us together?
- Why are we motivated to act?

- Given our intentions, what crossroad are we at?
- What's in our heart about the issue at hand?
- To unpack expectations, what is on and off the table?

- With zero constraints, what would our ideal vision look like?
- With our vision, what is our shared purpose?
- What creative tensions are calling out to be discussed?

- Do we have sufficient clarity in our goals, roles and rules?
- How do we sense Life guiding us? What does our intuition say?
- On a scale of 1-10, how committed are we to our vision?

Collaboration blocks and enablers through the lens of nature

Speaking of the voice of Earth, let's conclude with what she teaches us about collaboration blocks and enablers. The natural world offers many insights about the aforementioned issues: victim-thinking and self-empowerment, conflict and power-sharing, hierarchy and co-creating vision.

Starting with victim-thinking, the natural world does not succumb to this consciousness. Each being knows its place, value and role in the ecosystem. When people walk in an old-growth forest, it's easy to feel the majestic nature of trees. They remind us to embrace our power while adjusting to what's around, to stand tall yet not be rigid. Trees are adaptive by nature, pun intended. When we look up at the crown of a forest, we see trees basking in the glory of interdependence. They grow their branches in between and around tree friends so that all benefit from direct sunshine. When they fall due to old age, disease or a windstorm, they cause the least damage to their neighbors. Each living being is significant to the web of Life.

Furthermore, trees radiate empowerment in living their purpose without questioning their worth. As co-creative social beings, they are intricately interwoven into the living nest around them. They literally nourish others. Trees collaborate with their neighbors, their leaves break the force of rain so water percolates into ground-level plants, their bark offers shelter for insects and their roots feed from the soil. Even mother trees send extra nutrients through their root system to baby trees.

> *"The best and most beautiful things cannot be seen or even touched. They must be felt with the heart."*
> Helen Keller

Ecologist Suzanne Simard offers fascinating research about the miles of fungi filament in a forest. As it turns out, dying trees send phosphorus and nitrogen to healthy trees to "transfer its legacy" across generations and across species. A study showed that if two friend trees have roots that are closely intertwined, when one dies or is cut down, there's a good chance the other one will die soon thereafter. Butterflies depend on flowering bushes to feed on and, in turn, cross-fertilize other plant species. Plants lean on animals for nutrients, pollination and seed dispersal. After death, animals decompose to become natural compost for trees and plants. And so, the cycle of existence turns. Every healthy forest is a beautiful exhibition of *empowering interconnection*.

In the domain of conflict, trees occasionally deal with interspecies attacks. When this occurs, forester Peter Wohlleben explains that trees use their fungal root network to carry news of attack from one being to the other. Using this "Wood Wide Net," trees send electrical impulses to the other trees to warn them of the threat so that other trees can react by biochemically changing to protect themselves. Trees also produce airborne compounds that attract the natural predators of those pests. In the natural world, all beings align with the intention of equilibrium and harmony. For billions of years, nature's strategy consistently manages to effectively keep the ratio of predator and prey in balance. Ecological symmetry has withstood the test of time. It's a wondrous miracle to witness how interspecies conflict becomes a harmonious colorful interplay.

While humans tend to resort to violence and war, nature offers a collaborative path. Author Mehran Banaei states that nature offers much wisdom in the realm of sociopolitical conflict intelligence. For example, inter- and intraspecies disputes are settled in an efficacious manner. The sole criterion is rebalancing the ecosystem. As Banaei remarks, "When it comes to a territorial dispute or mating rights, birds communicate with each other and to other species in magnificent style. Among most birds, singing a musical song is the weapon of choice to resolve conflict." Banaei points out that nature does not settle disputes with judges or juries. There's no mitigation or litigation, no bargaining or appeals. Police are not needed to enforce the verdict. The participants are the judges themselves. In the absence of arrogance and egoism, defeat (for lack of a better word) is accepted graciously. A dispute does not result in the destruction of a habitat or the decimation of species. To the contrary, the relating of interspecies contributes to harmonious sustainability. Nature's model is all about *collaboration*. She creates conditions that are conducive to Life, not to destruction.

> "When we pay attention to nature's music, we find that everything on Earth contributes to its harmony."
> Hazrat Inayat Khan

In the animal world, there's a growing body of evidence that suggests that other primates also have effective behavioral tools to resolve conflicts. After two female baboons fight, for example, the winner approaches the loser with a soft grunt. The grunt signals her wish to stop fighting and enables her to interact peacefully with the one she just defeated. When bottlenose dolphins sideswipe each other in an act of aggression, the conflict is resolved with gentle headbutting and mutual close passing. Dolphins also present their belly to show vulnerability. Similar kinds of "reconciliation" behaviors have been documented in other primate species, such as spotted hyenas and domestic goats. *Power-sharing* is found throughout nature.

When it comes to hierarchy in the animal kingdom, some species display a social pecking order for the sake of survival, hunting, resource distribution and mating. Wolf packs and lion prides, for instance, depend on highly organized group behavior. Animals like stallion horses, male deer, tigers, bears, crocodiles and silverback gorillas exhibit a strong alpha presence. Yet, it's interesting to note that non-human primate research repeatedly demonstrates that dominance hierarchies decrease cooperation. In a similar vein, other research has found that social power among primates is *based on cooperation*. Chimp behavior focuses less on self-interest, strength and coercion and more on the ability to negotiate differences, enforce group norms and allocate food fairly. Primates who try to dominate others in a hierarchy by prioritizing their own interests will find themselves, in time, overthrown by peers. Given that humans share 99 percent of our DNA with chimps, our closest living relatives, these studies are illuminating. Once again, the research plugs into the value of working together collaboratively.

> *"There is something infinitely healing in the repeated refrain of nature—the assurance that dawn comes after night, and spring after the winter."*
> Rachel Carson

In countless ways, human collaboration can be greatly inspired and enabled by Nature's Laws. Resources are distributed to all the inhabitants. Healing and regeneration unfolds effortlessly. Her patient flow syncs up with the seasons. Life happens in its own time, pace and rhythm. There's no need to push anything to happen. When in her presence, we become present. The moment becomes sacred.

If we cultivated collaboration by holding the peace of nature in our hearts, our relationships would surely transform.

CHAPTER 8

RELATE GUIDING PRINCIPLES AND PRACTICES
R = RESPOND BY BALANCING
GIVING AND RECEIVING

*"Giving and receiving are different expressions of
the same flow of energy in the universe."*
Deepak Chopra

Constructing the bridge to RELATE effectively

In exploring collaboration blocks and enablers, we also highlighted the three bridge power pillars: empowering self, sharing power and co-creating vision. Now, we turn our attention to the six vertical ties that connect to and support the bridge deck. Each one is responsible for absorbing and rebalancing heavy traffic. With this metaphor in mind, I offer six guiding principles via the acronym RELATE to support the load of authentic collaboration. The principles are intended to uphold the bridge platform of mutual respect through times of ease and struggle.

These RELATE ties are principles because principles have robust staying power. Overall, I prefer principles over rules and inside-out change over quick fixes. Since collaboration is a comprehensive skill set involving psychology, sociology, social cues, organizational dynamics and change theory, no set formula nor framework can do the job. No single set of rules can be completely and consistently applied to another reality. Consequently, applying the six RELATE principles is not straightforward. Your application will depend on the context, relationship, perspective and culture. Relationship-building is an adaptive art, not a linear, undeviating process. Accordingly, the bridge's steel ties are both solid and permeable. They bend and flex with the winds of change.

As discussed, how we perceive reality shapes reality. Our unique background influences how we relate to the people and circumstances around us. Bearing this in mind, the RELATE principles act as a compass, pointing to relationship intelligence best practices even though the application may differ. While reading these next six chapters, I invite you to reflect on and experiment with these six principles. Note what works and what doesn't work for you in bringing the vision of authentic collaboration to your relationships.

> **When collaborating, to what degree do you RELATE?**
>
> **R** = Respond by balancing giving and receiving
> **E** = Empathize by connecting with heart
> **L** = Listen by uncovering feelings and needs
> **A** = Appreciate by welcoming different perspectives
> **T** = Trust by speaking authentically
> **E** = Equalize by valuing process and outcome

Applying the RELATE principles to your life

These RELATE chapters expound on the *what*, *why* and *how* of each guiding principle. Of these three aspects, the *how* is the most important puzzle piece. Building the muscle of authentic collaboration is far more challenging than understanding each principle and its value. The process speaks to our soul in exploring how resonant and aligned we are with the principles of bridge-building. Undeniably, introspection is deeply personal. As such, take your time with the practice exercises at the end of each RELATE chapter. Slowly meander the path of self-discovery: the mind-body-spirit exercises are lush with meaning, healing and growth.

To support a holistic approach, the *how* exercises strengthen all three lanes of the collaborative bridge: self, others and Earth. Each set of exercises starts with self—a limb of yoga called svadhaya. This means self-reflection, finding out who you are without the labels of who you *think* you are. Complementing the svadhaya practice are exercises that focus on how we relate with other people. For this section, I invite you to find a learning buddy, a small group or a book club. Many of the exercises can be carried out in-person and virtually. With the

AUTHENTIC COLLABORATION

Earth exercises, it's ideal to carve out time outdoors to feel into your connection with the natural world. Find a location to relax into the arms of Mother Nature. Note that all three levels pertain to relationships in general and authentic collaboration in particular.

When we apply the principles in our life, we activate our commitment to inner-outer whole-person development. By metabolizing our experience and integrating the learning, we embody a new way to RELATE. We augment our relational power by transmuting the energy that holds us back from authentic collaboration. Transmuting energy does not mean "getting rid of" blocks, fears and limiting beliefs but rather to enfold this contracted part of ourselves into our heart. This process of integration is what produces noticeable change. Integrated embodiment is the ultimate key to unlocking the door to authentic collaboration to live in ayni.

> *One of the most extraordinary powers people have is the capacity to change behavior at will.*

To be clear, the practice exercises herein support *voluntary* belief and behavior change. The prevailing wisdom is that people are motivated to change behavior by either seeking pleasure or avoiding pain. To put a fine point on this, human beings are driven to step beyond that which brings us discomfort. In the arena of collaborative relationship, the driver of pleasure can be meaningful connection, solace in nature, a sense of belonging, higher team performance, heightened well-being or a desire to be centered and grounded. The aim of relieving discomfort may include releasing the victim-perpetrator-rescuer triangle of interaction. Or to resolve conflict with greater ease. Or to let go of a co-dependent addiction. Or to support colleagues who are stuck in the quicksand of complacency. Whatever your motivation and wherever you sit on the pleasure-pain spectrum, bring some light-hearted humor to this practice. See authentic collaboration as a playful exercise.

While relationship soft skills are the "hardest" ones to develop, this process can be filled with inspiration and delight. Like any other growth opportunity, it takes commitment and willpower. Lasting change starts with incremental baby steps. If you commit to a habitual practice, your proficiency will exponentially expand. Find a way to incorporate this practice into your daily life. Ensure reflection time includes celebration. In the end, we are all worthy and deserving of experiencing greater love, joy and peace in our relationships.

R = Respond by Balancing Giving and Receiving
The minefield of reactivity

This principle starts off with the distinction between reactivity and mindful response. Reactivity is born in pain and lives in suffering. Mindful response is born in connection and lives in authenticity. While honoring the message of the former, relating from the latter is the zenith of healthy relationship-building—with self, others and Earth.

As discussed in the conflict intelligence section, reacting is normal—especially when we feel hurt, angry or attacked. To react is to "act back from" an experience without due consideration. We become like a rubber band, automatically snapping back when stressed. On a deeper level, reactivity is a sign of being disconnected from our body and inner wisdom. If this pattern of disconnection is ongoing, trauma may be at the root. Be it childhood neglect, domestic violence, attachment shock, abandonment, verbal aggression or physical injury, trauma-based reactivity is very much a part of the relationship terrain.

When trauma occurs, fragmented parts of us get caught in a circuit of disassociation. Undigested or unfelt emotion becomes trapped in our body like a hostage, waiting to be freed. Our nervous system triggers defense mechanisms. Our personality splits into two, with one aspect of vulnerability branching out in our consciousness and another aspect developing a coping strategy for self-preservation. When these coping strategies are set in motion, we present different aspects of our personality. It's like we have many actors playing out a predetermined script within our body. The script details our triggers and how our emotions become hijacked by our limbic brain. This limbic part of our brain, especially the amygdala, plays a vital role in controlling various emotional states such as fear, rage and anxiety. When automatic habits take over, our emotions seem uncontrollable and reactivity kicks in. Conscious choice contracts and aliveness shrinks. Authentic collaboration becomes very challenging.

Thanks to the pioneering work of neuroscientists, the neural biology of reactivity has now been well-documented. According to Dr. Daniel J. Siegel, when we have a conversation with someone, we know that our senses take in data via perceptual filters. These filters, designed to keep us safe, is what Siegel calls "an anticipation machine." Rather than being fully present with the speaker, we anticipate what's being said from either the conditioned past or imagined future. To counter this tendency, Siegel teaches people a meditation process that allows them to practice "open awareness." This is about resting in awareness, noticing what it's like to be conscious without paying attention to details. We let go of the need to concentrate and instead become aware of being aware of what's happening around and within us. In Siegel's book, *Aware: The Science and Practice of Presence*, he writes, "In everyday life, open awareness means approaching situations with fresh eyes, letting go of our habitual reactions and our expectations for the future."

> "As an advanced contemplative technique, open awareness has the potential of offering more freedom, peace and well-being in our lives."
> Dr. Daniel Siegel

Another helpful practice is to notice how confirmation bias affects our relationships. This bias has us create what we already believe and, as such, confirms our views. In other words, we attract circumstances that substantiate our beliefs and thus believe our perceptions to be accurate and complete. This neural net of activity is designed to help us survive. Yet, if we perceive someone to be a threat, real or imagined, our limbic brain generates a chain reaction. The prefrontal cortex, which is the rational, sense-making part of the brain, shuts down. Our stories become engrained with subcortical looping. We gather evidence and produce a circular feedback loop, generating one misperception after another. We're seduced into believing our thoughts to be the *whole truth*. This misperception wheel is the root of all suffering. That said, we can alter our perceptions by becoming aware, and thus begin healing our habit of reactivity.

> *How do you carry the misperception that you hold the "Truth" about a situation or person?*

With this awareness, we realize the irony of perception. We believe that our perception is the "Truth," yet, in actuality, it only offers one lens or viewpoint of reality. Everything we perceive is subjective by nature. A truly objective perspective is not biologically possible. This does not discount our experience, but rather acknowledges how we processed what happened. Perception is not reality yet it can become our reality because perception influences how we look at Life. With a perceptual reactive groove, we disconnect and no longer relate to others from a centered, integrated place. The uplink to our heart intelligence is cut off. When we're not able to be present, authentic communication is stymied.

When this maladaptive pattern arises, it's helpful to remember these energies are fleeting—real sensations but not true. This is the distinction between validating what's so while compassionately questioning our internal reactivity. In doing so, we discern our thoughts with self-empathy. With choice and meaningful connection, we come "home" to self and grow our capacity for mindful response.

The lifelong practice of mindful response

In a sense, reactivity gives away our freedom. When someone influences our reaction, this person determines our emotional state and shapes our behavior. Why not turn the tables and make our behavior our choice, not theirs? So let's look at *how* we can step into mindful response.

Mindful response is about creating space. In Tara Bennett-Goleman's insightful book entitled *Emotional Alchemy*, she writes about Dr. Benjamin Libet's neurosurgical experiments. He discovered that our brain experiences "a magical quarter-second" between stimulus and reaction: that's the amount of time between receiving sensory input into our brain and deciding how to react. This is the time lapse between feeling anger (impulse) and yelling (action). Do we follow the emotion-fueled impulse of our will or disregard it?

Tara explains that if we choose to pause, self-connect and consider what's happening, we can elongate this quarter-second of time and mindfully respond. Rather than automatically reacting, we can interrupt our habits. A micro-moment is all it takes to shift into skillful response and take constructive action toward authentic collaboration. Literally, this is about creating brain space within. Owning the moment is the choice-point of empowerment.

> *"Mindfulness is a way of befriending ourselves and our experience. The little things? The little moments? They aren't little."*
> Jon Kabat-Zinn

AUTHENTIC COLLABORATION

A mindfulness practice is not only inwardly focused but also outwardly oriented. As contemporary teacher Thomas Hübl wisely asks, "How can I experience you before I respond?" This involves self-awareness and discipline to remain in the moment to stay related. Mindfully engaging gives collaboration the oxygen it needs to breathe. By slowing down the conversation, we have the chance to play with and elongate space. Here, we can learn more about the feelings and beliefs behind what's said. We can inquire about the underlying motivation. Mindful, heart-centered communication is symptomatic of an enlightened way of relating. It's choosing to chauffeur the drive towards peaceful relations.

> *What is the why behind what was said or done?*

As one definition, mindfulness is becoming aware of our thoughts and emotions without interpreting or judging. As Eckhart Tolle teaches, it's about being present to make peace with the moment. In his book *A New Earth*, Tolle writes, "The present moment is the field on which the game of life happens." To support mindful presence, I often take periodic pauses to consciously breathe and to bring myself back to the moment of now. This simple action is like a soothing salve. My reactive brain calms down. This practice of emotional intelligence—leaning into uncomfortable feelings and allowing them to be as they are—dissipates uncomfortable emotions in its own time. If my angst continues, this is a sign that I have not yet been fully present with this energy. Perhaps a part of me is judging the emotion or circumstance. When I do self-connect and accept what's so, my authenticity bandwidth expands. I become self-nurturing and resilient.

For most of us, mindful response is a lifelong practice. In our family, workplace and community, it's a daily invitation to respect our own and other's feelings and needs; to notice our interior space and the group field; to pay attention to the content and process of what's happening. Balancing task and relationship is an ongoing check-in. Since every group has its own degree of resonance and dissonance, this is a high-level and-both mindset. It's a tall order, yet the outcome is worth the effort. Enhanced inner peace is the spin-off. "Peace is this moment without judgment," writes poet Dorothy Hunt, "this moment in the heart-space where everything that is, is welcome."

The power of intention

The power of intention also supports a mindful response. Setting an intention is an empowering declaration of commitment. It directs energy and frames the conversation in a positive manner. With an intention, we consciously think thoughts about the future we want. What we focus on is what grows. Stating an intention helps us tune in and be honest about what we desire *and* what the situation calls for. It's an act of veracity. Sharing it outright supports clarity, concentration and connection.

Giving ourselves even a few moments to reflect on our motivation makes a difference in how we collaborate. The intention shapes the approach which determines how others respond to us. This deliberate action influences the route from start to finish. It's how self-trust grows, which, in turn, builds trust with others. Our intention about bridge-building is as important as the end goal or destination.

> "You get what you intend to create by being in harmony with the power of intention, which is responsible for all of creation."
> Wayne Dyer

Truth be told, intention-setting is not always easy. A mentor once told me that, in any given moment, we typically have at least three intentions that drive our behavior. The surface or appearance level has to do with societal conditioning. If we inadvertently hook into the collective mindset, we start believing that it's what we want. We may even state an agreeable intention that we think others want to hear. The second level of intention is connected to our inner conditioning, reflecting what we believe is right, appropriate or beneficial. The third level reveals our deeper or sublime heart desire. If our mindful intention-setting extends from our heart, we discover that it's an alcove of authenticity, where love and wisdom converge.

TRY THIS: Bring to mind a collaborative dialogue that you anticipate having in the days ahead. Spend some time reflecting on your intention. Ask why several times to strip away the layers and source your real intention. Is your intention rooted in your egoic personality? What does your heart want? If this relationship is complicated, revisit your intentions periodically. Time may reveal subtle motivations bubbling beneath the surface. Honestly discern if your intention is only in your best interests or does it serve all involved?

A story of transforming reactivity with intention

When caught in the pitfall of reactivity, a dialogue about intentions supports a mindful response. An organizational team I worked for experienced a great deal of action-reaction conversation. One day, I was in a management meeting and a comment was made that triggered me. Without thinking, I contradicted the speaker and provided proof of his error. In embarrassment, he countered my reaction with criticism. The conflict escalated. Mercifully, someone called for a break. During this pause, I went outside for some fresh air and sighed while guilt swept through me. I knew that my reactive comment hurt this already fragile relationship. The incident punched a hole in the trust bucket, draining precious water of goodwill between us. After taking some deep breaths, I walked into his office to apologize but was told to leave before I uttered a word. The damage was done.

When the meeting reconvened, an awkward tension filled the room because this manager chose not to return. With a heavy heart, I said to everyone, "I've taken a lot of training on effective communication, but I still have much to learn. I want everyone to know that I regret the conflict that just happened. I tried to apologize, and now, I also want to apologize to you. My intention is to become more mindful in how I communicate so I can enhance, not detract from our collaboration." After this sharing, a long pregnant pause followed. This level of authenticity was counterculture. Then, someone spoke about her intention to reconnect to this team, admitting that she had been feeling disengaged for months. Two more managers followed suit in sharing their intentions. Our conversation became very revealing with uncharacteristic truth-telling.

At times, there's a difference between what we think we've done, what we intended to do and how other people experience what happened. In this case, my relationship breakdown sparked a breakthrough to break open team dialogue. I rediscovered that when we feel judged, heart walls go up, brick by brick. When we feel accepted, everything and everyone around us softens. Even when spinning in a cycle of reactivity, using the power of intention and shifting into mindful response can repair harm and bridge-build to something new.

Balancing giving and receiving

> "Balance is not a passive resting place—it takes work, balancing the giving and the taking, the raking out and the putting in."
> Robin Wall Kimmerer

With mindful response, we become aware of how we balance giving and receiving with all our relations. We sink into the realization that nature operates with a gift economy. She offers sustenance without any agreement on payment or trade in return. When communicating with people, we notice that we're at choice in equalizing how much we speak with how much we listen. Full, mindful presence helps us see our conversational patterns. We can ask, "Am I overly me-focused or other-focused?" If the dynamic is off-kilter, we can choose to restore the balance. This may require suspending the moment between someone's sharing to absorb what's been given. On the flip side, it may mean taking space to be truly heard and seen. In supporting mutuality, we endow our relationships with the message that, "All are of value." At the deepest level, heart-centered giving *is* receiving. There is no difference. This is a core principle of authentic collaboration.

Of course, every relationship will move through different stages whereupon each person will give more than receive. The back and forth oscillation depends on the situation. Balancing giving and receiving is not about maintaining a 50:50 dynamic but rather to come back to the center when possible. Indeed, our relationships would transform if we let go of the 50:50 ratio to take on 100 percent responsibility. Flourishing does not arise from half-hearted effort.

Feeling worthy and deserving of being fully seen is a struggle for many people. Including me. Worthiness is a state of being that says, "I'm enough." Receiving says, "My needs matter too." Believing we have the right to exist is central to allowing ourselves to be truly nourished in relationship. Low self-worth can lie beneath a reluctance to receive. A life coach gave me the distinction that lack of deservingness conjures up guilt, whereas unworthiness evokes shame. Each has its own brand and flavor. Building self-worth has little to do with the merit gained from accomplishment. It's a belief system that underpins identity, regardless of external achievements.

> "He had always known that to truly receive, you had to give. Now he understood the equal truth: that to be able to give with a whole heart, you had to be prepared to receive in turn."
> Elizabeth Rolls

Given how crucial self-worth is to authentic collaboration and to balancing giving and receiving, developing this aspect is essential. Tiny changes can have a big impact. For example, when someone asks you how you are, and they mean it, elaborate on your authentic truth. Learn to be comfortable with the attention. If you need to cry (and we all do from time to time), allow another to witness or hold you with compassion. If you need to break a promise, do so with gentle assertion rather than over-apologizing. Inquire into the voice of your inner critic. Be generous with daily self-appreciations.

In our Western culture, we're often taught to be "nice" or "polite" rather than authentic. This can translate into over-giving. We may find ourselves listening more than speaking. If we speak too much, we may judge ourselves as selfish in taking too much air space. Women hear this message repeatedly because we are esteemed for giving. Given the strong intuitive impulse many women have toward relationships, this conditioning can prompt women to take on a martyr syndrome. To self-sacrifice in the name of altruism can, in some circles, outrank self-care.

Over-giving can also translate into being over-responsible. Check-in and self-evaluate: are we taking on that which is not ours? There's a price we pay for over-pleasing. Taxing ourselves with the burden of other people's challenges—even in the name of empathizing—hinders authentic collaboration. Being over-responsible devalues the ethic of co-creation and the spirit of equal partnership.

At one point I had a business partner who was an over-giver. She put pressure on herself for fear of reprisal. This pattern gave her a fast ticket to burnout. Upon reflection, she became mindful as to why she said yes when she really meant no. She heightened her awareness of boundary-setting and why she evaded offers of support. We discussed how we could strengthen our authentic communication. When she felt an imbalance in her giving and receiving, she recalibrated by stepping out of servitude and back into right relationship with service. The upshot was a gradual building of trust within herself and between us as colleagues.

TRY THIS: Reflect on your own interactions in the past few weeks. To what extent is your giving whole-hearted? Do you carry a hidden agenda in wanting to be acknowledged or praised? Does a part of you want to alleviate guilt? In your giving, notice if you feel depleted or enlivened, frustrated or satisfied. How can you rebalance your giving and receiving to experience more collaborative fulfillment?

A life-changing story about receiving to give anew

When I think about balancing giving and receiving, my relationship with Earth or Life comes to mind. Until recently, my trust in Life would ebb and flow, depending on what was happening in my world. In times of happiness, I trusted her unabashedly. In moments of stuckness, I questioned Life's plan for me and experienced doubt at every turn. Even though Life's love for me was and is unconditional, the love I gave back was conditional. My hesitancy to trust Life affected my ability to authentically collaborate.

> *"None of us knows what might happen even the next minute, yet still we go forward. Because we trust. Because we have faith."*
> Paulo Coelho

Then, Life gave me a profound wake-up call. Literally. My father's physician phoned to inform me that my dad was dying. If I wanted to see him again, I needed to book a flight and hurry home. I did exactly that, yet, due to this last-minute booking, the trip included a brief stopover. When I left for the airport, the sky opened to release a heavy rainstorm. It felt like an omen of what was to come. En route, traffic was extra heavy and slow. I realized that I wasn't going to make my flight. In a moment of panic, I prayed and asked Life for a thirty-minute flight delay. Then I phoned the airline to check the details. Amazingly, I learned that my flight was postponed by exactly thirty minutes. I breathed a sigh of relief and expressed deep gratitude to Life. But the saga continued.

As my taxi approached the airport, a minor car accident had traffic snarled to a stop. The terminal was so close and yet so far. I tensed up and again asked Life for a flight delay. This time, fifteen minutes. With trepidation, I explained to the driver that my father was on his death bed. In sympathy, the driver stepped on the gas and drove on the gravel to bypass the accident scene. I arrived at the terminal, ran to check-in, only to learn that my flight was further delayed, by exactly fifteen minutes. I was astounded as I breathed another sigh of relief.

AUTHENTIC COLLABORATION

But lo and behold, more drama was to come.

When the plane approached the stopover city, ominous storm clouds prevented us from landing. We had to circle the airport again and again because clearance was denied. I felt a surge of panic when the pilot announced that we would be delayed indefinitely. I felt helpless, desperately wanting to be at my father's side but instead trapped in a plane that couldn't land. In that exasperated moment, I called upon Life for a third favor—to delay the second flight by twenty minutes.

To reassure myself, I recalled the two astonishing flight delays that had just happened. I intuitively knew that this was my moment to fully surrender and trust Life. My inner voice told me all would be well. With a heavy exhale, I let go and let Life take over. Minutes later, the pilot announced that the clouds had miraculously parted. A wave of elation washed over me when he said, "Buckle up for landing." After disembarking, I ran through the terminal and arrived at the connecting gate, panting with anxiety. The attendant greeted me with the words, "Relax, the flight has been delayed twenty minutes because of the storm." I stood paralyzed. It seemed incredulous that all three of my requests to Life had been granted *exactly* as I had asked. Floodgates of pent-up emotion burst open, and I started to weep. Upon seeing this, the attendant gently said, "Don't worry, dear, we'll be boarding soon!"

During these intense moments, Life took me by the hand and reassured me that I was seen, heard and loved. Despite my flip-flop trusting habit, I was supported at every turn. Yes, I had, on occasion, felt abandoned by Life by my own disconnection, but my heart reminded me that Life never abandoned me. With this unbelievable set of circumstances, I de-storied my long-held narrative. I cried tears of mourning for my father and myself. I decided to balance my giving by receiving grace. If I expanded my faith and harmonized my rhythm with Life, we would become powerful co-collaborators.

With this realization, I arrived at my father's bedside at the perfect time. We spent his last hour of consciousness giving and receiving love. As I looked into his eyes, I shared what was in my heart and said goodbye—for now.

> *"Death ends a life, not a relationship."*
> Mitch Albom

Practice the Principle: Respond by Balancing Giving and Receiving

Self-Discovery

Exercise A: A Mindfulness Sentence Completion

Our early childhood profoundly affects our adult relationships. The degree of closeness, nurturing, affection and recognition we experience from our parents and caregivers has an enormous influence on how we collaborate. The extent to which we develop healthy attachments is shaped, in large part, by our childhood experiences. This is when we develop schemas or mentally stored patterns of social behavior. Whatever our history, our memories can evolve. Our story isn't finished until our last breath.

This exercise helps you unpack early relationships and the meaning you attach to them, offering insight as to how you balance giving and receiving and why you react the way you do. This reflection may support you in shifting out of reactivity and into mindful response. The more we're able to respond versus react, the better able we are to authentically collaborate.

As you write your responses to these questions, pay attention to your feelings and self-talk. Consider sharing your answers to help you process.

Self-Discovery Questions

1. My earliest memory in relationship to my family is…
2. In my childhood, my needs were met by…
3. How I felt with my family was…
4. Growing up, I was triggered by… And now, I become reactive when…
5. The extent to which I held self-respect as a teenager was… And now…
6. My experience of collaboration growing up was…
7. What expands and contracts my ability to trust is…
8. One action I will take to deepen self-respect is…
9. How I balance giving and receiving in a relationship is…
10. To me, a healthy, nurturing relationship looks like…

Exercise B: Strengthening the Diaphragm: A Bodily Bridge

Sitting at the base of the lungs is the diaphragm, a large muscle that serves as our body's bridge. The diaphragm connects both the feminine left and masculine right sides and the lower three chakras with the upper four chakras. This muscle also represents our ability to balance receiving from Life via inhaling with giving to Life via exhaling.

To strengthen this biological bridge, practice mindful breathing by laying down and engaging with your diaphragm. With every breath, notice how tense or relaxed this muscle is. Are your breaths shallow in raising your shoulders or deep in expanding your belly? Is it easier for you to receive or give? Place one hand on your chest and the other hand on your stomach. As you inhale, slowly breathe in through your nose to the count of five. Imagine your breath is gently being pulled down toward your stomach. Exhale through pursed lips while your belly rises. Again, count to five. In both receiving and giving, try to keep your chest still so that a full oxygen exchange occurs in your stomach. Be present to the messages your body's diaphragmatic bridge offers you during this exercise. If emotion arises, allow the sensation to pass through.

If you practice diaphragmatic breathing for five to ten minutes each day, you'll notice your core muscles strengthen, your heart rate and blood pressure decrease and your body relax. How we attune to ourselves reveals how we do so when collaborating with others and Earth.

As another bodily experiment, recall a recent collaboration conflict. Practice using the bridge of your spinal cord to connect your mind's story of what happened to your heart and gut intelligence. Bring your focus, breath and energy down your cord to your heart and gut. Notice what insights arise in each of your body's power centers. Receive somatic wisdom by giving yourself the gift of inner bridge-building.

Exercise C: Opening our Hands to Receive

Lay down on a bed or a yoga mat and place your hands at your side. Notice if the palms of your hands are facing up or down. If your inclination is to place your palms down, you are likely a giver. To practice receiving, flip your hands over so they open to the sky. Breathe deeply. Create an intention to embody balanced giving and receiving.

Authentic Collaboration Practice with Others
Exercise A: A Dialogue about Giving and Receiving

With someone you care about at home, at work or in community, practice connecting with *both* yourself and the other person simultaneously. Notice where your attention goes and how your energy flows between you. Explore your relationship with the following prompter questions:

- Overall, how do we balance giving and receiving in our relationship?
- Generally, how much do I/you listen versus speak?
- What is the degree of mutuality I/you experience?
- Why do you think we relate the way we do?
- What are we afraid to give and receive in our relationship?
- If off-balance, how can we come into ayni or a stronger sense of mutual respect and reciprocity?

Exercise B: Noticing Reaction Habits in a Team

With a team you belong to, open a dialogue to discuss an issue such as purpose, structure, development stages, membership, rewards or challenges. During the conversation, uncover different viewpoints and notice reaction habits. Observe the seesaw of relationship—of independence and interdependence, of reaction and mindful response. Pay attention to how team members engage each other, encourage heart communication, actively listen, demonstrate flexibility, offer non-verbal messages and ask thoughtful questions. Pause and discuss how you are interacting.

Take note of the pattern of giving and receiving, with yourself and the team. What is your comfort zone? To practice giving, ask, "How can I support you?" or "Tell me more." To practice receiving, ask for sincere feedback or an appreciation. Drink in the acknowledgment. To what extent are members giving what they want to give and receiving what they want to receive?

Keep in mind the infinity symbol, which represents simplicity in balancing both giving and receiving. How does your team carry this energetic ribbon? How are you able to stay centered in the midpoint of this symbol?

As a follow-up, consider co-creating team guidelines to support authentic collaboration. Discuss what's important to each person and speak about commonalities. This exercise is about becoming conscious of what's important about team communication and interaction. Again, notice the extent to which your team holds all needs and perspectives with care. Develop a list of four to six team guidelines to start. Finish by exploring how to hold each other accountable. Regularly revisit these guidelines to ensure it's a living document.

Exercise C: Co-creating a Vision with the Power of Curiosity

Visioning, and successful negotiation, are based on two things: reciprocity and curiosity. This is what sits at the heart of co-creating something new with one person or a group.

With this in mind, review the questions in the collaborative template provided on the next page. With a partner, think about your respective work and choose a project that would benefit from working together. The project can be currently at play or in the ideation stage. It can even be imaginative to simply practice the art of co-creation.

Select the questions that resonate with you. Take a few minutes to first reflect on your responses as it relates to your own project vision or goal. Then, practice having an authentic collaborative dialogue together.

Consider this to be an exercise in growing your awareness of how you balance giving and receiving.

- How connected did you feel in your communication?

- How did you respect the needs of self and other?

- How would you describe the interplay of reciprocity?

Authentic Collaboration: A Co-creation Template

Before the Conversation: Becoming Clear on Intention
- Given my vision/project, what would success look like to me?
- If I was granted any wish, what would be my biggest, boldest dream?
- What does my vision really mean to me?
- What are my hopes and concerns?

Developing a Commitment
- Regarding this vision/project, what am I committed to?
- How can I distill this into a clear, one-line commitment statement?
- What am I willing to do and not do to support this goal?
- What's most important and non-negotiable?

Discerning Needs
- What do I want versus need?
- What's missing?
- What do I think is crucial to achieving success?
- What resources (time, talent, money) are required to achieve my goal?

During the Conversation: Exploring What's Possible
- I'm curious about your vision, project, goal, commitment. Tell me more.
- What is your story in bringing you to this collaboration?
- What issue or question keeps you up at night?
- What values and needs underpin this initiative?

Agreement-Making
- What is the echo in our stories? What's the natural fit or a common link?
- If we yield to the unknown, what do we sense Life wants us to do together?
- Does a partnership make sense in this context? If so, what's our goal?
- In our collaboration, what do we see as the benefits and risks?

Support Requests
- To move forward, how can we best support each other?
- Would you be willing to____? If this is not doable, what's another option?
- What actions will best move our agreement forward?
- How can we measure success and assess progress?

Promises
- What is the promise we're willing to make that constitutes a major shift?
- I commit to ____ by this time ____. Is that agreeable to you?
- Let's communicate by way of ____ on this date of ____ to exchange updates.
- How can we hold ourselves accountable to respect our partnership?

Collaborative Connection with Earth or Life

Exercise A: Giving our Beauty to Earth

Consider these poetic words by Toko-pa Turner from her book entitled, "Belonging: Remembering Ourselves Home."

"As we apprentice ourselves to the way of nature, we begin to understand that all of Life is in a continuous cycle of giving and receiving. It is the honoring of this cycle that makes us feel at home in ourselves and in relation to the rest of nature. In order to experience true belonging, we must not only acknowledge the gifts we are receiving, but also give our beauty away, no matter how it may be received by others."

Reflect on how you want to acknowledge the gifts you receive and how you want to give away your beauty to Life. What would bring you delight? It may be planting a native tree or tending to a garden. Decide on a meaningful goal. Use this action to become mindful of how you give to and receive from Earth.

Exercise B: Earth-Sky Body Movement

Ideally, try this exercise outside on the grass barefoot. In a tai-chi type of flow movement, begin by leaning over at your waist to reach for the ground. Hang like a ragdoll. In this bend, scoop the fertile, abundant energy of Earth into your hands. Cup this energy and bring it up through your feet, legs, hips and torso until your hands reach your heart. Pause here and feel the love from Earth.

Next, with your hands, bring some of your heart energy up through your neck and head to extend up to the sky. With your arms outstretched, give Life your love. Send gratitude to the vast sky, sun, moon and stars. After a couple of breaths, bring the sun's energy into your head with your hands, allowing the light to cascade down into your heart. Drink in the warmth. Finally, bring some of your heart energy down into your belly, legs and feet. Notice how your feet feel as they sink into the grass. When we send healing energy to the land, we also receive healing.

Conclude by sending a message of appreciation to Earth for all the ways she nourishes you. Repeat this movement of giving and receiving love for and from

Earth and sky for as long as you desire. Practice reciprocating daily as a way to strengthen the feeling of interdependence with Life.

Exercise C: Somatic Listening: To Give and Receive

Somatic bodywork is an emerging field in mind-body-spirit well-being. It's a well-researched mindfulness practice that calms the nervous system and re-engineers the body from trauma. Because we all hold trauma in our body, this somatic exercise explores the mystery of how our body parts interconnect, continually giving and receiving. On a profound level, we all have a relationship between our biology and biography.

This exercise may provide insight on how you open and close with others. How you flex from trust to distrust. Lay on the floor or a bed and bring your attention inward. Relax your mind by taking three deep inhales and exhales. Set an intention to listen deeply to the intelligence of your body. Note that the left side of your body is feminine and the right side is masculine. So this is an interaction between these aspects of yourself. Slightly bend your left leg and allow that knee to fall open to your left side. Permit your leg to rest open on the floor. Next, slowly bend your right leg and place your right leg onto your left so that both knees are stacked on top of each other. If you're unable to lay your right leg fully onto your left, honor your body for what it can do.

If you feel any tension or emotion in your right hip, breathe and allow the sensation to inform you. Know that you are endowed with instinctual awareness. Be still and know. Cultivate an empty beginner's mind and a compassionate heart as you feel into what your hips are saying. The hips hold repressed emotion. Lovingly meet the energy where it is without trying to make something happen.

After a few long breaths, slowly flip your legs to your right side, one at a time. Notice the difference, if any, in your left and right hips. How does your left hip feel as your knees attempt to connect? With this exercise, can you sense what the masculine side of your body is saying to your feminine? And vice-versa?

Afterwards, journal your insights. Notice that the union of opposites is found in the heart. Here, there is no separation, only giving and receiving with ease and grace. Thank your body for the miracle that it is.

CHAPTER 9

E = EMPATHIZE BY CONNECTING WITH HEART

"What is as important as the head?" asks the mind.
"To see and feel with the body," responds the heart.

Spotlighting empathy

Empathy is a gateway to relationship transformation. This relationship intelligence capacity is a universal need and a powerful prosocial building block to connection. Empathy enables us to share in and understand another's emotions. Although it's impossible to truly put ourselves in other people's shoes, we can imagine their experience and guess their feelings. In so doing, we dethrone ourselves as the center of the universe and place others beside us in a communal circle. We move from our head to our heart, as empathy can only come from that sensitive space. Whether we're collaborating in-person or virtually, empathy can be transmitted and experienced by the power of heart connection.

Different than sympathy, which is couched in pity, giving empathy is a bridge-building act of kindness. It's inclusive and contagious. Offering someone sincere empathy is like placing a warm blanket around a person's shoulders on a cold winter's night. As a sign of caring, it calls forth empowerment in acknowledging our humanity. The conditions needed for change ripen. As medicine to alleviate suffering, empathy is steeped in the energy of peacebuilding.

> *"Empathy is the medicine the world needs."*
> *Judith Orloff*

The great news about empathy is that it's a learned skill. Even if your childhood lacked this experience, we can grow our ability to be present and heart-centered. To practice, empathize with the part of you that wants to push away uncomfortable feelings that arise during some RELATE exercises. Step beyond self-abandonment by asking how you can best love yourself in the moment. Probe the depths of your self-worth. When you feel anxious, gently inquire about your perceptions and assumptions. When you feel frustrated, validate your underlying desire. Since empathy arises from presence, honor your innate nurturing capacity.

Empathizing is an in-built social skill because we live in an interconnected network. Proof of our empathetic wiring comes in the form of mirror neurons, a type of nerve cell that resides in the premotor cortex part of the brain. Neuroimaging experiments show that these neurons are activated when we observe movement, sensations or emotions felt by ourselves *and* others. If someone experiences disgust, happiness or pain, for example, it triggers an internal experience within the observer. Empathy can pour out of this energetic transmission. It facilitates a sense of belonging. This is why a baby who hears the cry of another baby will start to cry.

Mirror neurons are also known as "smart cells" and mimicry. This "smart" skill is Life's way of assisting us to understand, adapt and survive as social beings. If someone breaks out into laughter, we tend to follow suit. Sadness begets a similar emotional response. Conscious and unconscious mimicry enables people to connect and feel a sense of affinity. Indeed, empathy-inducing mimicry is a bridge unto itself.

> *"By listening, we can activate our mirror neurons and resonance circuitry to literally inhabit one another's emotional universe."*
> Bonnie Badenoch PhD, LMFT

In a similar yet different way, the term *respeto* is used in the Indigenous American communities in South America and Mexico. Akin to the English word *respect*, respeto points to a mutual consideration for other's activities, needs and wants. As a form of conditioned mimicry, socialization messages are passed on from mother to child. For instance, a common respeto message is to be courteous to elders. In these cultures, this thoughtfulness promotes empathy and shared understanding. As a learned skill, communal needs take precedence over individual pursuits.

Balancing the giving and receiving of empathy

> "Empathy lends my sense of them to them, thus helping people reconnect. It's a quality of presence that dissolves the blocks to action."
> Dominic Barter

Empathy is the elixir of relationship-building. In my social circle, I have friends who excel at empathy. It comes from a deep wellspring. I never feel it's forced or false. They teach me by example that empathy derives from the heart, where every cell is activated, turned on and focused on the other. When I am listened to with empathy from these cherished friends, I can source my inner wisdom. I feel seen. Whatever feels bound or stuck resolves itself within me because I can more readily self-connect. In their listening, my upset disappears. Confusion turns into clarity. Action may not even be needed. From these friends, I've learned that empathy is a full-bodied energy broadcast involving our ears, feeling, intuition, heart and both sides of the brain.

When we offer empathy to others, it's a gift that keeps on giving. It's typically appreciated more than unsolicited advice. Sincere empathy is a balm that soothes ruffled energy. Since no script nor grand plan can bring forth empathy, its author is authenticity. Empathy helps us intuit what may be happening if we're unsure how the other person is feeling. By presencing another person, we understand what's being communicated. We acknowledge what's so in people's world, connecting in silence or words. Silence is a superb transmitter of empathy. If I want to ask a question, I pause to notice if I am satisfying my curiosity or supporting the person. I challenge myself to simply accept someone's experience without wanting to change it or the person. On many levels, empathy has the power to uplift the human experience.

> "The highest form of knowledge is empathy, for it requires us to suspend our egos and live in another's world."
> Plato

Some people self-describe as an empath. In some cases, they become an emotional sponge in taking on other people's energy. While empaths have a compassionate, caring nature, empathizing does not mean absorbing other people's pain. For self-care, it's important to set limits or withdraw from situations that are emotionally draining. When asserting healthy boundaries, release the fear of offending people. Discern how to best use your endowment of sensitivity. Remember: Saying no is a complete sentence.

When feeling depleted, use Earthing to refill your well of empathy. This practice is about walking barefoot to feel Earth's medicine through the bottom of our feet. It's a way to ground, cleanse the body, renew the spirit and improve well-being. Thanks to science, we're learning what our ancestors knew long ago: Earth has an abundant supply of free electrons. When we ground into the soil, these electrons organically flow between Earth and our body. We reduce the free radicals in our system, purge static electrical charge, reduce inflammation and prevent health disorders. Given this insight, the next time you walk in nature, take off your shoes and declare that your body is a sacred vessel. It's not to be used to harbor other people's angst. The ideal way to serve others, paradoxically, is through nourishing ourselves.

When we give and receive empathy *in balance*, it's an investment in our maturation. When we trust in the abundance of Life, relational scarcity decreases. Mutual caring elicits caring responsiveness. When we do something to help another, the giving engenders receiving. If someone is there for us during a difficult time, with a listening ear and a compassionate heart, we are inclined to offer the same. The sweet honey of reciprocity is triggered. The heart-opening spirit of ayni is activated.

> *Honeybirds live in ayni. These birds are known to lead people to a beehive of honey, trusting that enough will be left for them to enjoy.*

Empathy in the workplace

In the workplace, leaders who excel at empathy hold a golden rod of galvanizing power. With mindful relating, they can discharge far more discretionary energy. While a percentage of staff activity is generated from must-do compliance, a larger percentage comes from discretionary energy. The latter comes from people's desire to opt in or out of full engagement *at will*. This discretionary part of the workforce is filled with creativity, enthusiasm, curiosity and a desire to make a meaningful difference. It's often an unbroached watershed of potentiate. Empathetic leaders know how to catalyze this discretionary energy and inspire people into action.

Empathetic leaders also know that sound rational thinking incorporates empathy. In fact, empathy helps them see all sides of an issue to appreciate how a decision may impact people. Intuitively, they understand that balancing task and empathetic relationship-building is key to unleashing human talent. In a *Forbes* article written by Tracy Brower, extensive research ranked empathy as the most important leadership skill. Specifically, the positive effects of this competency include higher innovation, stronger engagement, lower turnover, greater inclusivity, enhanced cooperation and better work-life balance. In brief, empathy is good for people and organizations.

Because empathy is deemed to be a strong success driver in business, *Harvard Business Review* created an annual Global Empathy Index in 2014. Using various metrics, they assess and determine which companies have the strongest empathy-driven culture. In 2016, the top-ten companies in this index increased in value more than twice as much as the bottom ten. Furthermore, these same companies generated 50 percent more earnings as it relates to market capitalization. This correlation speaks volumes. Companies with empathetic cultures retain bright people, create collaborative environments for people to thrive and reap impressive financial rewards.

In Businesssolver's 2022 State of Workplace Empathy Report, 77 percent of CEOs say they fear they will be less respected if they show empathy in the workplace. Beyond that staggering number, 79 percent of CEOs say they struggle to be empathetic. These findings beg the question, "If we know that empathy is correlated with high performance, why does its expression leave some people uncomfortable?" Perhaps one reason is because we collapse giving empathy with taking on other people's problems. We then take the wheel of over-responsibility in trying to rescue others who are suffering. Subconsciously, this may be an attempt to receive love and validation. Bottom line: giving empathy is restorative, it's not about shouldering the burden for other people.

> *I feel your pain.*
> *And, your story is not my story.*

Connecting with heart—it all adds up

With this principle, empathy is sourced by connecting with our heart energy, an ethereal universal radiance that can transform any relationship. Our heart is not only a physical organ but the symbolic engine of love and the epicenter of our being. It's what drives our life story, our radical truth-telling, our deepest yearnings and creative aspirations. Our heart is a bottomless reservoir of compassion and forgiveness. I find it to be my guiding radar, telling me when I've diminished my integrity or expanded my joy. It also tells me when to devote energy to lifting others up. Deciphering our heart aches *and* heart wisdom is a doorway to empathy. Heart caring and empathy are natural companions on the bridge of authentic collaboration.

> "There is no exercise better for the heart than reaching down and lifting people up."
> John Holmes

The power of the heart has been extensively studied by the pioneers of heart math. The HeartMath Institute, an organization that explores the science of interconnectivity, defines heart coherence as: "The synchronization of our physical, mental and emotional systems. It can be measured by our heart-rhythm patterns: The more balanced and smoother they are, the more in sync or coherent we are. Stress levels recede, energy levels increase and our 'heart brain' works together. It is a state of optimal clarity, perception and performance." Simply put, heart coherence describes the purposeful alignment of our internal selves and our external actions. At the center of this alignment lies empathetic self-collaboration.

With over twenty-six years of research to draw from, HeartMath clearly shows how bridging the intuitive connection between the mind and heart is beneficial. Positive outcomes of this meditation and slow-breathing practice have been linked to mental acuity, body health and relational well-being. When we slow the cadence of our heart to match our rhythm, dopamine is released and our physiology changes. Our nerves begin to relax our organs. Serenity fills our inner state. As it turns out, the heart sends more information to the nervous system than the brain. By infusing heart energy into a collaborative dialogue, we are more likely to emit empathy and experience equanimity.

Heart vulnerability as a source of power

Our heart is both our superpower and a place of vulnerability. You might describe vulnerability as the core of the authentic collaboration onion. Risk is inherent in the process. We simply cannot experience meaningful connection without vulnerability. Vulnerability comes from the seventeenth-century Latin word *vulnus,* which means "wounded." Yet, the paradox of vulnerability is that our wound is also a source of strength, the bud from which we grow. Nature reveals this truth.

> "Vulnerability can be defined as uncertainty, risk and emotional exposure."
> Brené Brown

For instance, the growth spurt of a tree comes not from the bark but from a vulnerable, soft, green bud opening.

Learning to embrace vulnerability is central to the relational bridge architecture. Because our vulnerable heart is often experienced as raw, shaky and uncomfortable, it's a practice that challenges people from all cultures. Yet, embracing the emotional discomfort reaps rewards such as shared understanding and intimacy. When the vulnerable murmur of our heart meets the intelligence of our mind, we grow our self-connection and worth.

Allowing ourselves to feel and share our vulnerability cultivates not only empathy but also authentic power. Even though our Western culture conflates vulnerability with weakness, vulnerability is a sign of strength. Its expression allows for self-acceptance, learning and meaningful connection. As singer Saul Williams remarked, "Vulnerability is power."

Gandhi understood this when he chose peaceful non-cooperation to guide his freedom movement. His use of soft power had hard results. Soft power involves negotiating our own interests while validating others' interests to find a creative way to incorporate both. Underneath soft power is an open heart; it means seeing the humanity in others even when facing hurtful behavior. It's about responding with nonviolence, despite the harm. When we have the strength to show people all sides of who we are, it gives others consent to do the same.

When collaborating, whoever has the greater capacity to be vulnerable, real and transparent is the person who holds the most power in the room. This is because they relate with an undefended heart: nothing to hide, nothing to lose. It's highly attractive. Some say charismatic. Overall, people are more apt to trust those who are vulnerable than those who keep their cards close to their chest, so to speak. If we bear this in mind during conflict, vulnerability becomes the juice of bridge-building. In letting down our guard, we dare to live authentically. We relish the experience of Life, rather than attempting to control Life. In the eloquent words of author Mark Nepo, vulnerability is "the exquisite risk."

> *How would you describe your relationship to vulnerability?*

The vulnerability-strength paradox

When I first reflected on the vulnerability-strength paradox, I was doubtful that one could consistently live in this world from a tender, open heart space. The idea seemed beautifully ideal yet wholly unrealistic. I was drawn in by a desire to relate as though I had nothing to prove but I found myself backing away, afraid of being attacked, judged or rejected. Then, I remembered the words of a poem by Guillaume Apollinaire that my mother gave me. The hand embroidery read:

> *Come to the edge, no we will fall.*
> *Come to the edge, no we will fall.*
> *He pushed them and they flew.*

One day, I decided to fly off the edge. While facilitating a workshop, I took a leap to share my vulnerability with the group. When I revealed my story, my heart began beating rapidly and my whole body felt unsteady. In response, people leaned in, wanting to hear more. The listening changed and the space opened. My sinking into authenticity brought the conversation to another level of candid sharing. The empathy I received instilled in me greater self-confidence. Creativity flowed as the dialogue deepened. At the end of the day, the group commented on the remarkable connection that we all felt. As it turned out, decision-making was easier when we felt our shared humanity. We discovered that vulnerability evokes empathy which, in turn, becomes a formidable starting gate to authentic collaboration.

Vulnerable heart expression requires courage. The word *courage* comes from the French root *coeur,* meaning "heart," and *age* meaning "time": time of the heart. Even though the heart plays a role in generating courage, its expression sits in the throat chakra. This chakra energy vortex, located at the center of the larynx, revolves around speaking our truth. It takes courage to be in our truth and speak with radical honesty. After all, not everyone is ready for this level of honesty. Confict may ensue. Rejection may occur as relationships are a risk-taking venture. Confronting differences is a gamble. Given this, courage is about feeling fear embracing the discomfort and acting anyway.

> *"The greatest act of courage is to be and to own all of who you are—without apology, without excuses, without masks to cover the truth of who you are."*
> Debbie Ford

How would your relationships be different if you stretched your courage muscle?

Intimate relationships and the gift of grace

Relating empathetically with our family can be one of our greatest challenges, for this is where our deepest longing resides. This is when authentic collaboration ushers in a different type of risk. The stakes are higher. The choice for courageous heart expression is ever-present. Vulnerability is stitched into the fabric. Love, pleasure, anguish and pain all arise in our family—be it our family of origin, our created family, our extended family or our step family. Common wounds include abandonment, exclusion, feeling unlovable, deprivation, subjugation, failure and rejection. The effects are far-reaching. In the container of family, depending on the quality of empathetic relating, our potential is either tapered or nurtured.

Authentic collaboration with those near and dear has been my ultimate testing and learning ground. Even with deep love in the mix, there have been times when keeping my heart open required warrior-like resolve. With discernment, I've had to choose how to relate and when to step away. I find myself simultaneously holding a desire for authentic connection *and* autonomy. I want to be open-hearted *and* self-protective. I want to reveal *and* hold back. With these tender relationships, bridge-building to seek common ground carries more weight. My ability to see beyond my storyline to who is really in front of me is a continual challenge. Mother Theresa's words come to mind: "If we truly want peace in the world, let us begin by loving one another in our own families."

In truth, family relationships have a way of penetrating our Achilles heel, a place of weakness in spite of overall strength. During conflict, known vulnerabilities can be exploited in the heat of the moment. With multi-generational patterns at play, emotions can be highly combustible. Words can become venomous. Long-standing unresolved issues can haunt us from the past. In the core of our being, we hold love and know that we're wedded in connection, yet we succumb to separateness. Afraid of being hurt, we ask, "Can I count on them?" In our heart, we realize that what we're really asking is, "Can I count on me?"

> "I do not at all understand the mystery of grace—only that it meets us where we are but does not leave us where it found us."
> Anne Lamott

Authentic collaboration with loved ones is not for the faint of heart. To practice empathy, call on grace as a source of strength. Grace can help us touch the part of self that is never separate, and thus never afraid.

Showcasing the heart in the theater of collaboration

In effect, the principle of empathy is about bridging our mind and gut to our heart to inform our thinking and doing. When in our heart, we access a space that has no identity, no story, no ambition, no gender and nothing to possess. The push-pull impulse of bonding-rejection slows down with heart presence. As a natural intelligence, our heart helps us realize deeper truths. It is boundless and conscious. Herein, we understand that our reality is comprised of changeable perceptions. When we change our mindset to align with our heartset, how we collaborate transforms. To paraphrase Joanna Macy, "The core of Life calls us awake with the beat in our own heart."

Collaborative relationships are like a theater for the heart to know itself. As actors on the stage of Life, we play roles that invite self-discovery. With our individualized script, relationships give us an opportunity to explore those parts of self that need to be loved. When Life calls us to listen to the song of our heart, do we turn toward or away? Do we retreat upstage away from what's happening or move downstage to come upfront and close to others? The plot is never dull with authentic relating.

> "It is with the heart that one sees rightly; what is essential is invisible to the eye."
> Antoine de Saint-Exupery

In my own play, I've become well-rehearsed at pulling out the thorns of misperception with the tweezers of self-care. I've learned that being closed does not protect me nor anyone else from pain. Being closed *is* the pain. Courageously staying open to what is and making peace with the drama that unfolds is the tough love action our world needs. Truly, embracing all of self and others is the live performance that counts.

For the love of Earth: A story of heart-based empathy in action

When I reflect on heart-opening collaborative experiences, a forest council retreat comes to mind. This council of thirty eco-advocates gathered for a four-day solution-finding workshop to conserve and restore our intact forests in the world. Because of our shared love for Earth, we all held a desire to protect her. With this heart connection, I felt as though I had found my soul tribe.

Our constellation was both beautiful and sticky, with an undercurrent of different agendas, needs and expectations. At one point, a wise indigenous elder addressed this tension by calling for a different quality of dialogue. He invited the men to hold sacred space for the women to share. So, under a canopy of trees, we formed two concentric circles. The men held the outer-circle rim and the women sat in the inner circle. Within this loving container, I felt an energetic ring of heart-centered empathy around me. The honoring between the masculine and feminine was palpable. We were presencing Life.

Held in the tender arms of masculine solidarity, the feminine voice was heard. I tuned in and listened to the echoes of my sisters within me. Soon, a tidal wave of emotion arose in me that had to be expressed. When the dam broke, the words and tears poured out with great intensity. It felt as though I was releasing the pain of oppression over many lifetimes. I also sensed that I was speaking on behalf of Mother Earth. For she too is dominated. Of the world's land mass, only 3 percent remains ecologically intact with undisturbed habitat. This fact, along with many other grief-laden thoughts, coiled around my emotional release. My heart wall burst open.

In my sharing, I untied an energetic knot that was both personal and universal. I was reminded that in the healing space of compassion, everything dissolves and resolves. Herein, we can transcend the limitations of the mind and our tendency to compete, blame and compare. With meaningful connection, we can suspend conclusion-jumping. We can stoke the fire of curiosity with the kindling of calm inquiry, allowing the embers of judgment to burn.

During this experience, I no longer saw collaboration as a strategy but as a field of vast potential. I learned that when we attempt to problem-solve, there is great power in generative dialogue. When there are no roadmaps nor precedents to guide us forward, an emergent approach can bring forth unexpected personal *and* systemic insights. Above all, I realized that what really matters in relational bridge-building and solution-finding is how much heart empathy we offer.

> *"A heart full of love and compassion is the main source of inner strength, willpower, happiness and mental tranquility."*
> Dalai Lama

Practice the Principle: Empathize by Connecting with Heart

Self-Discovery
Relationship Timeline Exercise

A timeline is a grid-like picture that shows your life from a bird's-eye view. It's an empowering tool that reveals a series of events, trends, themes and pivot turns that occurred in your unique history. With this recorded picture, you can see the highs and lows and make course corrections, if needed. This timeline exercise will reveal key people and experiences that have influenced how you relate.

Dedicate a few hours with paper, pen, colored pencils or markers. Set your heart intention and light a candle, trusting the flame to illuminate your life path. Draw a horizontal straight line from one end of the paper to the other. Starting at one end of the line, mark your birth date and note your primary family. At every stage of your life, indicate the significant people and the role they played. Practice self-empathy as realizations come to light.

Relationship Timeline Exercise Questions

With each significant relationship on your timeline, reflect on:
- How has this person shaped my life?
- How nourishing or challenging was/is this relationship?
- At what points did I feel my heart open or close?
- How can I self-empathize when I consider this timeline?

When your timeline is complete, reflect on the story that is revealed:
- What patterns do I notice and what meaning do I ascribe?
- What connection milestones, changes and turning points are noteworthy?
- How did I receive empathy in my close relationships?
- Is there anyone I am purposely leaving out?
- How does my family and ancestral story influence how I relate?
- From this timeline, what different choices do I feel inspired to make?
- If friends described my timeline, what would they say?
- Five years from now: how would I like my important relationships to be?

Bonus follow-up exercise

Given this timeline reflection and where you are now in your life, carve out some quiet time to reflect or meditate. Tune into your heart. When you feel self-connected, take out some pencil crayons and paper and draw what you see at the center of your heart. Offer yourself empathy as you allow your intuition to guide you in your drawing. Hold the picture with tenderness and honoring. Attempt to see you, behind the you.

Authentic Collaboration Practice with Others
Exercise A: Experiencing Layers of Authenticity

Sit across from a partner or learning buddy knee to knee, without a table between you. Each person takes a turn to share what they do in their work life. Prompt with, "Tell me about your role/job." Both receive five minutes of uninterrupted time to elaborate, with no clarifying questions or comments made by the listener. If you or your partner are currently not working, speak about your last employment experience. If studying, ask about your schooling experience.

When complete, repeat this same conversation again with the same partner. Yet, first go within and connect with your heart. Take three deep inhales and exhales. Follow your breath into your belly and feel the well of empathy within. Breathe your heart home. Connect to what truly inspires your heart as it relates to your work. When you both have touched this soft place inside, ask each other, "About your role, what do you really care about?" Take another five minutes to share your response to the same question.

Afterwards, debrief how the second sharing was different for both of you—as a speaker and listener. What did you observe? Discuss how empathetic heart connection transforms communication. How can you bring this essence into your relationships at home, at work and in community?

Exercise B: Group Mix & Mingle Empathy Exercise

When organizing an in-person group event or workshop, ask people to only write their first name on the name tags. Leave off titles, department and any other work-related information. In an opening introductory exercise, invite everyone to mix, mingle and introduce themselves with no mention of work. Instead, select empathy-evoking questions that invite heart connection. Examples include:

- What excites you about Life?
- What's alive in you at this moment?
- What is your heart hoping to learn from this gathering?
- What's one thing that really matters to you in life (or in your work)?

Exercise C: Ho'oponopono Reflection

A powerful way to activate our empathetic heart is with the beautiful Hawaiian ho'oponopono prayer. This simple mantra states, "I'm sorry. Please forgive me. Thank you. I love you." Since this prayer for forgiveness and reconciliation is about taking responsibility for our feelings and experience, it's helpful to share even if you are the one who feels hurt. It's healing to acknowledge that there was a hurt. Coming into right relationship is not about trying to erase what's been done—or not done—but rather validating the experience itself.

With a partner you are experiencing conflict with, repeat these universal phrases again and again while looking into the other's eyes. If it's not safe to do so in person, close your eyes and do this exercise in your mind's eye. Start with two minutes each and then build to five minutes. Notice the effect on your heart and your shared energy field. Repeat this prayer to yourself in the mirror to support self-forgiveness.

Collaborative Connection with Earth

Exercise A: Core Compelling Question

Create a quiet space, close your eyes and relax. Feel the love and empathy of Life being gifted to you. In this space, reflect on what your core compelling question is pertaining to either relationships in general or to authentic collaboration specifically. Take as much time as you need to intuit what question is calling you.

Write down this question, post it on your fridge and revisit for a month. See how Life responds to your heart inquiry.

As a bonus exercise, reflect on a recent collaboration upset and/or success. Write down all the beliefs you have that may have contributed to how this dialogue unfolded. While reflecting, conjure up empathy for yourself and the other. Ask Life for insight. Open your heart to receive what comes to light.

Exercise B: Expanding Perception

In the Laika wisdom tradition, shamans live by the power of "percept" rather than "precept." Our culture operates on precepts—society's rules, dogma, laws, mandates and doctrine that shape our behavior. Perception, on the other hand, is choosing to act based on how we sense and interpret our experience of Life. It's about being self-directed versus other-directed.

With this lens of understanding, *perception is reality*. For example, illness can be perceived as a set-back or a set-forward healing opportunity. By changing our perceptual filter, we alter our attitude and shift our collaboration experience. It's like taking off a pair of short-sighted glasses to broaden our view of reality. In the shaman world, the power of perception is used to shape-shift or bend reality.

This perception-shifting exercise is inspired by The Four Winds Society, a leading school of energy medicine and healing founded by Alberto Villoldo. Start by selecting an issue, challenge or relationship angst you are currently dealing with. Write down the issue in a one-sentence summary headliner. Next, call upon the energy of serpent to help you tune into your first chakra to see the issue at the literal physical level. Chakras are circular vortexes of energy that hold and distribute Life energy, or Qi or Prana. Allow serpent to guide you in deeply listening to how your body holds this issue. Lean into the discomfort to gently hold what you instinctively want to turn away from. Allow the upset to say what it needs to say. Notice and record the insight that arises from your intuition.

When complete, bring your attention to your second chakra—located beneath your naval at the perineum. Our second or sacral chakra is our relationship zone, which holds primitive emotions and beliefs associated with how we relate with others. While focusing on this sacral chakra, feel into the issue again with the energy of jaguar. Receive this animal's courage, strength and integrity. Rather than get caught in the story, step back to see this issue from a different angle. Empathetically listen and record the thoughts and emotions swirling within you.

AUTHENTIC COLLABORATION

Next, focus your attention on your heart chakra, located in the middle of your chest. This perceptual heart filter holds prudence and compassion. It has greater subtlety, like the delicate petals of a blossoming rose. Call in the energy of hummingbird to help you drink the sweet nectar of wisdom. Feel into this level of heart perception with tenderness, note the difference and record the insight.

Lastly, move your attention to your third eye chakra, the place between your eyebrows. This is your spiritual center and the seat of clear perception. It holds abundant intuitive capacity in breaking through the veils of illusion. In Sanskrit, this illusion is called Maya. Call upon the energy of eagle-condor to help you rise above the issue. Perceive from a helicopter stance. Tune into your eternal spirit, soar above the level of separation and feel into unity consciousness. Notice and record what comes to your awareness.

Conclude by offering gratitude to the different aspects of your being and to these wise spirit animals.

CHAPTER 10

L = LISTEN BY UNCOVERING FEELINGS AND NEEDS

*"One of the most sincere forms of respect is actually
listening to what another has to say."*
Bryant H. McGill

Deep listening: The oxygen of authentic collaboration

Deep listening is vital to effective communication. Indeed, it's the secret to a fulfilling relationship. This is not a news flash for most people, yet it implores us to ask, "Why does deep listening elude so many of us?"

Well, it seems that most human beings listen not to understand what someone is saying but rather to reply. Yet, with intentionality and presence, we all can improve our listening skills. If we listen to understand, and show that we understand, our relationship connection strengthens. If we listen with the sole purpose of allowing someone to be fully expressed without judgment, transformation can take place. If we toss authenticity, love and acceptance into the mix, relationship miracles can occur.

Listening is our most primal sense. Starting at around 18 weeks, we listened to our mother's heartbeat in the womb. Listening is as crucial to our growth as milk is to a baby. It's also said that listening is the last sense to go in the dying process. There's nothing sweeter than the voice of a loved one whispering in the ear of someone who is leaving the body.

In the art of authentic collaboration, listening involves words and silence. Often, the non-verbal cues speak the loudest. In Dr. Albert Mehrabian's pioneering research, he found that the interpretation of a message is 7 percent verbal, 38 percent vocal and 55 percent

> *"Deep listening is experiencing heightened awareness or expanded awareness of sound and of silence."*
> *Pauline Oliveros*

visual. His conclusion was that 93 percent of communication is nonverbal in nature. We add richness to our interactions when we turn up the listening dial and pay attention to body language, facial expressions, tone of voice, pauses, sighs, shallow breathing, hand gestures, fidgety behavior and the like. In doing so, we can better unpack values, needs, assumptions and desires. Intentional listening is how we discover common linkages, areas of concern and shared commitments.

In practicing mindful listening with other people, we can also extend this to our own heart and to Earth. After all, both communicate with us minute to minute, hour by hour. This possibility brings a whole new level of connection with self, others and Earth. Communication can then open into communion, forging an appreciation for the message and the messenger. With good reason, this principle is a celebrated vertical tie on this unique bridge. It's a Life-giving element of authentic collaboration.

Hearing versus listening

While we are born with an inherent ability to deeply listen, many blocks prevent us from consistently doing so. One block is the inability to distinguish between hearing and listening. People may show up to collaborate, ready to hear the words, but not willing to listen and grasp the meaning of what's being communicated. Hearing is a sense organ function that uses our ears and brain, whereas mindful listening is a full-body experience. The latter is about activating our mind, body and spirit to engage with presence.

Recently, I worked with a team who admittedly practiced hearing versus listening, a habit that prevented them from making progress. In fact, they were stuck. When we untied the knots of listening, one person said she expected others to mind-read what she meant. She hoped others would just "know" what she wanted rather than check for understanding. Another person confessed to rehearsing her words rather than being present while listening. A newcomer to the team realized that he was attached to certain views so he filtered what was said to meld with like-minded colleagues. One manager divulged that she was often in a hurry, so she rarely paused long enough to validate what was said or to absorb the meaning and connotation. Another manager confessed that he continually

> *"To listen, there must be an inner quietness, a freedom from the strain of acquiring, a relaxed attention."*
> Jiddu Krishnamurti

interrupted or found the flaw in an idea. During this honest sharing, I disclosed my own occasional habit—jumping to the conclusion that I've heard this before. In thinking, *I already know this*, I disrupt my ability to listen and my attention swings in and out. Inner quiet was missing. All these listening habits were a type of learning disability. Each habit dis-abled people from opening to something new: to listen and learn with a beginner's mind.

In considering these blocks, let's explore more listening distinctions to better understand this fundamental bridge-building skill.

Seven Levels of Listening

To appreciate the multifaceted nature of listening and to support self-development, I've developed a framework entitled Seven Levels of Listening. This spectrum is cumulative, with one level building to support the next. It highlights listening distinctions that weave into the bridge vertical ties. Just as brain surgeons understand the distinctions of the brain, with all its regions and functions, we too can expand our understanding of listening to support the health of collaborative relationships.

In considering these seven levels, we see that listening is not a black-and-white skill. It's a highly nuanced competency in facilitating authentic collaboration.

If self-judgment comes up when reading this list on the next page, realize that listening blocks are universal. Regardless of race, gender or background, most human beings experience listening challenges to one degree or another. In many cultures, listening is filled with biases, labels, pre-set conclusions, limited knowledge or an already-formed response. That said, our habits have intelligence. Behavior serves a purpose. For instance, background self-talk may be a way to self-protect and even survive. Further developing our ability to listen includes compassionately seeing why we do what we do.

As you review each level of listening, assess your own capacity. Spotlight your habits and improvement opportunities while applauding your strengths.

- If you rate yourself, which level is your common way of listening?
- What expands and contracts your ability to listen?

Seven Levels of Listening

1. Distracted
Distracted listening reveals a scattered or unsettled mind. The listener tunes in and out while thinking of a response. The speaker feels distant. What is communicated is only partially received.

2. Background Self-Talk
More attention is given to self-talk than to listening. Background self-talk includes assumptions, judgment and dualities such as right-wrong, good-bad, agree-disagree, dominate or submit, scarcity-abundance, attack-defend and win-lose. This listening filter takes precedence over what's said.

3. Heart Presence
By connecting with heart, the listener becomes aware and present to lean into what's communicated. The interaction is held with care. Validating what's said allows the speaker to be seen and heard. No-fault listening is demonstrated, even if there's disagreement.

4. Active Listening
The listener slows down the conversation by reflecting back what's heard for shared understanding. Phrases include, "What I hear you saying is…is that so?" "Did I understand correctly that you meant…". As interpretations are set aside, the mind becomes open, curious and receptive.

5. Empathetic Listening
By sensing into the speaker's underlying feelings and needs, the listener understands that people are emotional beings and behavior is an attempt to meet needs. Empathetic listening tunes into the music between the notes or the meaning beyond the words. With empathy, blocks to action dissolve.

6. Emergent Listening
With pauses, emergent listening patiently waits to see what wants to come forward. Since communication is "pregnant with meaning," listening becomes generative. Something new can be born such as an idea or insight. Nonverbal or meta-messages are honored as in silence, tears or a big exhale.

7. In Service to Life
A reflection practice bridges the listener to the soul. Source is channeled—a vast field of consciousness where there is nothing yet everything. As a sacred witness, the listener becomes an empty vessel in service to Life. Self, others and Earth are seen with new eyes. Oneness becomes a felt experience.

Evolving to presence people and Life

The big leap in listening occurs at level three— heart presence. The word *presence* comes from *pre,* meaning "what comes before," and *sense,* meaning "the space of our being." Therefore, presence is about bringing to light that which existed before our personhood—our soul energy. Since our essence is love, presence is love. It entails groundedness to stay in the moment rather than allow the mind to drift to the past or future. Connecting with our heart supports our capacity to be present with others, especially during the tough times. It's an ironic twist—by deeply listening to someone's heart-breaking story, we open and heal our own hearts.

TRY THIS: To practice being present, close your eyes. Tune into your senses. What are you hearing, touching, smelling, tasting and seeing? Be with this awareness. Of the three human time zones—past, present, future—notice where your mind tends to be the most. With patience, bring your mind to rest in the present moment and enjoy this listening space. Accept what is here now. See how this listening exercise correlates to your willingness to accept others as they are.

Quality listening is, in essence, about compassionately receiving people as they are. To do so, it's helpful to become mindful of mental chatter: to notice the noise and calm the inner babble. To presence ourselves, one tip is to pause periodically throughout the day. If we stop, pause and notice ourselves feeling scattered, we can be at choice. We can suspend the reactive impulse by creating a gap between what's being said and our reaction. In the interval, there's quiet in the space. By decluttering and emptying the mind, we can reach beyond the intellectual mind and allow for greater understanding and compassion to surface. This quality of presence generates stillness.

> *"The deepest listening is presence—it's consciousness itself. It is space, an open heart, compassion and a deep receiving of someone."*
> Thomas Hübl

Listening with an empty mind allows collaborative creativity to emerge. When a thesis is offered, and an antithesis is given as a counterpoint, the only way to move into synthesis or a new insight is listening with an empty mind. The neocortex has the space to entertain other options. A yes-and response becomes possible. If the teacup of the mind is already full of busy noise, then whatever is added overflows into the saucer. As the mystic Jiddu Krishnamurti writes in *The Book of Life*, "Real change can only take place when the mind comes to the problem afresh, not with all the jaded memories of a thousand yesterdays."

Another way to practice presencing is by listening to our intuition. Many people only tune into their gut occasionally or in the event of a crisis. To normalize this as a habit, notice how you distract yourself. Given that the gut is a highly tuned sensory organ that continually releases information to our brain, it serves us well to develop a healthy collaborative relationship with this part of our body. Presencing our gut provides clarity and direction as Life speaks to us via our intuition. Our sense of safety resides in our belly. Because there's more serotonin hormone in our gut than in our brain, it can also boost feel-good emotions. While the belly is only one gauge of emotional information, it's a way to expand awareness. If you feel disconnected, ask Life for guidance.

> *To what extent are you able to listen to your gut intuition as you read this paragraph?*

Listen to the messages that appear around and within you. The signs will be there. In time, you'll develop heightened sensitivity to not only your inner reality but to others as well.

Emotional intelligence: listening to uncover feelings and needs

In our modern era, human beings have devalued the act of listening to feelings. People are typically not taught emotional literacy to articulate what they feel. Case in point, a common response to the question, "How are you feeling?" is "I feel good, bad or fine." None of these responses are a feeling. According to Plutchik's Wheel of Emotions, there are eight core emotions: joy, trust, fear, surprise, sadness, disgust, anger and anticipation. All other emotions derive from one of these or a combination thereof. To expand your emotional vocabulary, create an inventory of feelings to label and assess your range.

As a pathway to developing emotional literacy, consider the highly esteemed work of Dr. Daniel Goleman, a Harvard professor who popularized the theory of emotional intelligence (EI). He defined EI as "…the ability to recognize our own feelings and those of others, to motivate ourselves and to handle our emotions well so we have the best for ourselves and our relationships." This framework has four domains of teachable skills: self-awareness, self-regulation, social awareness and relationship management. While emotional self-regulation was previously discussed in chapter 7, we'll now focus on social awareness and relationship management as these domains revolve around listening and responding to feelings and needs. This EQ competency encompasses level 3 listening and beyond. It's a baseline enabler for relationships to thrive.

Let's rewind to unpack the word *emotion* because its meaning speaks to the essence of emotional intelligence. Emotion comes from the French word emovare, which means "to move." When we experience something that evokes feeling, we say that we've been moved. This word also points to the ever-changing nature of emotions. Emotions are not meant to be repressed but rather to *move* and fluctuate. It's imperative to our well-being that we express and release our emotions in some way, be it through conscious breathing, speaking, dancing, singing, writing, stomping or exercising. Just as babies do not hesitate to express their feelings, adults also need to follow suit.

Emotions are an instinctive aspect of relating. These energies are natural, neurochemical, adaptive responses to the world around us. Like waves in the ocean, emotions rise and fall, moment by moment. In their own time, space and intensity, these sensations unfurl in our body to help us get to the kernel of the truth inside the feeling. This process has its own pace. Our job is to listen, name, acknowledge and validate our feelings to fully release the energy. Doing so helps us attune to our body's felt sense to understand what we need and what support requests we can make. Creating the space for empathetic self-listening is central to healthy relationship-building.

> *"Feelings are something you have; not something you are."*
> Shannon L. Alder

It seems that I had to learn this EQ lesson the hard way. One awakening experience came during an argument with an ex-partner. Upon hearing that he withheld significant information, I felt angry and betrayed—like I was kicked in the gut. Despite my intense feelings, I only expressed a part of my truth. I feared that divulging everything would end our relationship. So I covered up my feelings. I put aside my need for honest disclosure. At that time, I didn't see how my partner and I were a mirror to each other.

On the heels of this conflict, my body reminded me that it has memory. My health began to deteriorate. I soon developed a chronic cough: my anger needed to "bark." My stuffed feelings also affected my intestines. Because I wasn't metabolizing the emotion, I suffered with poor digestion.

On an inner child level, I was afraid to fully feel and voice my anger because I grew up watching the harm caused by toxic anger. With this reflection, I dug up a subconscious no-win belief conundrum: If I express my anger, I damage or lose relationships. If I bury my anger, I betray myself, leak my power and harm my relationships. It was a distressing catch-22 dilemma. Since feelings and needs are inseparable, this inner dilemma had me discount my needs. I was disloyal to myself.

> "When we go deeper into every experience and emotion; especially, the painful ones, we tap into the source of our greatest hidden gifts."
> Ulonda Faye

Additionally, I noticed how my anger carried righteousness. In being "wronged", I could sit on the bench with the gavel of being right. And I did, at the expense of my well-being and freedom. I also saw the damage of judging my unpleasant feelings. Another layer of thoughts and feelings had to be teased apart. Slowly, I renewed my EQ practice of empathetic self-listening and dissolved this belief thread. I realized that I could express anger *and* have an open heart.

To rebuild trust with honest communication, I re-initiated a conversation with my partner. With trepidation, I stretched into a new zone of authenticity. As our connection rekindled, my anger released. I concluded that authentic relating involves being known. To love is to be vulnerable. When we share the naked truth of who we are, the conversation may be uncomfortable, but we *move* the energy and maintain the connection. Best case scenario, intimacy matures and our relationships grow.

Listening to feelings equates to whole-person living

Listening to our feelings is a brave act toward restoring our body to natural flow and equilibrium. It's an essential capacity for whole-person living and relating. As my story shows, when we clamp down on our emotions, we suppress our immune system and diminish our well-being. For example, research shows there is a correlation between holding onto anger and heart attacks. Chronic pain and stifled emotions are also interlinked. The word *de-press-ion* implies a "pressing down" of emotions or a lack of listening.

When we press down or deny our feelings, we run the risk of numbing our life experience. As Dr. Brené Brown stated, "You can't numb those hard feelings without numbing the other affects, our emotions. You cannot selectively numb. When we numb those, we also numb joy, gratitude and happiness." The practice of authentic collaboration is deciding to not anesthetize ourselves: to dare to bring more of who we are to our interactions. It's choosing to heal, feel, express and be here, in our body, to experience the fullness of our humanity.

Since our human experience evokes both pleasant and unpleasant emotions, ignoring half of our experience is like deciding to swim in only the shallow end of the pool. I once heard that addiction is the choice to not feel what needs to be felt in that moment but instead to reach for whatever offers relief. This is to stay in the shallow end and not experience the depth of who we are. It's common to find ways to distract ourselves from our emotional landscape by grasping on to food, sex, a substance, a state of mind (worry, anxiety), video games or the Internet. Many of us have stories of stuffing emotions, bypassing or pretending. Listening to our body is a step to reversing course and befriending ourselves on a new level.

> *What is the feeling you are not willing to feel?*

Brain hemisphere collaboration, co-regulation and healing

In the burgeoning field of relational neuroscience, we're learning that the left brain is task- and behavior-oriented while the right brain is oriented to relationship, emotions and connection. Yet, we live in a "left-shifted world." According to the research of social psychologist Barbara Fredickson, 75 percent of us are living in the left hemisphere most, if not all, of the time. With this left-brain reliance, separation and isolation permeate our life experience, even when surrounded by people. It thus becomes difficult to cultivate a felt sense of community.

That said, human beings are wired for co-regulation. We're designed to be in caring relationships to help us process emotions. Just being in the presence of a calm, trusted friend who deeply listens can calm our emotional limbic brain.

As therapist Dr. Bonnie Badenoch shrewdly explains, "We need the leadership of the right brain, assisted by the left, to help us be in a ventral resting state." Ironically, both sides of our brain also need to collaborate to bolster emotional and social intelligence.

> *Yes, even both sides of our brain need to collaborate to live and relate whole-heartedly.*

Empathetic listening to emotions transforms and releases heavy energies. It's about being okay with ourselves and others, no matter what is felt. The US healthcare system translates this wisdom into promoting relationship-centered communication. This training, which revolves around active, empathetic listening, encourages healthcare professionals to interact with attentiveness, curiosity and positive regard. Doing so fosters co-regulation and shared meaning. Research has shown that these communication skills benefits not only patient well-being, but also healthcare teams and organizational outcomes.

Whatever and however feelings arise, love and accept them. In so doing, listening to feelings is analogous to surrender. Being present is a radical giving and receiving of love. The ego softens and defensiveness evaporates. As Dr. David Hawkins noted, "Letting go of negative feelings is the undoing of the ego, which will be resistant at every turn. Let the resistance be there but don't resist the resistance." The more we surrender into the resistance with empathetic listening, the more relational flow we experience. The ground for meaningful connection becomes fertile. There's no denying that the outward practice of authentic collaboration is dependent on the inward practice of listening.

Inspired by level 6 emergent listening

In the Far East, I witnessed an organizational group play at their edge with inward listening, empathy and authentic collaboration. They demonstrated level 6 emergent listening, and I was inspired by what unfolded.

This multi-stakeholder workshop was intended to build collaborative partnerships for the purpose of reducing poverty. As the facilitator, I set-up a simulation by asking the group to replicate a typical project management meeting. Participants self-selected to role-play a donor, a program advisor, a community-builder, a monitoring specialist, a government official and a program user. During the role-play, I noticed the program user was quiet as decisions were made *for* him.

In the debrief, I asked if anyone observed the silence of the program user and the group power dynamics. The advisor acknowledged that he was a "token poor person". The group assumed that he was illiterate, with no value-add contribution. In fact, they admitted that so-called poor people were not involved with program design, only evaluation. I inquired, "How do you create an effective program that does not involve the people it was designed to support?"

> *"Not everything that is faced can be changed, but nothing can be changed until it is faced."*
> James Baldwin

With this question, participants realized that their work culture displayed aspects of the rescuer syndrome, a subconscious pattern of "let's fix-it for them" set of beliefs. Programs were intended *for* the "beneficiary," implying that decisions were made for others' benefit. This parental attitude bristles with the belief, "I know what's best for you." This subtle block to authentic collaboration was imbued into the system. Due to unexplored assumptions, people perceived to be economically vulnerable were excluded from decision-making. Being resource poor and lacking resourcefulness were collapsed into one frame of reference. Most of all, they didn't listen to what was really happening in the group dialogue.

After we discussed the value of mindful listening, the participants decided to continue the role-play. They began with a reflection to quiet their background conversations and listen within. In the hushed workshop space, everyone tuned in on a different level. The program user was then invited to share. He revealed his own childhood experience of poverty with the pain of hunger, the embarrassment of unemployed parents and the helplessness of chronic sickness. He also spoke about deprivation and how this impacted people's mental health. Poverty produced widespread suffering in his community. His sincerity touched a chord with the participants. They offered supportive listening and affirmed his experience. They practiced attuning to the meta-messages of what was said and not said. The group paused to notice what was arising within as well as in the field. With self-reflective *and* empathetic listening, a constructive dialogue took shape. The group challenged their work norms and decided to adopt an inclusive, human-centered approach. Moving forward, they resolved to partner with all stakeholders to co-design a new program that focused on underlying issues versus symptoms.

From this role play, we concluded that a culture of listening is foundational to a culture of learning and authentic collaboration. We also realized that there's always a story in our hearts that wants to be heard. Unwrapping these tender stories elicits not only information but emotion. The process starts with mind-body-being presence and understanding the beneficence of people. With emergent listening, people *become* the space for new possibility.

A story about lion-hearted listening

I first experienced Level 7 listening in the heartland of South Africa. There, in Timbavati, I had the privilege of spending a month with a talented group of leaders and thirteen critically endangered white lions. This region is the natural habitat of the only free white lions in the world. Thanks to the Global White Lion Protection Trust, these lions are safeguarded from hunters as they are considered sacred by the local indigenous people. White lions hold a special role in the ecosystem as apex predators: they are keepers of balance and harmony. It's a magnificent sight to watch these majestic beings roam, play, hunt and rest in the bushveld.

> *"Until people learn to respect, listen and speak to the animal world, they can never know their true role on Earth."*
> Vangelis

In this nature sanctuary, our group practiced deep listening by spending every day—all day—outside. We were immersed in the beauty of this Savanna biome. During the first week, we learned the art of animal whispering to commune with the lions. With the assistance of lion-trackers, our daily jeep rides brought us to the lions so we could practice sending and receiving messages. I had many jaw-dropping experiences that convinced me that nature was not only listening but responding to my communication.

And I listened in return. With rapt attention, I watched and learned from this pride of lions who collaborated with ease. I was awestruck by their symbiotic connection with Earth. They lived in timeless mutuality with the land and each other. These lions demonstrated how to blend power with gentleness and fierce protection with play.

As the month unfolded, I relaxed into the ever-waiting bosom of Mother Nature. My body felt snuggled by the luxuriant green landscape and the presence of exquisite wildlife. The shockingly blue sky held infinity. Surrounded by this splendor, I began listening to my feelings and needs on a whole new level. At one point, my inner stillness was so fused with nature that I felt the mystical intimacy of oneness. When I took refuge in Earth, I sensed I was her conduit. During these fleeting moments, it felt as though the door between me and the eternal was ajar. There no longer seemed to be a boundary separating me from the natural world. My heart opened with solemn reverence and expansive love.

With lion-hearted listening, I experienced the rapture and joy of Earth dancing with all her tenants. Looking into the eyes of animals, I realized they were my teachers. The plants spoke to me of their medicine. I listened to the rain with new ears. The wilderness untamed my heart. Nature gave me a new perspective of love—space to be all of who I am, so that others can be all of who they are. This nature-based journey healed and fortified my core. I left South Africa ready to roar my heart truth.

My renewal would not have been possible without deep listening to Earth, self and others—in that order. When I returned home, I saw my relationships with fresh eyes. I noticed that we don't often make the time to deeply listen to ourselves, let alone other people and nature. When people comment that it's a low priority, I ask if they find the time to listen when the cloth of an important relationship has been torn and needs repair. If the relationship is valued, the answer is always yes. Deep listening is the supreme relationship gift that says, *I'm here and I care about you. Let's make the time to explore a way forward together.*

Practice the Principle: Listen by Uncovering Feelings and Needs

Self-Discovery

Exercise A: Journal Reflection about Listening

As a practice for this principle, I invite you to journal your response to one question each week. To slow down your writing and tune into your heart, I suggest placing the pen in your nondominant hand to write your response. This helps you tap into your feelings and subconscious truth. Listen to your inner voice to deepen self-awareness.

1. Overall, how would you describe your listening?
2. With the seven levels of listening, what are your growing edges?
3. What background conversation gets in the way of your listening?
4. Ask people for feedback on how you listen. What surprises you?
5. When you feel upset, how do you connect with your feelings and needs?
6. How do you listen to your unpleasant bodily sensations?
7. Practice level 5 listening with a friend. What did you learn?
8. What is the lie you continue to tell yourself?
9. How connected do you feel to Earth, your source of well-being?
10. Stop. Listen to your heart at this moment. What is it saying?

Exercise B: Heart Listening

For one week, set aside twenty minutes each day to deeply listen to your heart. Place your hand on your heart, quiet your mind and ask for guidance. Peel back the layers of authenticity. When an insight emerges, patiently wait for the body-felt sensation to reveal its tender truth, for the heart and body are talking buddies. As an ally, "be with" your heart. This is a path of direct revelation. It's like living inside your house rather than peeking in a window. The commitment levels are different.

When listening, notice if resistance crops up. Feel into the shadow and follow the impulse. Practice radical acceptance. Each day, complete a couple of these prompter sentences in a journal:

- Listening to my heart evokes the memory of…
- If I by-pass my feelings, I am afraid of…
- I am bad (good) because…
- If I express my anger, then…
- To release my judgment of _____, I need to…
- My deepest emotional truth in this moment is…
- My heart aches for…
- My heart rejoices for…
- What I want to shout to the world is…
- To revitalize myself, I need to…

Authentic Collaboration Practice with Others

Exercise A: Listening Self-Assessment and Sharing

This exercise analyzes how you listen in different environments, such as home, work/school or in community. It invites you to be radically honest yet kind with yourself. In dialogue with a partner, friend or colleague, become curious about what you do well and what you want to improve. Be open to new insights. Conclude by reflecting on how you want to build on your listening strengths to create meaningful connection with the people you care about.

Listening Self-Assessment Exercise

On a scale of 1 (low) to 10 (high), to what degree am I able to…

1. _____ avoid distractions to create space for deep listening?
2. _____ notice my mental talk as a neutral observer of self?
3. _____ set aside reflection time to tune in and observe my mind?
4. _____ tune into my body's sensations and receive its messages?
5. _____ listen and validate without the need to fix or rescue?
6. _____ listen to the meta-messages being communicated?
7. _____ self-regulate emotions when triggered?
8. _____ listen with empathy—with or without words?
9. _____ be patient in not interrupting or finishing people's sentences?
10. _____ rephrase back to check for understanding?

Exercise B: Level 4 Active Listening: Rephrasing Back to Validate

With a partner, friend or colleague, have an active listening conversation in rephrasing back what you hear. Add no-blame listening to the exchange in letting go of the need to judge, find fault or interpret. Give your mind a rest from the need to debate, assess, advise or rehearse what you will say. Both of you will have uninterrupted time to speak to a controversial angst-filled issue that you feel strongly about. It may be the same topic for both or different. Alternatively, you may decide to speak about your relationship, a recent conflict or the patterns you co-create. Discuss and agree to these three guidelines: use I statements, be succinct, pause in between sharing to reconnect with self.

Allow your partner to start. Offer the highest level of listening that you can. When your partner is done, acknowledge what you heard as the key message(s). Reflect back and validate what was said. No need to offer your opinion—just speak to what you heard. When you finish rephrasing back, your partner will respond to verify if what you said was accurate. Stop the exchange after this sharing. Pause to digest this communication.

Now switch. When speaking, give yourself the time you need to connect with your heart and body. Perhaps you will want to tune into a buried perspective or emotion, waiting to emerge. Afterwards, receive the gift of acknowledgment from your partner. Debrief the experience and your insights. Discuss the meaning of "shared understanding." Moving forward, experiment with a new discipline: Rather than (re)act first, speak second and listen last, try reversing this order.

Exercise C: Level 5 Empathetic Listening

In dialogue with a friend, complete these sentences to uncover your feelings and needs. Welcome whatever comes up intuitively. No preparation is needed. Notice the degree to which you authentically communicate. How present are you? It's said that the average adult attention span is 8 seconds. If your mind wanders, pause to bring yourself back to the conversation. Occasionally, connect with your belly. Notice what it feels like to be deeply listened to. When complete, reverse roles and have your partner respond.

> **Listen to what feelings and needs arise by completing these sentences:**
>
> - If I feel cared about in relationship, then _____.
> - If I lean into true interdependence and rely on others, then_____.
> - If I surrender into my heart, then _____.
> - If I let go of my need to know, then _____.
> - If I find myself in conflict with someone, then _____.
> - If I ask for what I really want, then _____.
> - If I am worthy of realizing my dreams, then _____.
> - If I support others in need, then _____.
> - If people don't follow through on an agreement, then _____.
> - If I feel loved and accepted for all of who I am, then _____.

Collaborative Connection with Earth

Forest Bathing

Forest bathing, an ancient Japanese form of eco-therapy, is about walking in nature and expanding our listening to the ecosystem around us. This type of experience reveals the magic and miracle of Life. As a full-body sensorial experience, research shows a clear link between well-being and forest bathing. Some of the benefits include reduced blood pressure, improved concentration, faster recovery in hospitals, better school performance and less violent behavior. At Tokyo's Nippon Medical School, scientists found that women who spent six hours in the woods, over the course of two days, had an increase in virus and tumor-fighting white blood cells. Interestingly, their noticeable physiological boost lasted for at least seven days afterwards.

With this insight, enjoy a slow forest walk for at least an hour. If a forest is not accessible, visit a community park. Engage not only your sight, but also taste, smell and touch. And yes, walk barefoot again if you can. Listen deeply to Earth as she communicates to you. Greet her as you would a new friend. Be aware that every mindful step you take is an interaction. Afterwards, journal how you felt as you strolled among the foliage and animals who inhabit that space.

Nature Visualization

In your mind's eye, sit at the foot of your favorite tree. As you lean against the bark, know that she has your back. Allow your breath to reach down into your hip bones and back up to your collarbone. Imagine the tree's timeless wisdom and feel into its unflinching strength. See the tree as a bridge between Mother Earth and Father Sky. In perfect symbiosis, she drinks in Earth's nourishment and gives away precious oxygen. Sustenance for humans and animals is generously provided. This is ayni or reciprocity in action: the epitome of balanced harmony.

Ask this beloved tree for support as you deeply listen to her wisdom.

- How can I become more grounded and fully present to Life?
- How can I embrace self-doubt and grow to new heights?
- How can I express my wild nature?
- How can I effortlessly change through the seasons of my life?

Like a forest of trees that bridge from one to another, imagine that you too are a bridge in this world, capable of giving and receiving in the flow of interdependency. You are also a connector, honoring the mind and heart, the ego and soul, the visible and invisible realms. Listen to your heartbeat and then merge with the tree's rhythm. Allow this tree to teach you about authentic collaboration.

When you feel complete, send gratitude for the tree's beauty, strength and enrichment. Imagine the tree branches embracing and appreciating you. You reflect each other's grandeur.

CHAPTER 11

A = APPRECIATE BY WELCOMING DIFFERENT PERSPECTIVES

"Out beyond ideas of wrongdoing and rightdoing, there is a field.
I'll meet you there.
When the soul lies down in that grass, the world is too full to talk about.
When the soul lies down in that grass, the world is too full to talk about.
Ideas, language, even the phrase 'each other' doesn't make any sense."
Rumi

Appreciating differences = Valuing diversity

Appreciation is a powerhouse word. I see it as the horse that pulls the carriage of gratitude. Appreciation is an expression of perceived value, whereas gratitude is more about feeling thankful. On the authentic collaboration bridge, appreciation is at the core of the central power pillar. Without it, the bridge deck sways in the wind. The hard parts of Life can sometimes bear hurricane-force winds, wreaking havoc on a relationship. It takes the calm, stabilizing influence of appreciation to augment connection and steady our course.

In the end, all human beings want the same thing: to be seen, heard and appreciated. Appreciation has the energy of rejuvenation. It invigorates a relationship with new lifeblood and makes people smile. When I'm working with groups, I often start and end the conversation with appreciations. This type of heart sharing is a wonderful way to inject feel-good emotions into the room. If any ruffled emotion lingers, appreciation has a way of rebalancing the group energy field. Sincere appreciations touch the heart, engendering a feeling of closeness, respect and trust. It also prompts

> *"What you appreciate, appreciates."*
> Lynne Twist

people to reflect on their strengths and how they want to express their gifts in their world. Instituting a daily appreciation practice fortifies any relationship.

Appreciating to welcome different perspectives is about responding to diversity in a respectful manner. It speaks to how we handle contrarian viewpoints. After all, bridges are intended to connect two terrains, enabling us to travel among different personalities, ideologies and values with ease. This principle entices us to approach differences from a state of curiosity, wonder and learning. When we do so, our relationships become warm and friendly. Positivity proliferates. Our interactive roadway becomes well-maintained with the bonding agent of appreciations.

> *"Happiness in relationship is not about getting what you want but about appreciating what you have."*
> Anonymous

In conflict, when unsettling differences arise and acceptance feels impossible, the bridge roadway becomes muddled with ruts and potholes. People may be tagged as enemies or antagonizing rivals. Dialogue becomes a minefield of explosive commentary. Strong opposing viewpoints shut down conversation. Sometimes, people take a stance of passive retaliation in closing their hearts. Learning stops and appreciation fades. This is when differences and alternative viewpoints offers us an opportunity to bridge-build. Turning this around starts with reminding ourselves that every person is worthy of respect, regardless of behavior. Taken further, we can adopt the idea that people are in our lives to help us awaken.

People tend to like people who like them. Although, in the practice of authentic collaboration, not everything said or done has to be liked, accepted or reconciled. It does, however, call for *receptivity*. This requires bridge-building with an and-both mindset. If we strive for mutual benefit in our relationships, then respecting a person's right to their opinion is fundamental.

Some ways to practice being open and receptive include:

- become centered and grounded before discussing something controversial,
- develop awareness of personal triggers,
- depersonalize by focusing on the issue at hand,
- defuse by acknowledging and validating what's being said, and
- perceive feedback as a gift, even if the words are divisive.

At the very least, we can thank people for their passion in speaking up about what matters to them. Their choice to engage with you may be an indicator of caring.

Essentially, this principle appreciates diversity not as an occasional circumstance but as the face of Life. The nature of who we are is diverse. By extension, relationships are diverse. Group conversations are designed to reveal multiple perspectives. What would it look like to truly *welcome* contrarian opinions into a dialogue?

> *"There's no key to great relationships, there's simply a well-worn welcome mat."*
> Curtis Tyrone Jones

Yes, those who display oppositional defiance can be frustrating. Disrupters and debaters can be annoying. Nay-sayers who consistently go against the grain can evoke stress. Yet perhaps these behaviors can remind us that healthy conflict is a part of collaboration. Maybe it's an opportunity to sink into deeper authenticity. Alternate viewpoints can elicit values and assumptions or even entice a group to refocus and explore an overlooked angle. That said, welcoming different perspectives is not about needing to agree. Rather, it's being genuinely open to other viewpoints.

Since we can only see something through our own set of eyes, our perspective is limited. Metaphorically, we each wear horse blinders. Our beliefs and perceptions cannot be full and complete. Opening our field of vision to consider other perspectives helps us deepen understanding. It helps us let go of the habit of demonizing or pigeonholing people. Thanks to diversity, authentic collaboration can be a mind-expanding, growth-inducing, creative process.

The challenge of groupthink

Welcoming diverse perspectives is not just a polite platitude. In some cases, it's a case of life and death. If people are not given permission to speak up, and groupthink takes over, calamity can occur. According to psychologist Irving Janis, groupthink is defined as "A mode of thinking that people engage in when they are deeply involved in a cohesive in-group, when the members' strivings for

> *"The psychological components of war have not gone away—groupthink, dominance, vengeance, callousness, tribalism and self-deception."*
> Steven Pinker

unanimity override their motivation to realistically appraise alternative courses of action." Put simply, groupthink takes place when conformity outranks critical thinking and when harmony supersedes disagreement.

The US Space Shuttle *Challenger* disaster is one such tragic example. In 1986, the decision was made to launch the shuttle even though engineers expressed concern about the performance of the O-ring seal under cold temperatures. These voices were dismissed in favor of a strong leader's preference to move forward with the launch. Apparently, the concerned engineers were isolated from the decision-making group. With management not welcoming different perspectives and seriously considering the merit of their analysis, seven astronauts died.

As a psychological phenomenon, groupthink is alive and well in all aspects of society. We see its harmful effects in the military, schools, political parties and the healthcare system. In some families, people are given the message that to get along, they must go along. In business, not allowing divergent viewpoints and ideas can lead to negative repercussions. If, for example, staff concerns are not responded to, overt or covert sabotage can take place. This includes sick leave, procrastination on projects, quality control issues, missed deadlines and even destroying company property or products. The incurred corporate cost can amount to millions of dollars. When people feel silenced or pressured to buy into a way of thinking, the integrity of the work culture is weakened. As business scholar Paul Gibbons remarked, "That which a team does not want to discuss, it most needs to discuss."

The group effect also extends into conflict. Discord can become infectious. Dr. Daniel Goleman and Richard Boyatzis's work on social intelligence speaks to the effect of conflict reactivity on our biochemistry. Stress triggers our brain circuitry, which, in turn, releases a surge of stress hormones that spike the heart rate from thirty to forty beats per minute. If groupthink, ostracizing or judgment results in social disconnection, the sympathetic nervous system releases hormones and lowers the immune system. One person's stress reaction can influence others via mirror neurons and oscillators. Given this bio-interchange, conflict can be contagious.

To counter groupthink, consider subscribing to deep democracy, a philosophy that values and includes all voices and perspectives. Rather than rely on popular consent or a majority vote, the intention is to co-create safe space for different voices to be heard. It's a sign of respect when people care enough to unpack group assumptions and needs. This takes time, but there's enormous payoff—especially if people who are marginalized are welcomed to join the collaboration. While this may be a challenging undertaking in larger companies, just the act of exploring what's possible can lead to greater inclusion.

> "When working with groups, it's important to check things out—that is, to check assumptions rather than assume."
> Linda Lehtonen

As a final point, it's worth noting that deep democracy is a spin-off from the principle of deep ecology: giving due regard to the whole living environment. In this belief system, every being, human and non-human, has an inherent right to live and prosper. Embodying this mindset is a bridge-building asset on its own.

The obstacle of attachments

Another obstacle that hinders the expression of divergent perspectives is attachment. When we cling to a certain way of thinking, rigidity can arise. With an unyielding attitude, people's tendency is to close, attack and attach to a position of victim or a stance of righteousness. We lose sight of the fact that if we're right, then someone else must be wrong. Rarely does this dualistic mindset result in a kind exchange of words. Being right implies *I know*, which makes this a double-loop attachment. Cleaving to knowledge as a source of power ends up making us feel unsafe. This is because power is then perceived as external to self. And, seeking knowledge is a never-ending mouse wheel.

Each attachment reveals how bonded we are to our beliefs and expectations. Disappointment becomes our shadow. The more I cling to right-wrong, good-bad thinking, the more I avoid myself, stay in evaluator mode, keep my walls up, correct the wrongness in others, cover up my own shame and shut down compassion. It's a primitive, polarizing relational block to meaningful connection. As Buddhist philosophy teaches, attachments lead to suffering because everything is transient and impermanent. Since loss is inevitable, attachment is against the fluid nature of Life. It creates relationship

> "Attachment is the strongest block to realization."
> Neem Karoli Baba

stress. I've come to realize that what I cannot control is teaching me to let go. The way out of this trap is to live from the heart space of humble awareness and mindful non-attachment.

Living with non-attachment does not mean people and things have no value. Rather, it's recognizing that grasping is a sign of an unhealthy emotional dependence. Insecurity may be swimming in the undercurrent. When we loosen our grip to attachments, we create space for other people's perspective to be welcomed and appreciated. The ground of authentic collaboration becomes lush and productive.

In the scenario of collaborative family relationships, we may confuse attachment with love. These are two entirely different animals. Attachment is me-focused and revolves around anxiety and dependency. It is separation-oriented. Love is we-focused and pertains to acceptance of what is. It is unity-oriented. Love without attachment offers a quality of connection devoid of limitation, neediness or scarcity. With an open yet non-attached way of relating, respectful collaboration becomes effortless.

Common Attachments

Reflect on a recent conflict. Which attachments were evident within you?

- an agenda or a set of rules
- perfectionism or overmanaging how things get done
- controlling how people behave

- distrust and cynicism
- playing the role of perpetrator, victim, rescuer or bystander
- being right or looking good

- withdrawing or avoiding to stay in your comfort zone
- deflecting self-responsibility or being over-/under-responsible
- fear of commitment

A story about handling different perspectives with care

As a social and eco-justice activist, my attachment to certain perspectives often comes to the table. When I deal with controversial issues, I sometimes hold this lightly and other times with churned-up heavy emotion. Years ago, I was involved with a community-based environmental group. We routinely welcomed other volunteers to support eco-protection and restoration efforts. We acknowledged the need to grow our movement and include diverse perspectives, talents and resources. Then, one day, the conversation took an abrupt turn.

An oil company representative contacted us to request a meeting and explore the possibility of collaborating. Some people perceived this as a door-opener. They wanted to expand our circle of eco-champions, gain insight about the fossil fuel industry and influence change. Others were adamantly against a partnership and criticized the company's environmental track record. They noted the risk of greenwashing and being exploited for PR benefit. Without having met the oil company representative, some questioned the real motivation of this person in wanting to join our group. Different perspectives generated group upset.

In response, we decided to talk about these delicate issues and sense into the collective wisdom. I began the dialogue by declaring my attachment to inclusivity as my top priority. As a community-builder, I stand for a we-orientation, not an us-versus-them approach. My belief is that Earth is our shared home and, as such, we need all heads, hearts and hands on deck to turn this climate ship around. Others, however, held a fear of being taken advantage of. They concluded that people who work for polluting companies were adversaries to the eco-friendly movement.

> *"Hold your ground yet also let someone in. The former is debate while the latter is dialogue."*
> Dr. Esther Perel

As the conversation unfolded, we all listened carefully. Slowly, an and-both solution surfaced. With care, we explored a shared value or super truth that could unite us. We resolved to appreciate diverse perspectives *and* uphold our commitment to associate with sincere Earth stewards. To help us know if newcomers shared this value, we created a volunteer pledge and a sign-off declaration, along with instituting an informal interview. Our goal was to balance inclusion, neutrality and values alignment with a statement about intention. As a healthy boundary, we asked that volunteers have no corporate affiliation. We welcomed anyone willing to serve as an advocate, regardless of their political, religious, work or gender identity. Lastly, we agreed that respecting self, others and Earth had to be front and center as a core value. Our authentic power was connected to our integrity and group alignment.

The role of healthy boundaries

This eco-story not only highlights the power of an and-both orientation but also the role of healthy boundaries. I see both as key elements of appreciating different perspectives. The word *healthy* is used because sometimes boundaries are so loose that they are easily set aside when pressure is applied. Alternatively, boundaries can be so rigid that people are spurned in the process. Collaborating then becomes an attempt to relate through a barricade of defenses. Boundaries may also be a sign of pseudo-strength, rooted in anxiety. As someone who has taken years to drop my own heart armor and proverbial sword, I can attest to how boundaries have a light protective side and a dark foreboding side. Only your heart knows your relationship with boundaries.

With boundaries, there's an inherent contradiction. On the one hand, we are all energetically interconnected and unified in a field of consciousness. At this level, boundaries are obscure and unintelligible. Perhaps, in this space, boundaries stem from a fear of not being able to wisely discern and self-protect. On the other hand, human beings live in separate bodies, with ego personalities and a potential to be violent. At times, boundary protection is necessary. Disrespectful behavior, for example, may warrant a clear line in the sand. If people are sensitive empaths with the proclivity to take on others' "baggage," then boundaries are of value here too. Even nature shows us that coexistence includes boundaries. Trees have bark, animals have fur, humans have skin, plants have pubescence (hairs) and birds have feathers.

As psychotherapist Terri Cole reminds us, most people are not taught how to effectively communicate their needs, preferences, desires or deal-breakers. Rather, we tend to deny our feelings, play small, resort to passive-aggressive behavior and even damage hard-won trust in our relationships. If we're

> *"Take baby steps towards establishing boundaries that are aligned with the way you feel and, before you know it, talking true will become your new normal."*
> Terri Cole

conditioned to be "polite" at all costs, we may people-please and collude rather than speak up in the face of unacceptable behavior. We may also dismiss our intuition when red flags appear or over-accommodate when people are in need. Boundary-setting includes learning when to extend support to others and when to stay on our own side of the fence. If we listen, our body will tell us when we've crossed the line.

When we relate with clear intentions and healthy boundaries, we are more open to varying opinions. If we're in our heart zone, it's easier to let go of bad-other images. Exclusionary thoughts begin to feel superfluous. We are more apt to welcome differing opinions, even if agreement or convergence is not possible. In the art of bridge-building, sometimes a strong no is a powerful yes to being true to self. Developing self-loyalty is knowing our non-negotiables and how willing we are to adapt and stretch.

Helpful Boundary-Setting Questions and Phrases

- Can you elaborate on your hard no boundaries? Now, here's mine…
- Let me consider your offer and get back to you by…

- I'm grateful for this opportunity, yet I will decline because…
- To be clear, I'm saying yes to this decision because…

- To move forward, I need your support. Here's my request…
- In considering the workload, how can we share the responsibility?

- I'm sensing resistance in our conversation. What are you noticing?
- How can we best help each other to succeed?

Validating when not in agreement

In my past relationships, I found myself acknowledging people's perspective only if I agreed. It was an egoic posture. If I disagreed and still acknowledged the viewpoint, I assumed this meant I was supporting the expressed opinion. I mistakenly collapsed validating with condoning. Then, a colleague offered a distinction. Acknowledging what someone says is not necessarily agreeing, but rather supporting the *validity* of the perspective. It's a sign of respect. Doing so does not diminish the value of my own perspective. In truth, a person's words have nothing to do with our own beliefs. The expression is only one path in a jungle of possibility.

> *"We cannot judge the lives of others because each person knows only their own pain and renunciation. It's one thing to feel that you are on the right path, but it's another thing to think that yours is the only path."*
> Paulo Coelho

With this in mind, note that this appreciation principle refers to the universal need to formulate and articulate one's thoughts. Validation is a celebration of our uniqueness and the beauty of human diversity. Sinking into this understanding enables us to collaborate with an open, welcoming attitude.

In studying with John Welwood, a clinical psychologist, teacher and psychotherapist, I gleaned many insights on bridge-building. One mind-bending exercise he offered was called the Fourfold Truth. When relationship differences arise, this exercise invites people to explore how viewpoints have validity *and* distortion. In acknowledging the fourfold truth of the situation, greater truth-telling, clarity, humility and understanding is possible. I've found it to be insightful when opposing perspectives produce muddled or even acrimonious interpersonal dynamics. Since viewpoints are both "right" and "wrong" to some extent, we can step out of the paralyzing effect of dualistic thinking. This quality of dialogue has the power to shift a collaboration breakdown into a breakthrough. The conversation has a better chance of moving into flow, with mutual respect restored.

Dealing with opposition in an empowered, respectful manner

In our polarized world, many people feel the urge to speak up about their perspective in very challenging circumstances. The threat of hearing ridicule and criticism is real, especially with sensitive, controversial issues. When our opinion is counter to the collective consciousness, the fear of rejection is valid.

> *"An eye for an eye only ends up making the whole world blind."*
> Mahatma Gandhi

In social media, cancel culture is now a well-known phenomenon. This action is about publicly ostracizing or shunning an individual on media platforms for speaking their truth. It's downright painful. With this risk of reprisal, civic discourse and freedom of expression are discouraged. What's more, our family and cultural conditioning engenders fear with tribal tenets such as: don't rock the boat, conform to be accepted, stay silent to be safe and punish with an eye for an eye. These teachings, bound up in society's rule book, are passed down generation after generation. Undeniably, speaking up can incur hurt.

To minimize the risk, practice mindful communication. Pause before you react. Be honest about your intention. Choose your words wisely. Assume positive intent.

To further support mindful communication, consider these four important distinctions.

Mindful Communication Distinctions	Reflection Questions
A criticism versus an underlying unmet need	If I criticize someone, what is my unfulfilled wish or need?
Label the person versus describing behavior	Do I define the whole person as "bad" or focus on describing the behavior?
Judgment versus discernment	How can I let go of fear-based mind judgments to call in heart-centered discernment?
Projection versus seeing people for who they are	How do I project my own undesirable shadow traits onto someone else?

These distinctions encourage respectful communication when opposing viewpoints are evident. It's helpful to remind yourself that other people's opinions are just that—opinions. People's words do not define who they are, nor who you are. If it's their inclination, allow people to react and judge. You don't have to take it personally. Hurtful words reflect the speaker, not you. Besides, replying with fear-based judgment only feeds the flame of divisiveness, wedging people between a rock and a hard place. Be mindful of conflating judgment and discernment. The latter is about understanding and gaining insight. Do your words arise from judgment, accompanied by frustration and stubbornness; or do they reflect discernment, with a sense of inner calm, wisdom and compassion? Only you know.

When the winds of opposition blow your way, choose to be curious about differences to stay connected. Puncture the balloon of negativity with the principle of mindful response. Give up the idea that Life must look a certain way and people must behave according to expectations. We don't have to be manipulated, retort with unkindness or move with the masses. Step beyond the notion that there is only one "good idea" or "right way." In the dance of relationship, we're always at choice in how we respond and declare our views. Stand for self-sovereignty, express compassion, assert with confidence and trust your truth. Anchor into your love center and reconnect with the energy flow between your heart and others.

> "For every great idea, the opposite idea is also true."
> Adam Kahane

When faced with contrasting perspectives and values, this question can be empowering: "How can we meet both sets of needs without resorting to demands and control strategies?" When we express a boundary that serves us yet triggers the other person, how can we hold space to tease apart what's really happening? Reflect on our internal operating system; what does it take for both people to feel safe, heard and seen? We don't have to believe that when some take their space at the table, then others will lose their space. This thought is based in competition. Let go of the scarcity belief that the table size is limited. We can co-create whatever table size we want. There's sufficient space for all needs to be held with care. Everyone's light is welcome to shine in this world.

All these points to ponder are intended to reclaim our power. In doing so, we slow down the conversation, open into curiosity, feel our feelings, speak our truth, explore needs and take responsibility for our choices. With heart listening and intentional speaking, our common humanity is served. We may even be left wondering what it would be like to never make anything or anyone bad or wrong ever again. How liberating would it be to let go of judgment so people can fully express and be who they really are? Freeing ourselves from these suffering-laden mind traps is a doorway to greater happiness.

The aptitude of resiliency

Even though our personality wants to stay in control, authentic collaboration is, in large part, about letting go of control. When the control tendency arises, dive into the disturbance to interrupt the mind spin. When we question our limiting beliefs and pivot towards life-affirming insights, we're creating a new resilient skin. With a heart-centered approach, we can rise above the fray of relational conflict. When we throw water at a dysfunctional relationship pattern, we change course. This is the power of resiliency in action.

Given the nature of collaboration, anticipate a variety of opinions. Developing inner resiliency is having the ability to bend, flex, adapt and adjust to different circumstances or alternative ways of thinking and living. It's an aptitude that enables us to bounce back and navigate through the crunchiness of Life. If we feel triggered or irritated with different perspectives, resiliency gives us access to self-discovery, understanding and empowered choice.

> *"Everything that irritates us about others can lead us to an understanding of ourselves."*
> Carl Jung

Here's a story that spotlights the correlation between leaders who demonstrated resiliency and the impact this had on their work success. When working abroad, I coached five private sector waste management companies who decided to put aside their competitive past to collaborate. Their intention was to explore ways to reduce, reuse and recycle anew. This was a first in the history of this sector. I was impressed that their commitment to positive communal results was stronger than their fear of sharing information or losing market share. These leaders experienced a clash of strong opinions, yet they accepted the tension as a part of the creative process. Consistently, they put aside their egos, adapted as needed and refocused on the greater good.

I was delighted to see the elegance by which these change-makers welcomed different perspectives. Like a river that finds another way around a log jam, they navigated their relational eddies. Curiosity was used at every turn as they opened to uncertainty and new possibilities. They expressed interest in both their inner experience and the world of other companies. By appreciating and learning from diverse viewpoints, this group developed the first recycling program in the country. They also cooperated to institute the first public environmental educational program. Success was measured not only by outcomes but by the spirit of collaboration within their team. By all counts, it was a watershed milestone.

At the end of the project, in celebration of their achievement, one of the team members quoted John F. Kennedy: "If we cannot end our differences, at least we can help make the world safe for diversity. For, in the final analysis, our most basic common link is that we all inhabit this small planet. We all breathe the same air. We all cherish our children's future. And we are all mortal."

Looking in the mirror of inter-being

As with all the RELATE principles, welcoming different perspectives starts within. The standing invitation is to reflect on how you greet the different parts of yourself. When you experience inner conflict, how do you hold competing energies? Assess how congruent your mind and heart are when resistance is experienced. Looking in the mirror never fails to bring us face to face with the intricate tapestry of authentic self-collaboration.

> *"We live within and beyond our own skin at the same time."*
> Bonnie Badenoch

Many moons ago, I went to France to study with Thich Nhat Hanh and his spiritual family at Plum Village. At this beautiful countryside hermitage, thousands of people gathered each summer for daily teachings. I was mesmerized by Thay—the name of "teacher" given to Thich by his students: his spiritual depth and authentic heart power were obvious. One of Thay's stories that impacted me was about a house roofing project. He explained that handling tools was not his forte, yet he wanted to help a friend in need. On the first day of construction, Thay fastened on the tool belt and climbed up the ladder. He attempted to pound the nail with the hammer but missed. Instead, the hammer hit his left thumb. A yelp of pain rang out. Immediately, Thay noticed that his right hand dropped the hammer and held his left hand with gentle compassion, caressing the sore finger with great remorse. His left hand felt comforted and soothed. Not for one second, Thay said, did his left hand judge or scold. There was no admonishment such as "How could you be so clumsy? Get away. Don't touch me." Rather, there was immediate forgiveness between his hands. The love offered was graciously accepted.

In sharing this, Thay challenged us to step into curiosity, to defy our conditioning and ask, "How can we let go of judgment and welcome in the different parts of ourselves with an open heart, regardless of what pain we experience?" In our interconnected universe, the more we're able to be curious and compassionate with ourselves, the more we can offer this to others.

> *"Curiosity is the wick in the candle of learning".*
> William A Ward

This interconnection is at the root of *inter-being*—a concept that Thay coined to describe the coexistence of all Life forms. One day, I hope inter-being will be commonly known around the world. Perhaps then, we will embrace diversity as our superpower. As a human family, we will meet other people who are different from ourselves, only to see…ourselves. Just as nature welcomes different species to co-create its luxuriant beauty, we too can expand our perspective to see the beauty in all.

To quote Sun Tzu from *The Art of War*, "There are not more than five musical notes, yet the combinations of these five give rise to more melodies than can ever be heard. There are not more than five primary colors, yet in combination they produce more hues than can ever been seen. There are not more than five cardinal tastes, yet combinations of them yield more flavors than can ever be tasted." It takes the combination of different talents to produce the magic of collaborative synergy.

Practice the Principle: Appreciate by Welcoming Different Perspectives

Self-Discovery

Exercise A: Journal Reflection Questions

1. How can you expand your appreciation for self, others and Earth?
2. On topics that matter, how open are you to contrasting attitudes?
3. When triggered, what helps and hinders you to stay connected?
4. What do you find difficult or embarrassing to share with others?
5. How can you stretch to be a bridge-builder in the face of difference?

Exercise B: A Self-Assessment on Dealing with Differences

Welcoming Different Perspectives: A Self-Assessment

With honesty, rate yourself on a scale of 1 (low) to 10 (high) to ramp up your self-awareness. Place an *S* to acknowledge your strengths or a *G* to signify areas of growth. When complete, journal about your story as it relates to holding all needs with care. Reflect on how your ability to do this with others is a mirror to how you do this with yourself. Conclude with an act of kindness for someone you care about and for yourself.

To what extent are you able to...

1. _____ clearly articulate your needs while respecting others' needs?
2. _____ engage in affirming dialogue in a group?
3. _____ authentically express while being open to other perspectives?
4. _____ validate when viewpoints are contrary to yours?
5. _____ say "let's agree to disagree" during a values clash?
6. _____ explore change in an important relationship?
7. _____ assess FEAR (False Evidence Appearing Real) during conflict?
8. _____ notice attachment to looking good and being right?
9. _____ reground and recenter when feeling upset?
10. _____ appreciate and leverage the diverse strengths of others?

Exercise C: Reflecting on Judgment

Bring to mind a person in your life who you want to change. Reflect on these questions and journal your insights.

- What is your motivation in wishing this person was different?
- Without self-judgment, what is your judgment about this person?
- What are your feelings and unmet needs in this relationship?
- What is the impact of you not accepting this person?
- What part of this person is you?
- If you saw this person from your heart, how would *you* change?
- How might your relationship change if you let go of your judgment?

Authentic Collaboration Practice with Others
Exercise A: Welcoming Divergent Viewpoints

With a trusted collaborative work partner or friend, sit across from each other and look into each other's eyes for a full two minutes in silence. Then, invite a dialogue that focuses on the questions from this list. Practice mindful listening and authentic speaking.

1. When we have contradictory viewpoints, what happens for you?
2. What do you need from me to support you in standing in your truth?
3. How would you prefer we communicate during emotional disagreements?
4. What am I/you devoted to? What's the common thread?
5. I observe _____. How does this match up with your perspective?
6. How can we meet your need for _____ and my need for _____?
7. What promises and requests do we want to put on the table?
8. What agreement are you willing to make?
9. If option A __ is not acceptable, what else might support your need for __?
10. I acknowledge your perspective and feel grateful for _____.

Exercise B: Bridge-building by Responding to Differences with Care

With a partner, discuss a topic that both of you care about yet hold different perspectives. When each says something that sparks disagreement, defensiveness or the impulse to interrupt, pause and tune into what your body is saying. Slow down the conversation to actively listen. Respond with care by rephrasing back what was said. Without evaluation, consider using bridging statements such as:

- Are you saying...
- What I heard is...
- What do you mean by...
- It sounds like the values you hold include...
- It seems to me that you think...
- I'm confused, can you elaborate on...
- I'm curious if you have considered...
- Although we have different viewpoints, I respect your...

Exercise C: Yes-and Exercise

In a trio conversation, practice listening by appreciating and building on what the other two people speak about. Rather than say, "Yes but," say "Yes and," each time you and the others communicate. Whatever is said, respond by starting with this phrase. Choose a divisive or conflictual topic that raises various opinions. Set aside at least twenty minutes for this conversation to sink into this way of listening, validating and speaking. Afterwards, discuss what this experience was like. How did the phrase *Yes and* resonate with you and your partners?

Exercise D: Uncovering the Positive Intent

Uncovering the positive intent behind someone's words is a powerful bridge-building skill. It's about suspending judgment while noting needs and values. While the positive intent may not be explicitly revealed, it's embedded in every communication. This capacity is especially helpful when opposing viewpoints surface. Acknowledging the positive intent can diffuse or de-escalate tension when emotions run high. When done skillfully, the speaker will feel heard, respected and validated.

To start this partner dialogue exercise, select a controversial, emotional issue that you both want to discuss. It's ideal if you hold different perspectives about this issue. Alternatively, you can choose a different topic from your partner. Invite the other person to express his/her point of view for a full two minutes. Your role is to deeply listen. When finished, speak to what you heard as your partner's positive intent—the value or beauty underneath the perspective. If you're unsure, guess or imagine what the need or value is. Your partner can agree or disagree. When complete, switch roles and repeat the exchange. Debrief the experience by sharing what struck you with this way of communicating.

Here's a demo...

In speaking about the issue of clear-cutting wild intact forests, I feel anger and grief related to loss. I feel sad about the loss of biodiversity. Nature's rich storehouse of nutrients and medicines is rapidly diminishing. I feel bereft about human beings destroying these last remaining beautiful ecosystems that we all depend on. I am also concerned about the plight of indigenous forest tribes. Many people are not aware of how we are degrading our precious Earth, let alone understand the implications for future generations. Collectively, we do not consider the ripple effect of harm we are complicit in.

After listening with empathy, my partner mirrors back the positive intent of my message by saying, "I hear you care deeply about our forests and the value they carry to sustain and enrich life. It also sounds like you want people to take responsibility for our serious deforestation issue—both individually and collectively—for our own sake and those yet to come. It sounds like your heart cares about those most vulnerable. You want people to become aware of this issue, reclaim their power and take action."

Collaborative Connection with Earth
Listening to Earth's Wisdom to Heal Adversarial Thinking

This activity can expand your ability to hold divergent points of view while healing adversarial thinking. For one month, dive into the world of your so-called enemy. If you consider yourself a capitalist, read socialist pieces in the media, watch documentaries or listen to podcasts. If you are a climate activist, consider articles or video interviews written by climate deniers. If you're a rationalist, review and discuss spiritual principles and ideas. On the political front, move to the other side of the spectrum from where you now sit. Choose a topic that triggers you.

AUTHENTIC COLLABORATION

Feel into the discomfort and the working of your mind. When judgment arises, venture outdoors to listen to what Earth has to say in response. What does the wild in and around you say about adversarial thinking? How does a plant, for example, deal with an invasive insect infringing on its space? How does she balance interdependent flow without aggression? Observe her benevolence expressed in every leaf, insect and flower. With surgical precision, notice what expands and contracts your ability to feel safe in the world.

Take the time to study your assumptions about those you label as "wrong" or "bad." Observe your mind trying to sense-make another construct of reality. Notice these are perceptions. Since all angst is based in misperception, how does your mind report "fake news"? What prejudice do you hold? What do you not want people to say about you?

During these thirty days, as you learn about alternate worldviews, you may be surprised at what happens. You may see other viewpoints as valid. You may conclude that taking sides is unproductive. The borders around the so-called "other" may even become blurry. Share your insights with a friend.

Sample questions to reflect on and discuss:

- How do I try to convince others from ego and personality?
- How do I impede collaboration by being attached to a viewpoint?
- How can I influence without force?
- How can I entrain my mind with my heart?
- How can I demonstrate respect, even when I disagree?
- What does nature say about how to hold all needs with care?
- How can I embody the unifying message of the eagle-condor prophecy?

CHAPTER 12

T = TRUST BY SPEAKING AUTHENTICALLY

*"Trust is the glue of life. It's the most essential
ingredient in effective communication.
It's the foundation principle that holds all relationships."*
Stephen Covey

Roaring the truth about how we trust Life

As I reflect on the role of trust in authentic collaborative relationships, I'm reminded of a true story about a lion cub in a zoo. Given my fondness for lions, my heart hurts when I imagine the trauma that lions and all wild animals experience when caught, trapped, transported and held in small compounds. That said, this account underscores the slow process of trust-building.

Years ago, when a beautiful lion cub arrived at a zoo, he was kept in a small cage—about fifteen-by-fifteen feet. Zoo patrons fell in love with the lion. They realized that this small cage would soon be inadequate. An adult lion needs large swaths of land to meander and play. In response, the patrons launched a fundraising campaign to raise money for the purchase of more land. Soon thereafter, an amazing multihectare forest park reserve was prepared for this lion to roam.

On the day the lion was to be released into the park, a large crowd gathered with great fanfare. Yet, when the zookeeper lifted the door of the cage, the lion did not want to leave. Much to everyone's surprise and chagrin, he simply sat down in the cage and gazed at the swarm of people. Eventually, this magnificent animal had to be coaxed out of the enclosure with food. After consuming the meal, the lion retreated back to his home. This pattern repeated for many days. The cage had become his comfort zone. It took considerable time for the lion to adjust to his new surroundings before he finally experienced the bliss of running free.

Human beings are like this lion. We are caged by years of conditioning. Bars of mistrust, made from the steel of limiting beliefs, inhibit us from stepping out and into our full potential. These mental patterns hold us captive until we outgrow the old belief container. Eventually, we may come to realize that there never was a container. Even then, it takes a willingness to trust and patient guidance to lure us away from the safety of what's known.

Trust is the operative word in collaboration. But what does it really mean? I've come to realize that trust derives from meaningful connection. Our propensity to trust starts with our primal relationship with Life. Connecting with Life occurs in an infinite number of ways, both seen and unseen. On one level, it's about connecting with the organic movement and flow of Earth. When we let go of mental chatter and become quiet within, there's space to be present to feel the subtle shifts within and around us. We are more apt to tune into our intuition and hear Life's messages. When we allow the energy of nature to move us, a sense of ease is felt. When we surrender to the current of Life, and release the need "to make things happen," new insights, people and resources come into our awareness. We're likely to follow our hunch. When we experience deep connection with Life, we sense that we are her manifestation, we hold her potential and, as such, we are continually supported. We effortlessly trust in the stream of Life.

> *Trust and meaningful connection are symbiotic. Connecting involves presence just as a hug involves embracing.*

To build trust in Earth or Life, consider these playful tips. For one minute, plunge into a pool or a body of water and float on your back. Allow Earth to uplift you with her buoyancy. Have faith that she has your back. Notice if you feel relaxed or tense. For one hour, contemplate why anyone, including Life, should trust you. For one day, notice the generosity of Earth and how she supports your whole being. How does Earth gift you with strength, inspiration and resilience? For one week, take daily mindful nature walks to notice the degree to which your feet fully land on Earth. Feel how grounded you are and how that correlates with your trust in Earth. For one month, consciously say yes to Life. Whatever and whomever offers you an invitation or opportunity, agree to the experience (within reason). See how that feels as you expand into newness. These actions, in effect, elongate and widen our inner collaboration bridge.

> *"Faith does not need to push the river because faith is able to trust that there is a river. The river is flowing. We are in it."*
> Richard Rohr

Ultimately, trust is a decision. Developing a relationship *is* deciding to trust Life. After all, relationship is an unfamiliar field saturated with risk. It's a brave choice to enter the perilous terrain of relationship. At times, it's tempting to retreat and stay in the cage. The more we connect our heart with Mother Earth, the more we fuel our courage to authentically relate. This is a starting point to deepen trust with the optimizing intelligence of Life, come what may. To be sure, the journey of trust-building involves the grit of fortitude and the grace of presence.

To what extent do you trust Life?

Taking a leap of faith

Some people move through Life taking trust as a given, until its lost. This can happen in a flash. It takes a long time to build and a minute to destroy, sometimes irrevocably. Yes, trust is a decision but it's also a leap of faith. While people want reassurance that it's safe to trust, there are no guarantees. Trusting is a gamble no matter what action we take. Even with the most detail-oriented plan and rational decision, Life will have the final say. This brings up vulnerability, a sense of being susceptible to potential hurt and harm. It takes self-collaboration to bridge to our heart and reignite our courage.

Deciding to experiment with authentic collaboration is a trust practice. With every exchange, we are, on some level, choosing how much to open and trust. Our capacity to trust is affected by our style of attachment. As previously noted, how we attach is dependent on how our caregivers related with us as babies. Psychologists contend that there are four predominant attachment styles: ambivalent, avoidant, disorganized and secure. Each style is shaped by certain beliefs and emotional patterns. Our style influences how we collaborate and depend on people, how we are triggered, seek approval and how we navigate closeness and distance. The band of trust encircles it all.

For me, an aspect of my trust journey is overcoming the fear of being fully seen. Being exposed can mean subjecting myself to a verbal attack or rejection. This conjures up resistance, as though I'm walking through Life with one foot on the gas and another foot on the brake. I'm leery of having my vulnerabilities laid bare and being judged. I need to remind myself that my strength comes from the flow of Life. It's an ongoing exercise to quiet my mind chatter, listen to my heart and trust this guidance. In these moments, I am able to let go of fear. The heavy weight of separation drops. I am free to express my authentic truth. My heart has space to breathe. The wingspan of my potential expands so I can fly.

> *"Until you spread your wings, you will have no idea how far you can fly."*
> Napoleon Bonaparte

TRY THIS: How do you feel about opening to a new level of trust? Notice how you experience constriction in your body. Stay with the sensation. Slowly and gently pry open the cage to reveal the inner metal bars. What beliefs arise in the dark corner of your mind? Presence this truth and trust that freedom is on the other side.

Behaviors that enhance and drain trust

Through daily interactions, trust lives and breathes as an ever-changing dynamic. It's elusive and delicate. With age and maturity, we learn about the nuances of trust through the full spectrum of relationship-building. Trust rises and falls with the contrast of positive trust-enhancing behaviors and negative trust-draining communication. There are countless intricacies that influence this intangible virtue. It's a crucial social bonding glue that's sticky in every sense of the word.

While it's commonly known that trust is essential to healthy relationships, have you ever considered how and why you add or deplete this element? I see trust as the by-product of certain behaviors and beliefs that enable us to have confidence and faith in something or someone. While some behaviors depend on culture and context, there are universal threads as

> *Trust is an ever-changing belief in the reliability, truth, skill and strength of someone.*

well, including integrity, follow-through on agreements, confidentiality, fairness, consistency and reliability through tough times. Many of these trust-building behaviors are rooted in the principle that frames this chapter: building trust by speaking authentically. With authenticity comes clear communication, transparency, vulnerability and honesty. This, of course, does not mean disclosing every thought or feeling. Nor does it involve remaining static in how we relate. Instead, it takes wise discernment to feel into what's genuine and appropriate for self, our relationship with others and the situation at hand.

Trust as mindful innocence

Trust and wise discernment go hand in hand. When it comes to crossing the bridge of authentic collaboration, our trusted guide is the intelligence of our inner guidance. Like emotional and relationship intelligence, there's no formal schooling in listening to our inner guidance. The art of trust-building is a "feel-as-you-go" self-awareness exercise. Spend time in solitude and silence to access this deeper knowing. Pay attention to what stories are in the mind. Our past stories shape our future and how willing we are to trust.

Some believe that we live with a destiny plan already written in the stars. Fate has already cast the future. Consequently, for these folks, trusting is about yielding to Life. Others, however, contend that trust is a moment-to-moment choice. It's a gift given when earned. This positions trust as a lever to use at will, depending on our perception. With this narrative, choosing to trust is continually amped up or short-circuited in reaction to what happens.

I sit in the camp of granting trust with the spirit of mindful innocence. This is about recapturing the feeling of innocence that we had as a baby, trusting that Life supports our needs. Of course, we have great power in shaping our experience with our choices and actions, yet living with open-hearted innocence is freeing. If we blend wonder with curiosity, and innocence with attentiveness, we can more readily collaborate with our heart. From this vantage point, we stay open yet aware, realizing that hurt is a part of relationships. We actively manage our tolerance of risk, our investment of energy and our perception of threat while being present to whatever arises. We balance our heart desire with the situation at hand. When we care

> *"Lead with your heart. The rest will follow."*
> A.D. Posey

about people and lead with that as our core value, meaningful connection can blossom.

Self, others and Earth—three equal sides of a trust triangle

A wise man once told me that it's an illusion to believe that we can trust ourselves but not others or Earth. In fact, all three trust levels run parallel because all originate from the same energy field. If we distrust ourselves to set and respect boundaries, this pattern will be evident in how we relate with others and Life. If we trust people to follow through on agreements, this is linked to our own ability to honor agreements. If we trust Life to support us no matter what the circumstance, this reflects how we support ourselves through tranquil and turbulent times. Self, others and Earth are three equal sides of the trust triangle.

Building the bank account of trust with others is facilitated by making ongoing deposits in our relationship with self. As we practice listening to and following the guidance of our heart, we're able to listen to others when they share their vulnerability. If we're accustomed to ignoring our intuition because "others know better," then we'll experience doubt about what we truly value. If we don't keep our word, then others cannot trust what we say. If we don't take risks for fear of failing, then understanding what we are truly capable of will remain a mystery. If we blame instead of taking responsibility for our actions, then we admit to being powerless. Building our self-trust bank balance begins by believing we are worthy of owning our power and standing in our truth. On a core level, this degree of self-trust and confidence is our *true wealth*. Trusting relations follows an investment in self-trust.

> *"The best way to find out if you can trust somebody is to trust them."*
> Ernest Hemingway

A no-plan trip to deepen intuition and trust in Life

Once, I decided to take an eight day no-plan vacation. I only packed one intention in my suitcase—to deepen trust. With playful anticipation, I spontaneously hopped in my car with no destination, no booked accommodations and no map. I asked Life to guide me based on her GPS. Every day, I sensed the tug of Life as I came to intersections, forks in the road, open field highways and apparent dead ends. I slowly unwound the cord of stress in my body. As I let go of all agendas, obligations and must-do messaging, my spirit skyrocketed with joy. My days were filled with magic. I was enchanted by the enigma of Life.

On day six, I ended up in a small village nine hours from home, a community where two of my dear relatives formerly resided. It was a hamlet that I hadn't visited for over three decades. I began to reminisce about all the times I felt nurtured and nourished here. The scent of love-filled memories doused my being. My car automatically drove directly to the church where my relatives worshipped. I lit a candle of gratitude for them and called to their spirit. My heart was full of adoration. With tears rolling down my cheeks, I heard their voices softly say, "This is the sweetness that comes from trusting Life and being willing to be supported. Speak your authentic truth then trust, relax and let go."

Listening to Life's guidance reveals our authentic truth. It's an inner voice that beckons us to trust our intuition. The word *intuition* derives from the Latin word *intueri*, which means "knowledge from within." It's about tuning into the interchange between our conscious and subconscious mind. We all have these types of experiences.

> *"There is a voice that doesn't use words. Listen."*
> Rumi

Here are a few examples:

Recently, while walking in nature, I contemplated my attachment to an unfulfilling work project. I debated whether to hand it off to a colleague. Suddenly, a snake slithered in front of me on the path. I smiled with the message. Just as a snake effortlessly sheds its skin that no longer serves, my intuition told me to let go of this project.

On another occasion, I felt an ocean wave of grief for a loved one who died. At that moment, a cardinal flew over and dropped a feather right in front of me. A sense of comfort filled my aching heart. My intuition told me his soul was now at peace.

Last year at an airport café, I left my wallet behind, filled with money and my ID. When I discovered my wallet missing high up in the clouds, my inner voice told me that I needed to let go of my "old identity" and prepare to receive in a new way. Throughout the trip, I was mystified. My every need was looked after.

I sensed that if I surrendered into receiving, I would reunite with my wallet. And that's exactly what happened. Upon returning home, I found my wallet intact at the airport security desk.

All these experiences have expanded my trust in Life as my steadfast companion. Life does not happen to me but *for* me. Deeply trusting our intuition can be a collaboration game-changer.

How we engage: buy-in versus enrollment conversations

Intuitively, we know that the act of engaging people can either expand or reduce trust. Be it at home, at work or in community, I find people typically use a buy-in strategy to solicit acceptance or approval. They say, "I need this person to buy into this idea, project or goal." A buy-in conversation is often a one-sided sales pitch to convince people to "buy" what you want to sell. Rather than foster collaborative co-creation and trust, the approach reveals a pre-set agenda with an intention to get someone to change or perform the way you want. Ironically, buy-in conversations can elicit resistance and, in some cases, be perceived as disrespectful. The unspoken message is, "My perspective, needs and ideas are more important than yours." Buy-in conversations are especially thorny during virtual collaboration when trust-building rapport gives way to the business at hand.

Buy-in conversations may also take the form of persuasion and cajoling tactics. Organizations frame it as the carrot-stick approach. Assumptions are made about performance incentives and what motivates people to "buy" an idea. If not handled carefully, people can feel manipulated. In a manager-employee relationship, a power-over dynamic can easily surface—in an overt or subtle manner. I've witnessed many buy-in conversations that unwittingly reinforce the domination power structure. This is when control is used to move an agenda forward, no matter the means. The short-term result may be a win via compliance, but the long-term health of the relationship erodes. Trust is forfeited in the name of expediency. The spirit of co-creation is compromised when force is the underlying energy. The conversation is counter to co-creating a reciprocal agreement.

An enrollment conversation, on the other hand, consciously engages people with the collaboration principle of deep listening. The focus shifts from "me" to "we" as each person's values and needs are heard and respected. It involves sharing vision while letting go of an anticipated outcome. Enrollment is a mindful response of slowing down the conversation to really understand what's being communicated—in words and non-verbal cues. There's space to patiently explore intentions and assumptions.

When people enroll others in a vision or mission, the engagement process is about revealing shared interests. If tension is felt, there's sufficient safety to explore risks. People can say no to an idea without fear of reprisal. Negotiation moves to a higher plane with compassionate acknowledgment. To solidify the agreement, accountabilities are teased apart. People sign on willingly. The action that follows an agreement is a testament to the quality of connection. We develop the *conditions of trust* when people are approached with inclusiveness, inquiry, empathy and humility. You might say that building trust is the new currency of power.

> *In an enrollment conversation, there's a mutual desire to explore shared interests and balance needs.*

Trust in a romantic collaborative relationship

In a romantic collaborative relationship, an enrollment conversation takes authenticity to a whole new level. The vulnerability of sexuality thrusts trust-building into another dimension. We learn that trust takes time to marinate. Many of us need to feel a certain degree of trust to open into love and intimacy. Incredible highs and devastating lows occur in this domain of connection. I think it's safe to say that love relationships are framed by both disappointment and pleasure. Sexual intimacy calls us to explore our darkest shadows and our deepest sense of oneness. It's a powerful path to experiencing and revealing the truth of who we are.

In the arena of couplehood, Dr. John Gottman is a world-renowned expert on intimacy and trust. Through decades of research, he identified four communication modes that predict with 90 percent accuracy which newlyweds would remain married and which couples would divorce within four to six years. Gottman called these the "Four Horsemen of the Apocalypse." The "horsemen" are criticism, defensiveness, stonewalling and contempt. These four habits have proven to be the most reliable communication methods for predicting relationship dissolution. Each damages trust and, by extension, any attempt at developing a collaborative relationship. If you notice these behaviors within yourself or others, disrupt the pattern. Get curious and uncover what's underneath. Nothing dark survives in the light of compassionate inquiry.

> *"Trust is rarely absolute, but rather is restricted to particular situations."*
> Paul Thagard

One of my partners gave me a powerful learning experience related to trust. When I met this gentleman, I dove heart first into the sea of intimacy. I swam with wild abandon and happiness, without a life jacket. In time, the buoyancy I felt waned when I discovered that he suffered from a commitment phobia. He spoke about our future together, but I found his behavior contradictory. I saw myself using a "horseman of the apocalypse"—namely, criticism. My reproach weakened our trust bond. Our push-pull conversations pitted commitment against autonomy. These conversations revealed new insights about my own commitment mold. I assumed that commitment would provide some degree of security. Yet the future is never promised, even when wedding vows are in the mix. I struggled to articulate my stand while supporting my partner. I wrestled with reconciling my need for stability and certainty with his need for flow and freedom. We were stuck in an either-or conversation. His childhood attachment wound was suffocation, whereas mine was abandonment. With this complementarity, we were perfectly coupled for our healing journey.

At one point, exhausted by our dynamic, I left the country to experience a ten-day silent nature retreat. I wanted to step back, process and explore my own commitment issues. It didn't take long to discover the unloved parts of myself. When I listened to my heart, the image of a mountain kept appearing in my mind's eye. Earth told me that I needed a strong, grounded base to rise to the summit. The path to the peak was through the valley of my fears. In the quiet of meditation, I realized that my partner's fear of commitment reflected my own. I too had one foot in and one foot out. I discovered a deep-seated belief tucked away in my mind: intimate relationship meant being trapped.

In seeing this projection, I owned my fear of commitment and forgave myself for my part of the suffering. Mistrust began to dissolve as I flooded my system with self-acceptance. Interestingly, this choice toward self-love had a delightful recoil effect on my partner. Upon my return, he sensed my renewed heart. Our love strengthened and we enjoyed a deeper connection. I bolstered my self-trust every time I spoke my authentic heart truth. With unsteady footing yet resolve, we slowly climbed back up the mountain of trust. Together, we weathered the blue skies and storms of our collaborative relationship until it ran its course. Even today, I still feel grateful for this lesson in trust.

> *"Have enough courage to trust love one more time, and always one more time."*
> Maya Angelou

Dissolving distrust with forgiveness

In intimate relationships and beyond, the bridge-building process towards greater trust gives us many opportunities to lay down the stones of forgiveness. Each stone is a choice in acceptance. When our trust has been violated and we perceive people to be untrustworthy, do we hold onto anger or come into a state of forgiveness? If we choose to be resentful and forego forgiveness, the fallout is great suffering. As Buddha noted, "Holding onto anger is like drinking poison and expecting the other person to die." This bitter potion keeps us ensnared as a prisoner. Avoidance, ambivalence and retaliation, as reactions to hurt, are also poisons that weaken trust. I've learned that it's possible to accept and forgive a person without condoning what happened.

When a hurtful situation has occurred, clean up the mistake soon after, if possible. If this doesn't seem doable create some distance to support the passage of healing. There is no such thing as rushing forgiveness. If we do so prematurely, we risk inauthentic bridge-building. For a time, it may be wise to only connect energetically at the heart level to restore some semblance of peace. The stones of forgiveness come in all shapes and sizes.

On my forgiveness journey, I've noticed that I sometimes hold a mental script: *If I do _____, then you ought to _____.* It's a should conversation that carries an expectation or a demand. Forgiveness is thus conditional; it's chained to someone else's choice. If I rewrite the script by leaving out the other and place myself at the center of the story, enemy thinking dissipates. If I don't own my buried treasure trove of distrust stories, it will come back to haunt me. With loving self-responsibility, I see no villain. It's a lesson in offering mercy and accepting imperfection.

> "Forgiveness says you are given another chance to make a new beginning." Desmond Tutu

It takes skill, care, compassion and time to repair broken trust. Growth potential lies in these tender conversations. New beginnings are possible, even if the person is not willing to reconnect. This is the distillate of authentic collaboration.

Growing our ability to speak authentically

With this principle, we may ask the question, "How can I authentically speak to build trust?" I used to believe that authenticity was black or white. It was either apparent or not. Now, I've come to understand that authentic expression is multilayered. Just like honesty. And courage.

Occasionally, I test my authenticity boundaries. I notice that the degree to which I relate authentically depends on the trust I feel in the relationship. If I feel a high level of trust, it's easier to be open and raw in my sharing. If not, I cling to my comfort zone and tie my authentic expression to the safety of silence. I've come to realize this is conditional honesty. In some circumstances, this may be needed for self-protection yet it's still a shallow level of authentic expression. If I decide to only speak my truth when I perceive favorable consequences, I set myself up for a strategy game. I'll be in assessment mode as what may or may not come to pass. Or I may be tempted to manipulate others to respond how I want.

I am curious about the nest of limiting beliefs that accompany authenticity and honest expression. For example, I once held a belief that my ability to trust and feel safe depended on other people's behavior. This kept me guarded and powerless. Subconsciously, this belief had me relate in a cautious, reserved manner. I communicated to conceal rather than reveal. It also took me off the hook, so to speak, since I assumed that power was outside of self. With this belief, I chained myself and others to a set of self-prescribed rules. I began to wonder, what would it look like if authentic communication was not tethered to the behavior of other people?

> "We create our own security by trusting in the process of life." Louise L. Hay

With this in mind, I decided to take a trust leap. In turning around this limiting belief, I reclaimed my power as a co-creator and collaborator with Life. Now, I believe that my sense of safety comes from within. This new understanding has given me greater trust in Life. As I practice connecting with my solar plexus power center, I feel more grounded. My self-trust continues to grow.

The horse sense of developing trust

Fortunately, I've had an opportunity to learn from horses about trust and authenticity. Equine therapy is an amazing experience because horses hold up a mirror to how we think, feel and behave. Every contact with a horse, no matter how subtle, is a conversation. As social herd animals, horses use distinct body language and ear twitches to communicate their preferences, fears and boundaries. They have defined roles in their pack and collaborate in inexplicable ways. Horses have authenticity bred into their bones.

When I first met with a statuesque horse named Red, he showed me the incongruency between my words, thoughts and feelings. I told Red that I trusted him, yet when this incredible thousand-pound animal approached and nuzzled me in a very intimate way, tension filled my body. He seemed to wait for me to set a boundary, but I just stood there, silent. In that moment, I tried to convince myself that I was fine. I repeated that I didn't need any boundaries, but he saw right through me. Red picked up the truth of what I was feeling. A horse has profound self-trust: he sensed dissonance and responded. It's not in his nature to pretend otherwise. My lack of authenticity was an integrity breach. I did not earn his trust in me, nor trust in myself, because my communication was not credible. A horse, as a prey animal, looks for a leader they can trust, respect and follow; and I wasn't measuring up. Red refused to walk with me around the pen until I came back into alignment and acknowledged my truth.

> *Trust develops when thoughts, words and actions align.*

With the help of this astute animal, I was reminded that enhancing trust is about consistent, transparent communication. Even if my authentic truth is, "I don't know what to do or say," that is an honest expression worth sharing. Otherwise, we offer a Trojan horse when collaborating, appearing one way yet being another.

Reclaiming our birthright of a trusting heart

If we come into this world with an open, trusting heart, then the challenge is remembering our essence. Assuming trust is in our nature, we have an ever-available opportunity to let go of what blocks trust. By confronting our trust fears, we can regenerate a deeper sense of empowerment and belonging. This means walking on Earth with a *chosen attitude*, not an inherited one. I've come to see Life as benevolent. I hold the axiom, "Life illuminates my path forward. I trust the future will take care of itself." I find it uplifting to *see everything and everyone as sacred*.

> *Our beliefs about trust become a self-fulfilling prophecy.*

This attitude does not always give me favorable circumstances, but it's my preferred way of living. By growing my capacity to trust, I've been able to travel to foreign lands independently, live on another continent, rise in love repeatedly, start my own business, trek in the Himalayas, scuba dive in the Great Barrier Reef, enjoy a hot air balloon ride, expand my social circle and experience different cultures. Writing this book is itself an act of trust. I had to question the comfort level I felt with self-revelation. In moments of anxiety, I was spurred on by the desire to authentically communicate with you, my beloved reader.

Practice the Principle: Trust by Speaking Authentically

Self-Discovery
Exercise A: Exploring Trust

With these questions, discern the degree of trust you hold in your important relationships. For ease, start with one relationship. Either journal your responses or, as a bonus self-discovery, initiate a trust-building authentic dialogue with a partner.

1. How would I describe my relationship with trust?
2. To what extent am I genuine and self-revealing?
3. What am I willing to let go of to strengthen trust in my relationships?
4. What do I need for emotional safety so I can express my vulnerability?
5. As a trust-builder, what is my quality of listening?
6. In a hard conversation, can I be trusted to hold the tension with care?
7. When I make a commitment, do I consistently follow through?
8. If not, do I clean up the broken promise and renegotiate?
9. How do I repair broken trust?
10. Do I openly discuss ways to grow trust?

Exercise B: Future Self Conversation

Have you ever wondered what your Future Self would say to you? This time-oriented exercise gives you an opportunity to glimpse this wisdom. According to physicists, time is a theoretical social construct created by humans for their own purposes. While this may seem counterintuitive to our learned notions of time, experiment with this time travel exercise to expand your mindset and heartset.

To represent your current self, select a visual reference like a photo. Place it in front of you. Next, choose an object that symbolizes your fully resourced, wise Future Self. Center yourself with deep breaths. Imagine a beam of golden light pouring down from the sky into the top of your head, slowly filling your entire head and spinal cord with warm light. When the beam reaches your tailbone, continue to beam out the light into ground. By rooting into Earth, see yourself connected to the vitality of Life.

AUTHENTIC COLLABORATION

In reviewing the following list, identify which questions you want to ask your Future Self. Dovetail in whatever inquiry is meaningful to you. Sample questions include:

1. Future Self, how would you describe my relationship with my heart?
2. How might I best expand my self-awareness?
3. Which of my significant relationships need extra care and why?
4. How can I ramp up mutual respect in my relationships?
5. What is an important growing edge I have now related to trust?
6. When faced with uncertainty, to what degree do I really trust Life?
7. What does forgiveness really mean to me?
8. Given that trust-building is a process, how can I develop self-trust?
9. Since authenticity is layered, what would it take to deepen my sharing?
10. Future Self, how can I strengthen my ability to authentically collaborate?

In your journal, write one of these questions at the top of the page. Hold your Future Self object and tune into this wise voice. When you feel ready to record, write the insight on the page. Trust the voice that wants to be heard. When complete, read what you wrote out loud. How does your body feel? How motivated do you feel to bring this wisdom into your life? Repeat this process with the other questions, as you wish.

Authentic Collaboration Practice with Others
Using Conflict to Repair Trust and Speak Authentically

Many people want harmony in their relationships yet also desire authenticity. Peace and honesty sometimes feel contradictory. This exercise, inspired by Nonviolent Communication, helps us reconcile this common either-or conundrum. Rather than slip into passive-aggressive behavior, this practice enables us to step beyond inner judgment and outer criticism. Experiment with "carefrontation"—gentle, caring, honest assertion. Try on an and-both way of communicating. This collaborative dialogue process is an attempt to heal, expand or enhance one relationship that you now struggle with.

Decide on an interpersonal conflict that has not been resolved. With a learning buddy, share a few details about what happened. In this conflict situation, what did you and the other person say or do? Notice if the words you use are observational or judgmental. The latter is not bad or wrong, simply understand that our judgments generate relational resistance.

As a next step, feel and communicate your emotions and unmet needs. Did you feel shame, guilt, fear, powerlessness, grief, frustration, disappointment or anger? Did you need trust, communication, understanding, clarity, to be heard/seen, appreciated? Elaborate on your experience.

Lastly, role play a trust repair conversation. Ask your partner to imagine what the other would say or do. Practice authentic collaboration by respecting yourself *and* your partner. Periodically pause, acknowledge, empathize, validate and become curious. Notice how comfortable or uncomfortable you are with vulnerable truth-telling. Imagine what the other person is feeling and needing. Of your judgments, assumptions and conclusions, which ones are you prepared to revise or let go of? How do you feel inspired to restore connection? What strategies might support the needs of both? Authentically express how you feel about moving forward.

Collaborative Connection with Earth
Journal Exercise A: Broken Trust

Start this exercise by reading a quote by A. H. Almaas:

> *"Your conflicts, all the difficult things, the problematic situations in your life are not by chance nor haphazard. They are actually yours. They are specifically yours, designed specifically for you by a part of you that loves you more than anything else. This part has created roadblocks to lead you to yourself and to a new, healthier direction. It may be pricking you in the side, telling you, 'Look here—this way!' That part of you loves you so much that it doesn't want you to lose the chance. It will go to extreme measures to wake you up; it will make you suffer greatly if you don't listen. What else can it do? That is its purpose."*

Reflect on a time when your trust in Life was broken. Recall what happened, how you felt and what needs were unmet. Find the tension in your body related to that incident. When ready, fast-forward to now and look back with different eyes. Why do you think Life offered you these circumstances for your healing and growth? What do you see now that has you realize the gift or learning from that experience? If you do not see the gift nor learning, how can you bring greater compassion to yourself? Journal your insights. Reflect on how you can rebuild the bridge of trust with Life.

Journal Exercise B: What If?

In thinking about Earth as our ally, play with the mind using what if questions. This line of inquiry can "trick" the mind into new awareness. Start by thinking about a trust breach in a relationship you care about. Recall the story and feel the stress in your dynamic with this person. Then, invite the grace and open flow of Earth to carry you in considering the following questions:

1. What if I saw this person in a completely new light?
2. What if we both have positive intentions in this situation?
3. What if this person was helping me by reflecting my blind spot?
4. What if I had the power to transform this situation and rebuild trust?
5. What if I was fully responsible for my own happiness?
6. What if my mind was able to let go of suffering and be at peace?
7. What if I was completely in charge of my own emotional landscape?
8. What if I trusted myself whole-heartedly to speak my truth?
9. What if I asked for and received wisdom from Earth?
10. What if Earth has always been my constant source of support?

Accompanying these empowering questions are feel-good emotions and an impulse to act. Figuratively, you are filling your well with the water of reconnection. Your expanding trust basin can help you deepen into the joy of authentic collaboration, with self, others and Earth.

CHAPTER 13

E = EQUALIZE BY VALUING PROCESS WITH OUTCOME

*"It is good to have an end to journey toward,
but it is the [relationship] journey that matters in the end."*
Ursula K. LeGuin

From sacrificing process to honoring process

Recently, I went on a road trip with friends. The two passengers seated in the back seat were children. Every few hours, they would ask, "Are we there yet?" It was obvious that the kids were not enjoying the journey. They were in a hurry to arrive. Our destination was more important than the process of appreciating the landscape and the experience of togetherness. Can you relate to this?

In our rushed, fast-paced Western culture, process is often sacrificed at the altar of an end goal. It's easy to forget that all Life experiences are a process. We skip through the hustle-bustle of our days without being fully present and miss the miracle of the moment. At work, our post-industrial efficient way of operating is largely and sometimes exclusively goal-oriented. Action outflanks relationship. Co-learning is secondary to our need to check off our "to do" list and accomplish. At school, some teachers are more focused on preparing students for tests rather than on the value of experiential learning. At home, many families do not process the highlights and lowlights of the day during dinner together: they quickly eat to get to their next activity. In romance, if a couple skips foreplay, love-making can feel transactional. With friends, attending an event may be seen as more imperative than connecting and seeing what's alive in the relationship. All these

> *"Life is a process. We are a process. The universe is a process."*
> Anne Wilson Schaef

scenarios can translate into missing the moment of now. The anticipated outcome or future task takes our attention, more than the act of relating itself.

Unless carved out, quiet reflection time and slow dialogue are rare. Life feels fast with one engagement after another. The "days fly by" as we wonder "where time goes." It seems that in today's harried world, we think too much, want too much, work too much and strive too much. Consequently, we lose touch with the contentment that comes from just being. We lose trust in the process itself. Our need for control outweighs the value of patiently wading into the mysterious unfoldment. What would it look like to adopt a "less do, more be" way of relating with Life?

So, the final bridge-tie principle—equalize by valuing process with outcome— reminds us that *process* offers a definite value proposition. It shores up the other five hangers. If we mindfully respond, empathize, listen deeply, appreciate different perspectives and consciously build trust, the fabric of authentic collaboration strengthens. We are enriched by the process of becoming curious, challenging viewpoints, learning and growing together. At the very least, we have more space to bask in the glory of our journey.

> *It's all rigged in your favor. Trust the process.*

When we look at how people manage successful pursuits, we see process honored at every turn. As every farmer knows, success requires diligence in the cultivation of crops. Italian chefs understand the process of slow cooking and eating. University graduates celebrate the process of learning as they walk across the stage to receive their degree. Olympic athletes are super aware that winning a medal is tied to the discipline of rigorous training. Business change-makers use design thinking as a process to innovate. Lawyers adhere to due process: the Latin legal principle *audi alteram partem* means "hear the other side." An inventor must meticulously learn from many failed experiments to adapt and achieve the desired goal. Thomas Edison apparently embarked on over one thousand experiments to create the light bulb. There are countless examples we could reference: all point to the value of equalizing process and outcome. In valuing both, we have an opportunity to mindfully develop the art and skill of authentic collaboration.

Fleshing out the value of process

What does a process consist of? A process involves reflecting, analyzing and learning from a series of thoughts, behaviors, actions and steps to achieve an outcome. It's implanted in the question, "how do we do this"? So process speaks to the desire for activity and movement.

> *Literally and symbolically, a bridge itself represents the value of process.*

Even the symbol of a bridge is a structure that represents process. The bridge deck represents movement from one fixed point to another. Bridge-building incorporates both process and the desired goal. If we only focus on the latter, the relational gradations are missed. If authentic collaboration is a bridge, the joy of crossing is the process.

The Value of Process

To highlight how this principle supports authentic collaboration, consider these five beneficial aspects of process. Each will be fleshed out in this chapter.

1. On the level of self, a daily reflection practice nourishes personal healing and growth.
2. On the level of others, facilitating an effective group process generates authentic connection and communal learning.
3. On the level of organization, process expands the bottom line by focusing on relationships *and* results.
4. On the level of Earth, acknowledging her rhythm, cycles and seasons creates space for creativity.
5. To support future generations, valuing and modeling process enables youth to see this in action.

---

1. Self: The process of healing and growth

Since personal growth is one of my core values, process is akin to how I live my life. One theme that I've processed over the years is that of pressure. The rushing, struggle and push-energy in our western society had left its mark. With the futility of over-efforting, over-pleasing and over-accommodating, my own heart rhythm felt alien. Overlaid into this pattern was cultural scarcity, a set of conditioned beliefs about lack. This mindset influenced my perception that I do not have enough: time, money, resources, talent or knowledge. At some point, I began to believe that *I am not enough.* This feeling of inadequacy generated a striving for "more-better-best." It was an attitude that left me estranged from the experience of ease and flow. I felt like I was carrying around barbells of heavy body tension.

> "Whether true or not, the thought of not enough occurs automatically before we ever think to question or examine it."
> Lynne Twist

It has been a long healing process to relax my over-stimulated vagus nerve, unlearn my conditioning and relearn a new way of being and doing. As I've shifted this pattern during my daily reflection practice, I discovered a new truth. My preferred and natural way of living is to balance "do-get-give" with "be-have-receive." This new inner dialogue motivated me to rebalance work and play and rejig my relationship with activity and rest. With the practice of yoga, a process-oriented exercise, I began using the bridge of my nose to consciously breathe and the arch bridge of my feet to reconnect with Earth. I adopted an and-both collaborative mindset to balance yin flexibility with yang discipline. This process continues to be my lighthouse in guiding me through stormy moments of self-relating.

In addition, I've incorporated the process of focusing into my reflections. Focusing is a practice developed by Gene Gendlin to allow our body to deepen self-knowledge. By using our felt-sense, we tune into what our body is saying on a regular basis. We ask questions like we would of a friend, listening to its messages and gaining insight. By virtue of focusing, I've come to see the body as incredibly adept at collaborating. Interdependence is its defining feature. Each cell is autonomous with a function, purpose and boundary yet also a member of the greater whole. Every cell affects and is accountable to the larger living organism. Understanding this interplay inspires me to distribute energy to the parts of my body needing attention to support the vitality of my entire system. Through a process of deep listening and presencing, I contribute to my well-being. This authentic self-collaboration practice is accessible to everyone.

2. Others: Facilitating process for authentic connection and co-learning

My exposure to Aikido, an ancient martial art, helped me understand the energetic nuances of process. Aikido is based on the premise of respect for self and others. The goal is not harming your opponent but rather using soft power to support structured control. I'm astonished at how this practice involves circular, dance-like, efficient movements that stabilize my center yet allows me to remain open to my environment. Literally, *Aikido* translates as "the way of harmony with Ki," which is the universal creative principle. This discipline balances the process of uniting Ki or Life force with the goal of neutralizing the other person. I see it as a form of grace. Aikido reminds to hold the tension with fluidity: to open to the flow of group energy yet not get mired in the muck. In looking for the middle way, this martial art enhances focus, self-awareness, discipline, perceptiveness and clarity. This skill can be especially useful when facilitating a tough process dialogue.

In any group, complaints tend to be a natural part of the process. Yet, many people resist responding to complaints because they lack the Aikido skill of holding grace under fire. Afterall, complaints can open the proverbial can of worms. If the complaint needs to be addressed with a solution-finding effort, consider these facilitation tips in supporting authentic connection and learning. Start by building process into a group gathering, dinner or agenda so it becomes a natural, normal, valued conversation worthy of allotted time. Be a convenor. With heart presence, listen to the complaint-holder as some people only need to be empathetically heard. Use a strengths-based approach in acknowledging the talents, contributions and wisdom in the group. As we all know, sincere appreciations generate positive vibes and rapport. Be explicit in clearly defining, owning and declaring the issue. In Alcoholics Anonymous meetings, healing starts with a personal declaration of an addiction.

> *"Defensiveness is the first act of war. When you are attacked, and you notice that you love them with all your heart, your Work is done."*
> Byron Katie

When finger-pointing crops up during a complaint discussion, notice how the attack is met with defensiveness. This is the moment to inject some love into the dialogue. Invite people to use "I" statements to acknowledge what's so rather than rationalizing, explaining or justifying. Recognize if it's a conversation of helplessness. If appropriate, suggest that the group look at how the system affects the issue at hand. Interpersonal dynamics do not exist in isolation. Before strategizing options, ascertain the underlying unmet needs. Slow down the process to absorb what's being shared: the act of caring and receiving is, in itself, a transformative process.

If you feel comfortable facilitating a group process, consider using participatory methods. Empowering process exercises include community mapping, scenario forecasting, focus group discussions, a nature reflection, a wisdom council, study teams, group problem-solving projects, theater play-back or a group mural drawing. If relevant, structure group work around a shared co-created vision. Inject casual fun into the dialogue. Stimulate co-learning so insights are exchanged. If the group is interacting from around the world, there are many web technologies and chat rooms to support asynchronous collaboration. With these tools, share knowledge, ideas, files and questions across time zones at your convenience. Whatever process is used, frame the dialogue with the RELATE principles. Respectfully balancing needs in a harmonious flow is an Aikido-friendly conversation.

TRY THIS: To curate some process-oriented questions, consider this list below. Each question is intended to foster authentic connection and communal learning during a debrief dialogue. With your group, brainstorm other questions that may support effective collaboration.

Facilitation Questions to Support a Group Debrief Process

- What is our contribution to the complaints we hear?
- How do we realign our desired outcomes to what's happening?
- To what extent are we truly engaging the people we are serving?

- How can we weave a collaborative dialogue into our gathering?
- What do we see as the prize and price of the change we want?
- How do we monitor our process and adjust course if needed?

- Looking at our change process, what conclusions are we drawing?
- What can we learn from this experience? What do we do now?
- How can we use these insights to improve how we work or live together?

3. Revisiting the organizational bottom line

At the institutional level, all organizations have some type of bottom line to indicate success. This may not only denote monetary profit, but also a balanced budget, new funding, effective spending of allocated resources, total services provided, client satisfaction and overall goal achievement. However the bottom line is touted, what would it look like to bridge the stated bottom line to the *relational profit world* as well? This means integrating two seemingly different value streams to recognize the importance of relationships *and* results. Indeed, results develop in the receptacle of relationships. Relationship-building is arguably the most important process in our life, let alone in the workplace. Organizational success depends on it. When we dig deep, we can see that it's impossible to sever relationships and results.

> *Relationship-building, by definition, is a process.*

In organizations, the means matter just as much as the end. Sometimes, leaders say that the means is a valuable end unto itself. Rarer still, progressive leaders say that the end reflects the means. This reveals an expanded understanding of how energy flows. *How* we approach a project, client or collaborative relationship influences what happens. This is seen by way of intention, attitude and communication style. For example, if I hold suspicions about my work partner, this doubt will be felt in our negotiation. If I believe a group is producing quality products in an ethical way, this will influence how I relate to them. If I feel impatient with how a group operates, this irritation will be sensed.

To discern if process is valued in an organization, notice if there's a collaboration framework available for staff. Ask management if collaboration support tools or a job aid exists. Guidelines may need to be developed to orient staff around the process of engaging clients, suppliers, stakeholders or shareholders. Inquire into the decision-making process. Notice how a group dialogue is set up, who is invited and what the process consists of. Pay attention to how listening is supported. Become aware of the *what*, *why* and *how* of process interventions.

> *"Dialogue is a process of genuine interaction through which human beings listen to each other deeply enough to be changed by what they learn."*
> Harold Saunders

One day, I hope to routinely see a quintuple organizational bottom line: planet, people, partnerships, peace and prosperity. Prosperity, I allege, depends on the four other process-oriented factors. Social, environmental and economic responsibilities are all key factors to sustainable development. In fact, the original Greek meaning of the word *economy* means "to take care of the house and all those who live in the house." Currently, our economic system in general and businesses specifically are failing to take care of our planet home. As such, we can no longer process what happens inside an organization without also considering the community of species on which it depends. It's time to reimagine corporate governance from a wider process lens.

Positive and negative workplace process examples

To paraphrase Dickens, my work experience has given me the best and worst of times. Over the past twenty-five years, I have experienced organizational teams who value relationship process and others who do not. The results were telling.

With respect to the best of times, I served a private sector global service company that had an engaging collaborative culture. We valued process by meeting weekly and communicating openly. The sharing was heartfelt. We convened in a way that inspired loving connection. This warm rapport greatly enhanced our motivation.

Beyond rapport, the company's governance structure was based on the principle of distributing authority according to roles and shared purpose. Changes were met with flexibility and ongoing, transparent dialogue. The boss-subordinate dynamic was replaced by empowered partnership. Agreed-upon boundaries reduced the need for the asking and granting of permission. We also received confidential leadership coaching, so we felt supported and cared for. Kindness was routinely expressed and reciprocated—something that counted yet could not be measured. According to managerial feedback, our team's performance was rock-star material. In fact, this office branch received global top sales awards week after week and set a new corporate record. Accolades came in from all corners of the world, with leaders inquiring about the "secret sauce"

> *"The most important things we need to manage cannot be measured."*
> W. Edwards Deming

of our team success. I chalked it up to the fact that we respected the process of building healthy collaborative relationships.

In hindsight, I see many commendable team process habits. Some include: awareness of enrollment conversations, starting our meetings with a personal check-in, ending with a check-out to get a pulse read on decisions, asking about—versus assuming—commitment level, building interdepartmental bridges to dissolve silos, encouraging innovation, streamlining redundant procedures and developing a team compact to respectfully deal with differences. Most importantly, we socialized after hours. Nothing replaces in-person relaxed dialogue over dinner to deepen trust. All these process-oriented practices were advantageous in helping us achieve extraordinary goals.

On the flip side, I also worked with a manufacturing company that minimized the value of process. This team struggled to foster a respectful team culture. I was hired to support a company trajectory turn. Right out of the gate, I noticed there was widespread team disenchantment. Relating felt mechanistic. People had orders barked at them as though they were in the military. Employees were excluded from decision-making on issues that impacted them. The culture was steeped in attack, defend, blame and punishment. Many told me they punched the time clock with an attitude of "doing time." Bare minimum performance to "get by" was the norm. Morale was low and turnover was high.

I worked with every departmental team to re-engage people with participatory processes. We carved out the time to relate as human beings, beyond our roles. On that basis, we were better able to tackle issues and identify new ways of working. Team process conversations were built into the production schedule to check-in personally, identify challenges and brainstorm solutions. Management took steps to share power, albeit reluctantly at first. We started with the decision to discontinue PowerPoint slide lectures. Instead, we used Open Space Technology to energize our meetings and engage everyone in the process. People voted with their feet, contributing at whatever conversational stations they wished to focus on. We experimented with reflective listening exercises, social icebreakers to build trust and circle dialogue to generate cross-functional collaboration ideas. Employees were asked how they would like to celebrate team accomplishments, how they wanted to be involved with orienting new recruits and how they wanted to engage in production design changes.

Over time, there was a sea change in this organization as more people came to value relationships and team process. It was a long journey yet this new way of working paid off with improved organizational performance. More importantly, we decided that we wanted a feel-good work experience. So, together, we set a new success standard around the amount of joy people felt at work. I've come to believe that cultivating joy is the marrow of collaborative relationships. It's a process that uplifts the human spirit.

4. Acknowledging the slow process of Earth or Life

Earth has her own process. Life has its own unfoldment. This was clearly revealed during the COVID-19 pandemic. During the first lockdown, I was able to see my own unfolding with new eyes. My pattern of overscheduling became glaringly apparent. I saw how my back-to-back commitments had me postpone creative projects. When the stressed, hurried energy of our world came to a grinding halt, I decided to tune into the slow pace of Earth. I began listening more intently to what she was communicating. With nowhere to go, no one to see and nothing to do, I had space to breathe deeply. I relished the peace. My body felt calm. For the first time in a decade, I felt as though I was floating down the river of Life rather than navigating the whirlpools and undercurrents.

Indeed, Earth never rushes process as each season and cycle has its timing and flow. She teaches us to value every moment as each contains wonder. When we spend time in nature, we remember how to genuinely connect. Her alluring rhythm supports the vivacity of Life. As Joseph Campbell eloquently noted, "The goal of life is to make your heartbeat match the beat of the universe, to match your nature with Nature."

> *"Nature does not hurry, yet everything is accomplished."*
> Lao Tzu

By definition, process requires sufficient space. It takes time to reflect on relationship nuances, process emotions and marvel at the wonders of Life. Embracing our full human experience is not less important than reaching a goal, but of equal or even greater importance. In the art of authentic collaboration, we slow down and pay attention to *how* we interact. Slowing down doesn't necessarily mean adopting a drawn-out, inefficient process with pointless conversation. Rather, it's about showing we care by becoming whole-heartedly present to what's happening in the moment. When we bridge-build from a space of meaningful connection, we recognize ourselves in the other.

Valuing a mountain-top eco-process

As a shamanic practitioner, I've come to understand that process is the path. As Earthkeepers, we draw wisdom from nature to better flow with the cycles of Life. We see that an acorn blossoms into a mature oak tree in accordance with the seasons, the weather patterns and the nutrients it receives. The mysterious Life force directs the unveiling of reality at will. Indigenous tribes understand that the warm moisture of the rainforest is absorbed into the atmosphere, where it condenses into rain. It's a well-regarded process because species flourish with rainfall. Shamans also see hardships as initiations, and, as such they create rituals to pay homage to the process of transformation. Disruption is welcomed as the precursor to new creation. An ego death is a transition into rebirth. Humility is cultivated by seeing everything in Life with the soft eyes of reverence.

During my twenty-one-day trek to Base Camp, Mount Everest, I felt a deep reverence for Earth. I had an extraordinary nature experience that connected me to the sacredness in all—a bigger world beyond the self. Enveloped by the clouds, I felt a devotion to the natural world. The silence of the Himalayas filled my heart. I surrendered into the mystery and allowed peace to envelope me. Even when I labored with low oxygen and heavy steps, I could feel Earth escorting me into the awe-inspiring expanse. For days, the only sound I heard was the call of birds. Above the treeline, nature had the last say.

> *"Pursue some path, however narrow and crooked, in which you can walk with love and reverence."*
> Henry David Thoreau

Each day, our team authentically collaborated. We discussed our hiking process and attuned to Earth—her landslides, water access, treacherous crossings and blizzard conditions. Yes, nature held the authority, and we were her servants. As my Nepalese guide said, "Everest is the mother of all mountains. We must bow to her timing of what happens when." Reaching the fluttering prayer flags of Base Camp became trivial to appreciating the power and beauty of Earth. On this unforgettable journey, creative insights filled my mind. I reprioritized what really mattered to me. In fact, the seeds of this book were planted on that mountain. That's when I embodied the truth that my voice matters, process matters and relationships matter.

5. Modeling the value of process so youth see this in action

Raising children to become curious, reflective, collaborative adults starts with paying attention to *their process* of being and doing. By engaging them in meaningful conversation, we can demonstrate communication skills such as expressing feelings, eye contact, deep listening, validation and turn-taking. Doing so helps young ones develop a mindful way of relating with self and others.

Open-ended inquiry is a simple yet brilliant way to deepen authentic connection with youth. Step beyond the quick yes and no questions to peek into their minds. Ask follow-up questions. From their experience, help them draw out new insights and conclusions. Young people want to be engaged on issues that matter to them. Attentive dialogue not only enhances self-awareness but also critical thinking and creative problem-solving. With the process of inquiry, we learn more about how youth think, speak, listen and interact. In turn, we also benefit from their wisdom.

I sense that the younger generation yearns for authentic dialogue. Social media posts and thumbs-up like icons does not equate to meaningful connection. This superficial way of interacting leaves many people feeling empty and lonely. Around-the-clock messaging in the digital space can be energy depleting. Open, honest sharing is what the heart longs for. It's the relationships that count, not the medium. Genuine communication is nectar for the soul.

In a conversation I had with teenagers, they shared a belief that arriving at some distant end goal is what constitutes feeling safe in this world. They felt anxious about their future in dealing with societal, peer and parental pressure. As such, they were in a hurry to grow up and have it "all figured out." Life's complications and uncertainties outweighed the thrill of the ride. They wished away the journey to reach "success," forgetting that success is self-defined and forever changing.

We all need reminders to slow down and smell the roses. It's seductive to air brush the moment of now as seemingly insignificant by anticipating what comes next. As a challenge, model the value of process by becoming present. If youth say they are bored and "killing time," inquire further. If they are in the habit of watching the clock at school or work, wanting to be somewhere else, ask why. If they seem withdrawn or frustrated, ask if the conversation is what they would like it to be. These small acts of caring demonstrate the value of process, not just outcome. The outcome, whatever that entails, will arrive in Kairos—the perfect timing of Life.

TRY THIS: Consider these two boxes of process questions. During the next month, ask the youth in your life several of these questions. Notice the extent to which they open up and share. Consider brainstorming other questions for both of you to respond to. Zoom in on different topics to conjure up questions on happiness, success or friendship. Enrich your relationship process with the pleasure and play of inquiry.

Questions for Parents to Ask Youth

- With your activity of _____, tell me why this inspires you?
- When you last had a conflict with a friend, how did you resolve the issue?
- When do feel the happiest?
- What helps you feel relaxed?
- How is your struggle helping you learn about yourself?
- Looking back, what got in the way when you attempted to _____?
- What is your favorite thing to do and why?
- In this situation _____, how can you make a different choice?
- What was your thought process?
- What goal matters to you? And how can our family support you?

Questions for Educators to Ask Youth

- What about that assignment was easy and challenging for you?
- What do you really care about and why?
- What do you enjoy learning about and why?
- If you had a magic wand, how would you choose to spend the school day?
- How can you develop discipline with your homework?
- What is a fun way for you to learn more about _____?
- How can we collaborate to solve this issue together as a class?
- If given the chance, how would you re-do this project?
- Describe a powerful learning experience this year. What made it so?
- What do you think supports healthy relationship-building?

Practice the Principle: Equalize by Valuing Process with Outcome

Self-Discovery
Journal Reflection Questions

1. To what extent do you feel connected with nature's rhythm?
2. How would you describe your ability to facilitate group process?
3. With the youth in your life, how do you value and model process?
4. During a conflict process, how do you want to grow your skill?
5. What do you do well with the process of self-care?

Exercise B: A Focusing Process to Heal the Pain of Colonialism

Around the world, the consciousness of colonialism is dying. The political system of authoritarianism, characterized by a lack of political plurality and the use of central power to enforce submission and obedience, is denounced in many cultures. Consider supporting this transition with the process of focusing. Touch into the felt-sense of how you, others and past generations have been controlled and exploited. How does this pain live in your body? Even if the pain and trauma was experienced years or centuries ago, the residue is still carried in our collective consciousness. Coming to terms with current and historical grievances is a part of our healing journey. Mourning collective trauma is a powerful way to heal reactivity and create space for mindful communication. On the other side of grief lies a new possibility—respect for all living beings.

To begin, reflect on an event or occurence that taps a sensitive spot in your heart. There's no shortage of emotion-filled examples of residual colonialism: South African apartheid, the First Nations residential school system genocide in Canada, the Holocaust, the burning of fossil fuels, African enslavement, the alarming current rate of biodiversity loss such as the recent extinction of the Indian cheetah and the Sumatran rhino, the Palestinian occupation, South American exploitation for silver and gold, massive coral reef die-off, world hunger or the neocolonial practice of global trade imbalances that leaves millions in poverty. In the twenty-first century, decolonization remains an unfinished business.

Initiate the process of focusing by closing your eyes and taking some deep breaths. Feel into the pain of colonialism that you carry. Validate whatever sensations arise. Recognize your story of oppression and your part in this saga, not from a space of fault-finding but compassionate self-responsibility.

Reflection questions include:

- How is dominance evident in your world?
- How does the weight of this reality sit in your body?
- Presence this sore spot and ask; what do you need?
- How do you project this pain onto others?
- How do you power-over others in your life?

Close your eyes and imagine yourself five feet in front of you. Attune to what presents itself. Quiet the mind and breathe out the labels, analysis and judgment. Allow the tears to fall. Be with whatever emerges: grief, sadness, anger or guilt. Tenderly embrace your sorrow. Allow the observer and the observed to unify.

This practice of ayni opens the heart, calms the nervous system, reduces reactivity and fosters self-acceptance. It also enables you to extend compassion to others. This is the authentic collaborative "we" space, when differences melt, dichotomies dissolve and creativity appears. On a deeper level, perhaps this is what Gandhi meant when he said, "Be the change you wish to see in the world."

Authentic Collaboration Practice with Others
The C Exercise

With a partner, choose one day as a "C-Alert Day." Discuss the C blocks and enablers listed below. When listening and speaking to people on that day, notice how these C blocks and enablers show up during interactions. How does it affect your communication process? Jot down your observations on paper. At the end of the day, compare notes and discuss what you noticed.

Blocks	Enablers
Criticism	Curiosity
Closed-mindedness	Compassion

When that conversation feels complete, reflect on a recent conflict each of you have experienced. How did these blocks and enablers affect your ability to resolve the conflict? Dialogue about what each of you wants to start, stop and continue doing when you communicate.

The P Exercise

With a group, invite everyone to dialogue about any provocative subject. After twenty minutes, stop the dialogue. Now, introduce a strategy developed by Art Costa and Bena Kallick called the three *P*'s—Pausing, Paraphrasing and Probing.

These powerful process skills enable a group to improve communication effectiveness. Demonstrate what each *P* might look and sound like. Pausing allows for meaningful silence after someone speaks so that people can reflect and digest what has been said. Paraphrasing ensures understanding by repeating back what was said using your own and the other person's words. Probing is asking clarifying questions to support understanding.

With these three skills in mind, invite the group to continue the dialogue while consciously interjecting the three *P*'s. Stop after twenty minutes and discuss the effect. What happened? How did these communication tools influence the quality of interaction? What struck you? What insights arose? How can you weave these insights into your collaboration process?

Group Process Rater Exercise

Consider creating a process rater questionnaire to open a dialogue about how your group functions. Invite people to rate themselves on a scale of 1 (low) to 10 (high). When completed, collect the anonymous rater sheets and calculate the average mean score for each item. Share the results with the group, allowing the feedback to surface reactions, feelings, appreciations and ideas to improve.

Sample rater topics include:

- degree of authentic communication
- degree of co-creation in developing a shared purpose
- ability to share power while building agreements together
- willingness to allow diverse points of view to be expressed
- degree of willingness to be flexible and adaptable

- ability to engage with respect when conflict arises
- ability to practice active listening
- ability to slow down to process a disagreement
- degree of trust

After you share the results of the questionnaire, ask some process debrief questions:

- What surprises you about the feedback?
- What are you noticing about our group?
- What feelings arise?
- What do you want to celebrate?
- What do you see as our top area for improvement?
- What ideas do you have for developing how we collaborate and function?

Collaborative Connection with Earth
A Home-Bound Process

Consider this quote from Ram Dass, *"We're all just walking each other home."*

This sentiment implies that we're on a journey. It carries the element of support and togetherness. Reflect on the multi-dimensional *process* of how you collaborate overall.

How are you walking others home...

- to their heart?
- to the arms of Mother Earth?
- to the profound truth of who they are?
- to the world of spirit?

An Ayni Ritual to Support Right Relationship

Living in ayni or right relationship with Earth is a guiding ethic to respect the natural world within and around us. It's about living in a reciprocal, harmonious and sustainable way, integrated into the larger whole of which we are a part. With ayni, we shift beyond self-interest to notice how our choices affect the greater landscape of Life. We ask how we can develop a deeper sense of meaningful connection with the natural world. The following nature-based ritual is intended to support you with this process of ayni.

Travel to a body of water near you—be it an ocean, river, pond or lake. If this is not possible, fill a bowl of water. At the water's edge, take some time to center and ground yourself, feeling the beauty around you. A collaborative relationship with Earth begins by recognizing her value as a living, sanctified being. Bow to honor Earth, your ancestors and all your relations. Call in the spirit of eagle and condor for support.

In your journal, on the left side of the page, detail the ways you currently do not live in right relationship with your environment. What habits are you ready to release? Radical truth-telling is important to healing. Allow the water to bear witness to your acknowledgment. If any emotions arise, notice them with compassion and allow them to float away. If you are right-handed, write this detail using your left hand and vice versa. This enables you to access a deeper part of your subconscious.

When complete, turn your journal page over to a new blank page to signify the start of a new chapter in your life. Again, with your non-dominant hand, write all the ways you feel inspired to come into ayni. Welcome the tide of emotion as it rises and falls. Write from your heart, as though this was a love letter to nature.

Next, find and select two stones near you. When you feel ready, bring one stone to your mouth and blow in all the energy associated with the left side of your journal entry. Do this three times. Read your words out loud to hear the earnestness in your voice. Release this by throwing the symbolic stone into the water. Ask how you can cleanse and purify your mind-body-spirit. Allow the flow to take your intention into her depth.

AUTHENTIC COLLABORATION

With the second stone, blow out that which you are prepared to promise Earth. Do this three times. Since commitments drive our actions, reflect on what changes you are willing to commit to. With an exhale, throw the second stone into the water. Be still. Listen to the message of the water by tuning into your intuition. Notice what's happening in this sacred space. Nature speaks to us if we have the ears to listen.

Conclude the ritual in whatever way Earth moves you. You may want to stroll in the flora and fauna around the water to drink in its medicine. Perhaps read a poem or say a prayer or touch the ground and send out love to all the four-legged and two-legged animals, the sea life, the crawlers and the winged ones. Express whatever sentiments of gratitude are within your heart. Nature rituals are an empowering way to bridge-build your connection with Earth.

CHAPTER 14

FLYING ON THE WINGS OF INNER GROWTH AND OUTER ENGAGEMENT

"Ultimately, our being is the bridge."
Abhijit Naskar

A grand invitation to let go and let come

Fundamentally, this book supports the fulfillment of the eagle-condor prophecy with the practice of authentic collaboration. When we expand into the consciousness of ayni, and come into right relationship with all our relations, we advance our capacity for sustainable living. With every mindful bridge-building interaction, we play a role in shaping the Great Turning.

Significant societal transitions are now underway and on their way. Extraordinary, volatile changes are being experienced on every level. Our global economic engine, with self-maximization as its goal, has revved up for over two hundred years. Dire consequences have come to pass with new challenges continually arising. Our relationship with Earth has been the sacrificial lamb. The environment has been deeply scarred by our insatiable consumer lifestyle and fixation with commercial growth. Moreover, the geopolitical landscape has been altered with social injustice, ecocide, the climate crisis, military and economic warfare and our global pandemic response. These issues are further complicated by corruption, racial inequity, cyber-attacks, extreme poverty, social tension and unstable governments. As a response to these complex issues and others, the bridge of authentic collaboration is a generative

> *"A powerful message—spoken in the language of fires, floods, droughts, and extinctions—telling us that we need an entirely new economic model and a new way of sharing this planet."*
> Naomi Klein

path forward. It's a passageway not only to meaningful connection, but also to communal wisdom and balanced solution-finding.

Truly, this is an era of shifting sands. For the sake of future generations and millions of living species, structural, systems, inter- and intrapersonal transformation is needed. Evolution necessitates disruption. Substantial change is a big ask for our generation, yet the status quo is no longer an option. It's time to forge a path of sacred activism and realign with peace.

One anticipated change will be the dying of the industrial growth model and its sidekick, the conventional collaboration paradigm. This worldview has served its purpose. When this mindset moves into its death throes, we will be called upon to hospice the macroeconomic policies and the relational model of the manufacturing age. With new eyes, we'll investigate the intended and unintended consequences of the systems we are a part of. Political, social and bureaucratic barriers will no longer be tolerated. Trail-blazing changes will be made in how we relate to the production of food, water and energy. The environmental, social, governance (ESG) agenda will take precedence. Supply chain issues will be amended. Technology and consumer behavior will deviate. I sense change is accelerating.

As we heal, shift and grow, we will slowly say goodbye to the old template of us-versus-them, either-or and win-lose. Entrenched dualistic thinking will fade into the annals of history. Our subject-object, separation-comparison orientation will have a reduced impact on the collective relational body. For many, ego death will result: self-importance will be replaced by a sense of union with others. In some circles, this process has already begun.

If we pay attention, intermingled with these sounds of dying will be birth cries. As enemy images and other addictions languish, we can practice healthier ways of relating. We'll exhale the societal trappings of role power, control, status, greed and habits of domination as we inhale new awareness. The pressure to perform, inform and conform will melt away as we embrace life-affirming values. We will re-envision the meaning of collaboration. Respecting self, others and Earth will become a meme. We'll stand for integrative bridge-building to bring all of who we are to social action. Just as the horse and buggy mode of transportation died to hasten the arrival of the automobile, I foresee our conventional habits making way for the practice of authentic collaboration. And so goes the natural cycle of life, death and rebirth.

Even though the future holds great uncertainty, let's work together to midwife this birthing process. Let's breathe through the pain and exhilaration. Let's anticipate miracles as we bear down and deliver on our commitments. The field of collaboration is pregnant with possibility.

This staggering moment of letting go and letting come is one grand invitation. It's a profound liminal space to honestly reflect on how we connect, work and live. We're at the cusp of breaking open a new seed of potential, with all the aliveness, messiness and bliss it holds. If separation is our old and current normal, meaningful connection can be our new normal. With the bridge pillars of empowering self, sharing power and co-creating vision, we can choose to find unity in diversity. With newfound attentiveness toward Earth, we can shift from ego-centricity to eco-centricity. We can care for our planet in the same way we do for our loved ones. Earth is knocking at our door. Embodied interdependency is peeking out from behind the curtain.

> *"What a caterpillar calls the end of the world, we call a butterfly."*
> Eckhart Tolle

This time of transition is ripe with opportunities. Clues on where to begin are all around. Given our multi-dimensional challenges, we can support positive change at the micro, meso and macro levels, namely with self-growth, relationship health and system functionality. They all run in parallel. One level does not have to precede the other. There is no "right" sequence of change, just growing edges and entry points. In our interconnected world, transformation in one realm produces a butterfly effect throughout the field.

We've reached a critical inflection point. While the contemporary global order undergoes restructuring and reform, we can't turn back. The train has left the station. To participate, let's escalate our sense of urgency for positive change. Let's question the assumptions that run our life. Like archeologists, we can gently examine the

> *"The strength of the forces of change will always be in proportion to the urgency of the need being championed."*
> I Ching 49

artifacts of our relationship history, noticing the remnants that still need love. Reconnecting with our heart never gets old. We can invite serpent energy to help us shed our old protective skin so that new authentic collaboration habits mature. We can practice with jaguar strength, bravely using the relationship-building RELATE tools provided in these pages. We can draw inspiration from hummingbirds who routinely drink from Life's sweet nectar. Together, we can fly on the eagle-condor wings of inner growth and outer engagement. By balancing both in our becoming, we can enact the change we wish to see in this world.

Diversity as a path to solution-finding and personal growth

Authentic collaboration is central to this societal transition because complex challenges do not have simple solutions. It takes the uniting of many diverse voices to co-develop an array of appropriate responses. How we support this interactive process is the padlock to the door. The key is reciprocated respect. Regardless if the response is global, regional or local, people notice *how* the collaboration process unfolds. Are groups marginalized? Are opposing ideas held with care? Is a third middle way considered?

Our challenges prompt us to value diversity. When we call for creative solutions, we ought to assume that differences will arise. As Frederick Ledelea noted, "The diversity of our being and our ideas can transform the entire world for the better." As a gift from nature, diversity is simply part of the landscape. So, we need to maintain respect even when intense conflict lures us into labelling others as bad or wrong. Avoid the temptation to quickly brand people and opinions. Question the accepted box of reality. Innovation and transformation can only stem from curiosity.

The quality of dialogue we need now *is* counterculture. Authentic collaboration is just that—an invitation to explore our societal norms. To notice what we typically shun. To embrace what emerges rather than run away. To listen with empathy rather than finger-point. To speak with humility rather than pretend we have the answers. The dialogue of solution-finding is bearing witness to each other's dreams and contradictions, attributes and flaws.

AUTHENTIC COLLABORATION

The rich diversity inherent in collaboration is full of golden opportunities to reflect and learn together. It's not helpful to relate as though some people "know" while others "don't know". Safe space is co-created by uttering those three vulnerable words—*I don't know*. Whatever knowledge and experience people bring to the table, let's rise to meet each other with mutual esteem, creativity and optimism. Doing so elicits beautiful synergy…if we all do our part.

> *"There is still so much in the world worth fighting for. So much that is beautiful. . . . It is not too late to turn things around, if we all do our part."*
> Dr. Jane Goodall

While humans have co-created serious challenges in the world, consider the idea that we engineered this chaos for the purpose of our growth. Consciously or unconsciously, our human family is seeking greater relationship intelligence as our quintessential, shared growth opportunity. The diversity of challenges are a means from which to grow. This is the order in the chaos. As an encouragement, remember that we already have the wisdom to authentically collaborate. The challenge is to unearth the golden wisdom nuggets buried in our hearts.

If we struggle to channel our wisdom, call upon the timeless part of ourselves to relearn the forgotten language that has always been within. The music of the mind-body-spirit relational dance can be heard echoing from long ago. Therein, we can find a reverberation of peace. We can embrace our wisdom and the world's beauty. We can enlist broken aspects of our personality to heal into wholeness *and* accept the magnificence of who we are. When our consciousness opens and expands, providence will be waiting to greet us.

A recap of the authentic collaboration vision

To support humanity's evolution, I offer a final summary of the Great Turning in the domain of relationship-building. While reviewing, imagine yourself walking across this three-lane bridge with your loved ones and Earth Mother by your side. Feel into which phrase resonates with you in this moment. Reflect on how you engage and connect with others digitally and in-person. Presume that partnership-building, relationship intelligence and authentic collaboration are now core citizen competencies.

AUTHENTIC COLLABORATION

> ### Authentic Collaboration: A Vision Recap
>
> **Evolving from…**
> - separation to meaningful connection
> - us versus them to interdependence
> - reactivity to mindful response
> - victim-thinking to self-empowerment
> - judgment and blame to curiosity
> - mind-sparked fear to heart-centered courage
> - power imbalance to power-sharing
> - one-way talking to reciprocation and co-creation
> - better-than, less-than thinking to respecting all diverse Life forms
> - exclusive focus on outcome to honoring relationships and results

To anchor in this vision, mull over what has touched you in this writing. Given your life experiences, what questions entice you? Maybe your inquiry revolves around a specific RELATE exercise. Perhaps you're wondering how to surrender into and live from your heart. Perchance, it may be a question about how to reconnect with the natural world, how to access heart intelligence or how to internalize the listening distinctions. Or, you may be curious about how to welcome in contrarian viewpoints to shake up your organizational culture. What's alive in you now?

Whatever your inquiry, know that questions are the engine of evolution. As a relationally responsive being, your questions speak to how you want to enrich yourself, your family, workplace and community. So ask big questions. This will signify your willingness to become an edge-walker. As David Whyte noted, "The marvelous thing about a good question is that it shapes our identity as much by the asking as it does by the answering."

> *"The power to question is the basis of all human progress."*
> Indira Gandhi

Integrating this vision with purpose

A line of inquiry that can help you integrate this vision is reflecting on your soul purpose, as it calls you. There may very well be shared commonality

AUTHENTIC COLLABORATION

between the vision of authentic collaboration and how you want to express your soul truth. In shamanism, it's understood that our soul speaks to us through symbols, metaphors, archetypes, poetry, animals, emotions, ritual and magic. For you, the process may be remembering why you came to Earth. For us all, it's about listening to our unique soul song. To access this deeper knowing, spend time outdoors to heed the messages of nature. Life offers a powerful source of guidance. Notice if you experience reoccurring themes that follow you like a shadow. Tune into what expands and elevates your spirit. Where does your passion lie, the spark that lights you up?

To discern your soul purpose, start by quieting your system. Beyond your mind, there is a tender space of yearning that wants to communicate with creation. Contained within the yearning is the possibility of joyful expression. This joy is an entryway to your higher soul intelligence. It's a voice that calls you to be of service to the greater whole. During moments of doubt, know that the world awaits your unique gifts. Hold onto the notion that Life has your back. Your soul dream is held by the arms of Life. In the field of interdependent belonging, your will and Life's will are actually one and the same.

> "[Find] the place where your deep gladness and the world's deep hunger meet."
> Frederick

Flying the vision into action with presencing

Flying the authentic collaboration vision into action requires two wings—inner growth and outer engagement. This translates into self-awareness and mindful interaction: communicating our feelings and needs while meeting others where they are. When we support ourselves and each other with care, realness kicks in. The residue of coaxing and convincing diffuses. A slow spiral of unmasking unwinds our defenses. An audible sigh of relief may be heard when we connect with others from a deeper space of our being.

What enables birds to fly is a unique pulley system located under their massive heart muscle. In human terms, the massive heart muscle of authentic collaboration is presencing. As a prodigious power, presencing facilitates inner growth and outer engagement. This involves reconciling the tension between the needs of self and others. It also means presencing the oscillating energies of sorrow and joy: they are two sides of the same coin. It implies developing awareness of how we walk in the world. Becoming fully open and available to self, others and Life—in the moment—is how we flex the muscle of meaningful connection.

TRY THIS: To practice presencing, recall the last time you experienced a relationship conflict. With this in mind, notice the extent to which you're able to "be with" your inner mix of thoughts and feelings *and* empathize with the other person. Do you err on the side of hyper-individualism or on the side of losing yourself?

Another presencing opportunity is to reflect on the notion of interdependence. Consider that each of us is a node in the web of Life and, as such, our thoughts, words and deeds ripple out to affect all our relations. Presencing this insight may evoke overwhelm. How people interface with the natural world, in part, is evident with these two statistics: our planet has lost at least nine hundred species in the past five centuries and over thirty-five thousand species are threatened with extinction today. Given these facts, how challenging is it for you to presence the emotion that accompanies this information? Whatever arises in your awakening, accept it with a tender heart. Even the tough stuff. It's said that grief escorts every jump in consciousness. To quote Natalie Goldberg, "Our task is to say a holy yes to the real things of our life."

> *"Humankind has not woven the web of Life; we are but one strand in it. Whatever we do to the web, we do to ourselves."*
> Chief Seattle

With a "yes" attitude, presencing can be practiced with every interaction. This includes the moments when we de-robe our hearts, speak with soft power, relate with esteem and activate meaningful connection. This habit may be pioneering for many but it's not foreign. Presencing in relationship is based on long-held values. What's more, we're born knowing the womb value of interdependency. The essence of this knowing has existed within us from inception. In the bowels of our being, we already understand the indivisibility of Life. The interdependent principle of authentic collaboration is like an old coat that's been tucked away in the back of humanity's closet. I invite you now to shake off the dust, try it on for size and feel the warm comfort of relational unity.

Inner growth: the noble path of personal mastery

To actionize the vision of authentic collaboration, let's explore the noble path of inner growth. Personal mastery is a tantalizing quest because we're always learning how to adjust to our ever-changing circumstances. As creative, organic beings, we're built to evolve and mature in our relationships. On the physical level, our body's adaptive capability is impressive: our intestinal track regenerates every five days, our liver every two years and our skin every thirty days. Since our body has this power, why not regenerate our mind as well?

Inner regeneration involves building self-awareness. With daily attention, our mental models gradually come to light. We start noticing how much time we spend seeking that which we believe we're missing, avoiding that which we don't want and clinging to that which we think we need. We begin to understand that perception is our dynamo leverage skill. Since the basis of Life is energy, and our perception is changeable, how we view and shape reality is also ever changing. As quantum physics teaches, it's all vibration. So, no obstacle we face is unmoveable, be it relational or otherwise. This understanding is intensely hopeful. The Newtonian notion that matter changes matter has been replaced by a more expanded truth: energy creates matter. This is significant in the art of bridge-building because the energy of new thoughts can resolve any stuckness. Every perspective shift precipitates some type of reality change. The beauty of the mind is wondrous to behold.

> *Try on this perception: To see the beauty in others, embrace your own beauty. It takes one to know one.*

Understanding and working with the power of perception is like owning magical fairy dust. Our mind is our personal talisman. A new perspective offers a pivot point to transform current reality to something once unimagined. With the power of the mind, we can shift out of our beta busy state to an alpha relaxed, creative state to even a theta inspired state. Eureka moments follow with great insight. When we hold this mind vibration along with loving kindness, we return to our true nature. Influencing becomes ease-filled. We confidently ask for what we want while giving consent for others to do the same. With radical self-responsibility, we heal from toxic relationships. We accept the universal law—we reap what

> *"One can have no smaller or greater mastery than mastery of oneself."*
> Leonardo da Vinci

we sow. Perspective change enables us to swim *with* the current of Life rather than paddle upstream. When our mind and gut power blends with heart intelligence, our self-mastery journey is well underway. Prepare for astonishing life changes.

Since everything serves the purpose of our growth and awakening, we don't have to look far for support. Conditions, resources and people emerge in their own time. Life is a bountiful school. Synchronicity surely finds us when we set a sincere intention. At the end of the day, the growth journey is a trust walk. Tomorrow is shaped by today's actions. Every choice informs how we evolve from getting, to having, to letting, to becoming, to relating in harmony.

To quote George Bernard Shaw, "Life isn't about finding yourself. It's about creating yourself." To add a caveat: Life is about creating ourselves *in relationship*. In an interdependent world, self-empowerment goes hand in hand with the upliftment of others.

Manifesting with embodied resonance

On the path to personal mastery, we become mindful about the process of manifestation. This is about creating something new via living in alignment with what we want. We do this by imagining that what we wish for has already come into existence. In doing so, we express a magnetizing energy that vibrates with our future identity. Our being and doing becomes consistent with our desired future. Spiritual teacher Michael Beckwith refers to this as the "law of resonance." He explains that what we create and attract resonates with our inner reality. So, if we want to manifest a new way to collaborate, reflect on what authentic connection means, who we want to be, the emotions we want to feel and what we want to offer. In other words, become clear on our dream and how this translates in our relationships. By creating a field of resonance, we send out an energetic broadcast. The hand of Life then presides in directing the magic of manifestation.

The law of resonance supports both the inner and outer circuit of energy. Like the infinity symbol, our inner loop of beliefs influences our outer loop of relationship-building. Our thoughts shape who we're calling into our lives and how we connect. Inner and outer change are symbiotic. We don't need to pound on the door because we're already standing on the inside. When we periodically upgrade our brain software and install a new belief program, we create a new relational path forward.

Put another way, our mind is like a tape recorder: when we rewind and re-record new inward messaging, our outward-facing life also shifts. Here is one belief thread that I am transforming to upgrade my vibration:

Life is happening to me. > Life is happening by me. > Life is happening through me. > Life is happening as me.

What new belief is calling you to evolve your relationships?

For those who believe it is self-indulgent to focus on self-mastery, consider personal growth to be *the* path to skillful action. How we think, speak and listen is how we refashion the world around us. The more we are willing to transmute limiting ways of thinking and behaving, the more we are able to change how we collaborate and alter the systems we are a part of. By developing our agency, we strengthen our commitment, our choice of language and our interpersonal connections. We then have greater agility to shift our narrative and approach. Our ability to effectively respond to complex issues exponentially grows.

> "We create our lives with our beliefs, and we broadcast those beliefs into the energetic environment around us. With that knowledge, we have the freedom to create whatever kinds of relationships we want."
> Dr. Bruce Lipton

In the living laboratory of relationship-building, it's tempting to believe that the power of change lies with others. It's seductive to think that if only others would change, then smoother waters would prevail. Trying to induce people to behave the way we want is scheming. These are fear-based fleeting thoughts. And it's an exercise in futility. Instead, gaze into the looking glass to empower self-transformation. Awaken the beliefs that free the soul, the latent energies that long to be expressed in our precious relationships. Become a seeker of the ageless wisdom within.

On the journey toward personal mastery, remember that we are *not the voice* in our mind but rather the one *aware* of that voice. Every time we take a step back and develop a relationship with our "observer self," we reinforce this truth. In noticing our patterns from this bird's-eye view, we issue a ticket to self-liberation. It breaks open a whole new panorama to learn that our past way of relating does not have to dictate our future. Our observer self is in the power seat. It is through meaningful connection, moment to moment, that we create a new destiny line, for ourselves and the world.

Outer engagement: transforming the habit of othering

Everything in Life is filtered through our lens of consciousness. As such, inching toward authentic collaboration and building community involves transcending our consciousness of separation and othering. Even though we're taught to separate from people we dislike or who are different, doing so does not make us safe. Excluding people only creates discord and divisiveness. This behavior originates from inner fragmentation, rooted in the suffering of separation. To solve challenges together, we need to transform the belief that "others" are the problem.

Whatever the symptoms of othering, the remedy is the same. Compassion is the prescription for the illness of animosity. Relating from the heart is the antidote to healing the self-other illusion. In taking daily doses of compassion, we no longer need to split the world into good and bad people. We begin to feel the urge to unify people. This is how we vitalize the life blood of authentic collaboration and create a new future. I see compassion as grace in motion.

> *"Grace is knowing that the future can rewrite the past."*
> Thomas Hübl

With every new positive belief, we co-create a world where, as john a. powell suggests, we each become a "belonging activist." In this reality, we extend respect to every diverse Life form on the planet and rejoice in inter-being. Differences become an invitation to learn. Rejection is seen as an opportunity to self-connect. Relationship breakdowns become a choice to self-empower and bridge-build with care. Distrust starts a heart conversation about what we need to feel safe. Curiosity translates confusion into greater understanding. When growing our consciousness, we need to let go of our self-imposed limitations. Doing so helps us appreciate the value of who we are, what we offer and what we're capable of.

As we practice mindful interacting, we note the difference between relating and relating consciously. The subtlety is like distinguishing breathing with breath awareness. Mindful communication is how we expand into and-both thinking. The veil of separation lifts as we discover what unites us. Even though we're taught to build a partition when afraid, trust that we are also well-equipped to build collaborative bridges. If we let down our guard with sincere communication, the journey is so much more satisfying. Warts and all, our beauty lies in our imperfection. As an insightful coach once told me: we don't need more perfection in the world, we need more authenticity. Consider so-called failed relationships to be an apprenticeship for what's to come.

When we dig inwards, we discover that we can meaningfully connect despite living in separate bodies. We may even realize that others live in us and us in them. As relationship neuroscience now shows, our mirror neurons create connection in mind-blowing ways. With this understanding, we can break our long-held attachment to individualism, along with its corresponding symptom of isolation. We can maintain individuality *and* wade in the water of unity. As a species, we can hold our autonomy amid diversity. The bridge of authentic collaboration is an uplink to supporting both our own interests while still caring for the greater whole.

> *"The essential challenge is to transform the isolation and self-interest within our communities into connectedness and caring for the whole."*
> Peter Block

Reaching out and developing a network of support

If you see this as a heavy elephantine journey, it doesn't need to be. We can walk with humor and a light heart, especially if a caring community surrounds us with support. And we all need support with the process of healthy relationship-building. Our well-being depends on our network of allies. Growing the vision of authentic collaboration alone is like looking for a corner in a round room. It's counter to the purpose.

Developing intentional networks enables us to connect across sectors, issues and constituency. With a broad cross-section of different worldviews, there is great learning available. Not only is continuous improvement and innovation stimulated but also broader understanding. When people are exposed to various

AUTHENTIC COLLABORATION

cultures and mindsets, the insights we gain tend to dispel negative stereotypes. Diversity nudges us to adapt to context.

Moreover, networks can arouse shared accountability, prodding people to take responsibility for issues affecting them. Together, results and consequences can be discussed, along with mustering the heart to commit to and own group decisions. Collaborative dialogue can address shared issues with new insights. Meaningful connection can generate abundant opportunities. Members can stay abreast of changes happening in their field of interest. Who we know expands what we know. In so many ways, these communities can be a powerful source of belonging and uplift. Purpose-filled partnerships are essential to growing a vision.

> *"May the frames of your belonging be large enough for the dreams of your soul."*
> John O'Donohue

Whenever we network and engage people with the spirit of authentic collaboration, we fire up the dandelion effect—we disperse the seeds with the wind of our energy. We root in the value of interdependence. With every budding opportunity, we nurture other pollinators and cross-fertilize a different quality of conversation. Passionate, courageous expression is contagious.

There's a plethora of possibilities to outreach and engage people. From this list on the next page, which idea inspires you into action? Use these ideas to reflect on who you want to become as a collaborative networker. Contemplate your power as a heart-centered communicator to open up dialogue about struggles, talents, worthiness, imperfections and bold action. Engagement offers a window on how much we trust and our willingness to reveal. Every relationship is an adventure for our spirit.

Whatever your desire as a network weaver, ensure that mutual respect frames how you engage. Alignment matters. Social change that has sticking power depends on mindful relating. It's the ring that marries the means and the end.

> **Engagement Ideas to Grow Authentic Collaboration**
>
> - Co-create a RELATE book club or a community of practice.
> - Begin a conversation with your own collaboration story.
> - Form a cross-functional work team around a question of shared interest.
>
> - Initiate a family dialogue about the two bridge graphics in this book.
> - Lead a nature hike with friends to consciously connect with Earth.
> - Explore ways to strengthen a local, Earth-friendly economy.
>
> - Become a super connector by setting up a peer-learning circle.
> - In an interfaith group, discover the spirituality of authentic collaboration.
> - Gather a group to discuss conscious coupling or collaborative uncoupling.

When resistance surfaces

When we fly on the wings of inner growth and outer engagement, authentic collaboration will still evoke resistance. It's an inevitable part of the landscape. Any vision worth manifesting will offer grist for the mill to test our resolve. Resistance is the grist of wanting something to be different than it is. These thoughts turn into feelings that we don't want to feel. In a sense, resistance is an avoidance of reality. Resistance may show itself in an inner conflict, an unfulfilling relationship, a boundary violation, broken agreements or a distressing partnership. We may even experience fear in being victimized, exploited or controlled by an oppressive system. Resistance takes on many shapes, sizes and stripes.

> *"When you experience resistance, you find the lessons that you are meant to learn."*
> Jon Gordon

When this tension arises, be aware that fear is not in the way: it *is* the way. Befriending our emotions to move us through the fog is like mountain climbers trusting that a fixed rope leads them to a new horizon. Similarly, we need to trust our emotional and physical sensations to be our teacher. They are invisible guiding signals. When we listen to and trust our body's truth, we morph our collaboration fear into courage. It is an act of bravery to embrace the detached and dissociated aspects of ourselves. For this personal healing work contributes to planetary healing. As within, so without.

When intra- or interpersonal resistance surfaces, develop the virtue of patience. We can only move as quickly as the most tentative aspect of self. Relationships move at the speed of trust: it's slower than we think. Just as an oyster makes a pearl in response to a sand irritant, we too can transform resistance into something precious with the gift of time. A mollusk will take anywhere from six months to four years to form an iridescent gem. It takes faith to relax into the rhythm of nature and wait for the magic of Life. In quieting our egoic mind, we see that resistance also carries the pearl of wisdom.

A story: learning to trust with nature as an ally

On a warm summer day, I reclined outside with a friend. Out of nowhere, a finch bird flew to me from a nearby tree, squawked in front of my face and then perched on my shoulder for at least two minutes. Crouching in the bushes, my cat sprang into action, prompting the bird to fly away. This left us perplexed; it's odd that a wild bird would do such a thing.

The next morning, what looked like the same bird flew over to me again. As she shrieked in my face, I sensed this winged one had a message for me. This time, the bird stayed on my arm for over *three hours*. Even my neighbors came over to witness this rare sighting. We were all flabbergasted.

Afterwards, I decided to meditate to connect with the bird's spirit. I wanted to understand what nature was communicating to me. In stillness, I heard a message that left tears streaming down my face: "If a vulnerable bird feels safe to trust and sit on your arm for hours, how can you risk opening your heart to trust and feel safe in the world?"

> "When I let go of who I am, I become who I might be."
> Lao Tzu

I see these empowering words as integral to manifesting the vision of authentic collaboration. To fly into our future, we need to deepen our capacity to trust and risk together. This means understanding our fears, including our resistance of interdependence. It's one thing to know that we all need each other, yet entirely a different matter to surrender into this truth. When we hold the vulnerability of someone's needs in our heart and allow others to do the same with our needs, we can rise as powerful co-creators.

To be sure, nature gives us many insights on embracing resistance. A beautiful lotus flower, for example, only grows in mud. Similarly, we too need the sludge of resistance and the dirt of unpleasant emotions to help us bloom into our fullness. We need contraction to recognize expansion. Maybe the happiness we're chasing has been in the mud of our relationships all along. At the very least, resistance provokes self-collaboration in returning us home to our hearts. At the very most, a new life may be waiting for us.

> *"Most of us have two lives: the life we live, and the unlived life within us. Between the two stands Resistance."*
> Steven Pressfield

Sometimes, we need discipline to breathe into the tension and prevent us from running away. *Discipline*, which comes from the word *disciple*, means "devotion." The discipline of inner growth and outer engagement is a devotion to regenerating and evolving. The next time resistance bubbles up, become devoted to the lotus of your heart in seeing the beauty beyond the mud. Take the risk and trust.

Final call to action

As a final call to action, I invite you to deepen your commitment to authentic collaboration. Do this by calling in the wisdom of your ancestors, for you stand on the shoulders of many teachers. Tune into their guidance as you move the RELATE principles into action. Blaze your own change-making trail. There is no glass ceiling to personal development.

With a soft heart full of wonder, reflect on the many questions and assertions in this writing. Communicate with integrity and the intention of unifying. Start with your own neighbors. Entice people to share their hopes and concerns. Allow feelings to cue up curiosity. Accord respect without exception. Relate with generosity of spirit. Allow your heart to be ripped open. Notice attachments to roles, rules and outcome. Understand the values that drive your choices. Become a devoted warrior to peaceful relations. Embrace the dimensions of yourself that are hiding. See what's behind the form, of yourself and others. Ask how interdependence lives in you. Move beyond defensiveness with a "yes and" response. Release the need to prove something. Make self-acceptance a habit.

Pause. Take a long, slow breath. Smile.

AUTHENTIC COLLABORATION

In the spirit of authentic collaboration, stand for win-win-win inclusion. Pay attention to the sound of silence. Invite the stories that need a voice. Search for commonalities. Realize that people's truth is often temporary. Weep and laugh together. Give thanks daily. Check in on people—just because. Let go of doing enough since you are enough. Embody the consciousness that there's only one hoop in Life. Awaken into Eros to reclaim your Life force of love. You are born to make a difference. The world is waiting for your talents.

> "Act as if what you do makes a difference. It does."
> William James

Earth as a way-shower

We can learn a great deal from indigenous people. Their wisdom is necessary to reinstate a reciprocal relationship with our planet...and thus each other. They trust Earth to be their way-shower. In the Amazon, tribes do not live in the forest, they are *of* the forest. Their accepted ethos is that humans and ants share the same origin and value. The Sioux perceive Earth as extended family. The Cree do not regard trees as "what" but rather "who". The Māori see the water and land as taonga or treasures. The tribal nations of the Kalahari have lived in harmony with others and Earth since the Stone Age. All around the world, our indigenous brothers and sisters hold great respect for the whole organism of Earth. Sourced from the same wellspring, they understand that we are all conduits for Life to experience itself. Collaboration is baked into their culture.

Beyond our indigenous friends, lessons are abundant if we listen to Earth. Nature always tells the truth. As our teacher, she places things in perspective. Her dance of reciprocity is deeply nourishing. When we detach our identity from our thoughts, things, roles, social media and mundane routine, our mind has space to learn from nature. It's humbling to acknowledge that everything we hold dear is from our shared mother. In uncanny ways, nature reveals the enchantment of authentic collaboration. By treating Earth well, we steward her *and* our own soul. We begin to rewild, feel our mycelia interconnectedness and celebrate our innate goodness. We remember that Earth lives in ayni.

> "Treat Earth well: it was not given to you by your parents, it was loaned to you by your children."
> Crazy Horse

When feeling lost, know that the ecology within and around us has answers. When feeling afraid, reconnect with Earth to feel her unwavering strength. When feeling confused, look to the ocean for calm. When feeling suffocated by others, look to the sky for relief. Allow her to be your trusted listening partner. The expansive splendor of nature recalibrates our system in minutes. She arouses awe and inspiration. Sinking into the bosom of Mother Earth is a beautiful way to be met with loving presence.

Crossing the bridge to a new tomorrow

With the vision of authentic collaboration, we have colored pencils to sketch our own unique storyline of relating. As we practice this with the orbit of our heart, the focus of our mind and the strength of our spirit, we disassemble our protective walls and raise our vibration. Offering respect and kindness, as an expression of love, is who we are. Just this one realization rotates us away from separation and toward belonging. Rumi said it best, "Your task is not to seek for love, but merely to seek and find all the barriers within yourself that you have built against it, and embrace them."

As we open our hearts even more, we can hear the clarion call of eagle-condor. Their unifying spirit encourages us to bring out the best within and among us. With the energy of love, their reunion reminds us that we can reconnect self-other, human-Earth, mind-heart, left-right brain and masculine-feminine. By owning our shadow, we release our light. By realizing who we really are, we find peace. By empathizing, we discover our shared humanity. By valuing all, we co-create a different future for our children. By interacting with altruism, we become the heroes we are waiting for. It's our cosmic destiny to soar on the wings of these spirit animals.

> *"We are the ones we've been waiting for."*
> June Jordan

When crossing the authentic collaboration bridge, trust that a new tomorrow lies on the other side. Each mindful interaction takes us closer to realizing the dream of nurturing homes, vibrant communities, enlivened workplaces, sustainable systems and a verdant planet. Perhaps, one day, we'll discover that we are the bridge.

NOTES

Prologue

xvii   **"When the eagle of the northern hemisphere flies with the condor of the south" (minute 1) and "write on the huge page in the sky" (minute 10:00):** video by Jaguar Bird, "The Eagle & Condor Prophecy: Elder's interpretations, From Several Nations," YouTube, January 25, 2018.

xvii   **Further reading about the Inca Prophecy:** Laurel Thompson, "An Ancient Legend Meets Modern Times: The Eagle and the Condor," *Threads of Peru*, May 13, 2016.

xviii   **Aang-Wang hello greeting:** Wisdom Weavers, https://www.wisdomweavers.world/aang-waan.

Chapter 1: Bridge-Building with Authentic Collaboration

1   **Shaman means "one who sees in the dark":** Colleen Deatsman and Paul Bowers, "Seeing in the Dark: Claim Your Own Shamanic Power Now and in the Coming Age," *Daily OM.*

1   **Links to learn more about shamanism:** To learn more about shamanism, see:

The Four Winds Society, https://thefourwinds.com;

Sandra Ingerman, https://www.youtube.com/watch?v=ZCjJURznqFA;

The Origins of Shamanism, https://www.gaia.com/article/how-much-do-you-know-about-shamanism.

2   **Further reading about Ayni:** Dorthe Steenberg, Sascha Amarasinha, Tina Monberg, and Gitte Larsen, *Common Ground* (USA: Editions and House of Futures, 2009).

4   **The meaning of relationship:** *Online Etymology Dictionary.*

5   **Dr. Daniel Siegel on relational attunement and feeling felt:** Daniel Siegel, "Culture of Empathy Builder," *Center for Building a Culture of Empathy.*

11   **Integrating the left and right brain hemisphere:** Unknown blog author of "Integrating The Two Hemispheres," *BrainoBrain.*

13   **Peruvian Q'eswachaka bridge-building:** "124-foot Bridge Woven by Hand," posted on Great Big Story YouTube channel September 5, 2017, video, 3:47.

Chapter 2: Relating Holistically with Self, Others and Earth

19   **Harvard Medical School research:** Scott Stossel, "What Makes Us Happy, Revisited: A new look at the famous Harvard study of what makes people thrive," *The Atlantic*, May 2013.

The Grant Study is part of the Study of Adult Development at Harvard Medical School. It is a seventy-five-year longitudinal study that followed 268 Harvard-educated men. George Vaillant's main conclusion is that the warmth of relationships throughout life has the greatest positive impact on life satisfaction.

20   **Integral Theory:** Ken Wilber, *A Theory of Everything* (USA: Shambhala Publications, 2000).

22   **John Hopkins University research about everything being subjective:** Eleanor Bird, "There's No Such Thing as an 'Objective View' of Something," *Medical News Today*, June 20, 2020.

26   **Quantum mechanics:** Serpil Opperman, "Are We Really Interconnected? Eco philosophy and Quantum Theory from a Postmodern Perspective," *Journal of American Studies of Turkey* 16 (2002): pages 51-64.

26   **Physicist David Bohm:** David Bohm, "Wholeness, Timelessness and Unfolding Meaning; An interview from the archives with physicist and philosopher David Bohm," *Beshara Magazine, Metaphysics & Spirituality* no. 14 (2020).

See also: David Bohm, *Wholeness and the Implicate Order* (USA: Routledge, 2002).

28   **Stockholm Resiliency Centre:** W. Steffen, K. Richardson, J. Rockström, S.E. Cornell et.al. "Planetary Boundaries: Guiding Human Development on a Changing Planet," *Science* 347, no. 6223 (2015), https://www.science.org/doi/10.1126/science.12598552015.

28   **Global Footprint Network:** The Global Footprint Network: Advancing the Science of Sustainability, *footprintnetwork.org*.

28   **419 parts per million of carbon:** Mauna Loa Observatory, Hawaii, (daily reading), *co2.earth*.

29	**Whole Earth thinking:** Sam Mickey, *Whole Earth Thinking and Planetary Coexistence: Ecological Wisdom at the Intersection of Religion, Ecology and Philosophy* (New York: Routledge Publishing, 2017), page 149.
30	**From Era of Empire to Era of Earth Community:** David Korten, "Seeking the Pathway to a Future that Works for All," Living Economies Forum.
30	**The Great Turning:** Joanna Macy, "The Great Turning," *Center for Ecoliteracy*, June 29, 2009.

Chapter 3: Unpacking Conventional Collaboration

33	**Collaboration dates back 200,000 years ago:** Coren L. Apicella and Joan B. Silk, "The Evolution of Human Cooperation," *ScienceDirect.com*, *Current Biology* 29, no. 11 (June 7, 2019), R447-R450.
34	**Apollo 11:** Apollo 11, United States Space Flight, *Britannica*;
	Steve Jobs and Steve Wozniak: "Steve Wozniak and the Story of the PC," *National Inventors Hall of Fame*;
	Montreal Protocol: "International Actions – The Montreal Protocol on Substances that Deplete the Ozone Layer," *EPA: United States Environmental Protection Agency*;
	Jubilee 2000: Ann Pettifor, "Jubilee 2000 Coalition," *Advocacy International*, 2000;
	Soccer Team Rescue: Pat Ralph and James Pasley, "This timeline shows exactly how the Thai cave rescue unfolded and what's happened since," *BusinessInsider*, June 24, 2019;
	World's Largest Orchestra: Reuters, "Venezuela claims Guinness World Record for largest orchestra," *The Hindu*, November 21, 2021;
	India's Uttar Pradesh tree planting: Biswajeet Banerjee, "Indians Plant Millions of Saplings Amid Mass Campaign," *AP News*, July 4, 2021.
44	**Family estrangement:** Robin Young and Serena McMahon, "The Depths of Estrangement: Why Family Rifts Happen and How to Heal," *WBUR Here & Now*, December 24, 2020.
44	**WHO estimation of women facing partner abuse and violence:** World Health Organization, "Violence Against Women," March 9, 2021.

44	**UN Office on Drugs and Crime:** United Nations Office on Drugs and Crime, *Global Study on Homicide: Gender-related Killing of Women and Girls*, unodc.org, Vienna, November 2018.
48	**Geopolitical affairs regarding inter-state coercive negotiation tactics:** Carsten K.W. De Dreu, "Coercive Power and Concession Making in Bilateral Negotiation," *JSTOR, The Journal of Conflict Resolution* 39, no. 4 (December 1995), 646-670. See also: Joseph S. Nye Jr., *Soft Power: The Means to Success in World Politics* (New York: Public Affairs/Perseus Books Group, 2004).
48	**Credit Suisse Research Institute:** Anthony Shorrocks, James Davies and Rodrigo Lluberas, "Research Institute: Global Wealth Report 2021," *Credit Suisse*, June 2021.
48	**Least Developed Countries:** UN Conference on Trade and Development, "UN recognition of the least developed countries," *UNCTAD*.
49	**The Guardian report of wilderness loss:** Adam Vaughan, "Humans Have Destroyed a Tenth of Earth's Wilderness in 25 Years–Study," *The Guardian*, September 8, 2016.
49	**Polluting waterways and infusing toxic chemicals into Earth:** SciNews, "Scientists Categorize Earth Toxic Planet," *PHYS.Org*, February 7, 2017.
49	**UN Intergovernmental Panel on Climate Change report:** "Climate Change 2021: The Physical Science Basis," *IPCC Sixth Assessment Report*.
49	**Scientists forecast a tipping point for the Amazon:** Ignacio Amigo, "When will the Amazon hit a tipping point?", *nature.com*, February 25, 2020.
49	**International Union for Conservations of Nature:** "Marine Plastic Pollution," *IUCN*, November 2021.
56	**Cherokee legend of Two Wolves:** "Two Wolves: A Cherokee Legend," *First People*.

Chapter 4: Envisioning Authentic Collaboration as a New Paradigm

61	**Wanderer, there is no road:** Antonio Machado, *Campos de Castilla*, goodreads.com.
70	**Thomas Lewis quote on relatedness:** Goodreads.com.

73	**People who spend at least two hours a week outdoors:** Jim Robbins, "Ecopsychology: How Immersion in Nature Benefits Your Health," Yale School of the Environment, *e360.yale.edu,* January 9, 2020.
78	**Six bases of power:** "French and Raven's Bases of Power," Wikipedia.org.
79	**Marianne Williamson uses metaphor of a lamp:** Marianne Williamson, "How to Plug Into the Universe," *Oprah Winfrey Network (OWN),* SuperSoul Sessions, November 6, 2015.
80	**We know that it takes a clear intention:** Joe Dispenza, *Becoming Supernatural: How Common People Are Doing the Uncommon* (USA: Hay House Publishing, 2017), goodreads.com.
84	**Neil Gaiman:** Neil Gaiman, "Make Good Art" (keynote address), University of the Arts commencement ceremony, May 17, 2012, *brainyquote.com.*

Chapter 5: Exploring the Nature of Relationships

87	**Psychologists confirm that, as babies and toddlers, we attach to our caregivers by how we are responded to and nurtured:** Kendra Cherry, "What Is Attachment Theory?: The Importance of Early Emotional Bonds," *verywellmind,* July 17, 2019.
87	**We all have the capacity to experience secure attachment:** Diane Poole Heller, "Understanding Attachment Styles and Their Effect on Relationships," *dianepooleheller.com,* February 7, 2022.
88	**In utero babies do experience the distress of mother:** Samuel Lopez De Victoria, PhD, "Emotional Trauma in the Womb," *PsychCentral,* (medically reviewed by Scientific Advisory Board), June 29, 2010.
88	**Research shows in utero babies do sense their mother's state:** Association for Psychological Science, "Can Fetus Sense Mother's Psychological State? Study Suggests Yes." *ScienceDaily,* November 10, 2011.
89	**Shimmer of motes:** Recorder, *Christ Returns: Reveals Startling Truth* (USA: A New Epoch, 2010), p 34.
89	**Non-dualism:** https://en.wikipedia.org/wiki/Nondualism.
93	**Etymology of the word patriarchy:** *Etymology Online Dictionary,* https://www.etymonline.com/word/patriarchy.

93   **Carol Gilligan on patriarchy:** Russell Bennetts, "Patriarchy's Paradoxical Persistence: Berfrois Interviews Carol Gilligan and Naomi Snider," *berfrois.com*, July 5, 2019.

See also: Carol Gilligan and Naomi Snider, *Why Does Patriarchy Persist?* (USA: Polity Press, 2018).

93   **Gary Zukav notes about power struggles:** Margaret Dill quotes Gary Zukav, https://margaretdill.com/archives/10325.

95   **Dr. Marshall Rosenberg pointed out:** Marshall Rosenberg, *Nonviolent Communication: A Language of Life, 3rd Edition* (California: PuddleDancer Press, 2015), 83.

97   **Carl Jung:** Mr. Purrington, "Carl Jung on the Effect of Projection," *carljungdepthpsychologysite.blog*, September 7, 2020.

98   **Earth is waking us up—species decline:** Rosamunde Almond, Monique Grooten and Tanya Petersen (Eds.), *Living Planet Report 2020: Bending the Curve of Biodiversity Loss* (Switzerland: World Wild Fund, 2020).

100   **Neuroplasticity research shows that we have the power to create new neural pathways:** Joyce Shaffer, "Neuroplasticity and Clinical Practice: Building Brain Power for Health," *National Library of Medicine, Frontiers in Psychology* 7, no. 1118 (July 26, 2016), www.ncbi.nlm.nih.gov.

Chapter 6: Exploring Why Authentic Collaboration Matters

102   **TED talk:** Simon Sinek, "How Great Leaders Inspire Action," *Ted.com* (TEDx Puget Sound), posted September 2009 on Ted.com, video, 18:35.

106   **Joseph Campbell's archetypal hero's journey:** Joseph Conrad, "The Monomyth: The Hero's Journey," *The Hero with a Thousand Faces*, https://www.allenisd.org/cms/lib/TX01001197/Centricity/Domain/1541/Heroes%20Journey%202015.pdf.

109   **David Tong, a quantum physicist**: David Tong, "What is Quantum Field Theory?," *University of Cambridge*.

109   **Centenarians exist in five blue zone regions in the world:** Laura Dan, "The Blue Zones: Lifestyle Habits of the World's Longest-Living Populations," *Fullscript*, October 19, 2020.

(FYI: A centenarian is a person who has reached the age of one hundred years. In 2015, the United Nations estimated there were almost half a million centenarians worldwide. In these blue zone regions, people statistically live longer, have fewer disabilities and experience greater vitality.)

111   **Robert Sussman and Robert Cloninger:** Washington University, "Humans naturally cooperative, altruistic, social," *phys.org,* September 8, 2011.

112   **Research published in Nature Neuroscience shows:** India Bohanna, "The Neuroscience of Belonging," *BrainBlogger,* September 17, 2012.

See also: N.I. Eisenberger and S.W. Cole, "Social Neuroscience and Health: Neurophysiological Mechanisms Linking Social Ties with Physical Health," *Nature Neuroscience* 15 no. 5 (2012), 669-74.

114   **Companies that promote collaborative working were five times as likely to be high performing:** Gaskell, Adi, "New Study Finds That Collaboration Drives Workplace Performance," *Forbes,* June 22, 2017.

115   **Gallup Poll results related to engagement of staff in the US:** Jim Harter, "Employee Engagement Rise in the U.S.," *Gallup,* August 26, 2018.

115   **Gallup's global engagement findings:** "State of the Global Workplace: 2022 Report," *Gallup.com.*

117   **Cloverpop research:** Erik Larson, "New Research: Inclusive Decision-Making Increases Performance of Diverse Global Companies," *Cloverpop*, September 19, 2017.

119   **Decrease in tween girls' self-esteem:** Ypulse, Katty Kay and Claire Shipman, *The Confidence Code for Girls: The Confidence Collapse and Why It Matters for the Next Gen, confidencecodegirls.com,* 2018 (Nationwide quantitative online survey of 1,394 eight- to eighteen-year-olds and their parents/guardians).

120   **Nineteen targets and twenty-five indicators for SDG goal #17:** United Nations Sustainable Development Goal #17: Strengthen the means of implementation and revitalize the global partnership for sustainable development. UN Sustainable Development Goals, list of targets and indicators: *unstats.un.org.*

Chapter 7: Examining Collaboration Blocks and Enablers

129   **Viktor Frankl's story:** Viktor E. Frankl, *Man's Search for Meaning* (USA: Beacon Press, 1959), p 12.

131   **Self-empowerment:** Inspired by the teaching of pioneer empowerment coaches David Gershon and Gail Straub, *Empowerment Institute.*

131 **Dr. Joe Dispenza:** Joe Dispenza, *You Are the Placebo: Making Your Mind Matter* (USA: Hay House Publishing, 2014), *goodreads.com* (quotes).

135 **All relationships follow a cycle of harmony, disharmony and repair:** Esther Perel, in an interview with Skavlan for SVT/TV 2, posted on YouTube December 5, 2018, video, 16:24, Comment is at the 30-second mark.

137 **Imbalance of power dynamics:** Caitlin Killoren, "3 Types of Power Dynamics in a Relationship (And How to Find a Balance)," *Relish*, December 23, 2021.

138 **Raphael Cushnir, ride the wave:** Raphael Cushnir, "The One Thing Holding You Back: Compendium of Emotional Connection Principles and Practices," *Raphael Cushnir*.

See also: Raphael Cushnir, *The One Thing Holding You Back; Unleashing the Power of Emotional Connection* (USA: Harper One, 2008).

138 **The RAIN practice:** Tara Brach, https://www.tarabrach.com/rain/.

See also: Tara Brach, *Radical Compassion: Learning to Love Yourself and Your World with the Practice of RAIN* (USA: Penguin/Random House, 2019).

139 **Elements of self-regulation:** Roy Chowdhury, Madhuleena, What is Emotion Regulation? + What is 6 Emotional Skills and Strategies, *Positive Psychology*.

140 **Nonviolent Communication (NVC):** Marshall Rosenberg, *Nonviolent Communication: A Language of Life, 3rd Edition* (California: PuddleDancer Press, 2015), page 83.

144 **The Sanskrit concept of anahata:** https://en.wikipedia.org/wiki/Anahata.

146 **Deming's quote:** The W. Edwards Deming Institute (note: the source is disputed by some), https://deming.org/quotes/10141/.

147 **Sergio Caredda's research on the first time the word hierarchy was used:** Sergio Caredda, "The True Meaning of Hierarchy," *Sergio Caredda*, May 19, 2020.

147 **Gylany:** https://en.wikipedia.org/wiki/The_Chalice_and_the_Blade.

See also: Riane Eisler, *The Chalice and the Blade: Our History, Our Future* (USA: Harper San Francisco, 1988).

151 **The hallmarks of circle communication:** Personal circle dialogue training with Christina Baldwin and Ann Linnea, PeerSpirit Circle Process.

See also: Christina Baldwin and Ann Linnea, *The Circle Way: A Leader in Every Chair* (USA: Berrett-Koehler Publishers, 2010).

152 **Jean Houston:** "Re-Storying Your Life," *Evolving Wisdom,* January 5, 2016.

See also: Jean Houston, *A Passion for the Possible: A Guide to Realizing Your True Potential* (USA: HarperCollins Publishers, 1997).

154 **Ecologist Suzanne Simard:** Suzanne W. Simard and Daniel M. Durall, "Mycorrhizal Networks: A Review of Their Extent, Function, and Importance," *Canadian Journal of Botany* 82, no. 8 (August 2004), 1140-1165, https://doi.org/10.1139/b04-116.

154 **A study showed that if two friend trees have roots that are closely intertwined:** Richard Grant, in an interview with forester Peter Wohlleben, "Do Trees Talk To Each Other?", *Smithsonian Magazine,* March 2018.

See also Peter Wohlleben, *The Hidden Life of Trees: What They Feel, How They Communicate–Discoveries from a Secret World* (Canada/USA: Greystone Books, 2016).

155 Ibid.

155 **Mehran Banaei:** Mehran Banaei, "Conflict Resolution Strategies: Lessons from Nature," *Scientific God Journal* 3, no. 4 (May 2012), 213-218, reposted on author's blog, June 12, 2013.

155 **Evidence suggests that other primates also have effective behavioral tools to resolve conflicts:** Joan B. Silk, "Animal Behavior: Conflict Management Is for the Birds," *Science Direct, Current Biology* 17, no. 2 (January 2007), R50-R51.

155 **Bottlenose dolphins:** Ann Weaver, "Conflict and Reconciliation in Captive Bottlenose Dolphins, Tursiops Truncatus," *Marine Mammal Science* 19, no. 4 (August 2006), 836-846, DOI: 10.1111/j.1748-7692.2003.tb01134.x, researchgate.net.

156 **Cooperation is impeded among chimpanzees:** Cronin, K., Acheson, D., Hernández, P. *et al.*, "Hierarchy is Detrimental for Human Cooperation," *Scientific Report 5***,** 18634 (2016).

Further reading on how humans and chimpanzees both have a bias for cooperation: "Research Shows Chimpanzees Cooperate First and Think Later," *Jane Goodall's Good For All News*, December 4, 2018.

Chapter 8: Respond by Balancing Giving with Receiving

161 **Dr. Daniel J Siegel:** Daniel Siegel, "How to Gain Freedom from Your Thoughts," *Greater Good Magazine*, August 22, 2018.

See also: Daniel J. Siegel, *Aware: The Science and Practice of Presence–The GroundBreaking Meditation Practice* (USA: Penguin Random House, 2020).

162 **Dr. Benjamin Libet's research**: Tara Bennett-Goleman, *Emotional Alchemy: How the Mind Can Heal the Heart* (USA: Harmony Books, 2001), page 143.

162 **The magical quarter-second**: Ibid, page 144.

163 **How can I experience you before I respond:** Thomas Hubl, "Healing Collective Trauma," interview hosted by @Banyen Books & Sound, posted on YouTube December 19, 2020, video, 1:38:31.

See also: Thomas with Julie Jordan Avritt, *Healing Collective Trauma: A Process for Integrating Our Intergenerational and Cultural Wounds* (Colorado: Sounds True, 2000).

163 **Eckhart Tolle on presence:** Eckhart Tolle, *A New Earth: Awakening to Your Life's Purpose* (USA: Penguin Books, 2005/2015), page 115.

Chapter 9: Empathize by Connecting with Heart

178 **Mirror neurons:** Lindsey MacGillivray, "I Feel Your Pain: Mirror Neurons and Empathy," *Health Psychology*, Volume 6 No. 1, 2009, page 16.

178 **Mimicry**: Peg Streep, "6 Things You Need to Know About Empathy," *Psychology Today*, January 23, 2017.

180 **Earthing grounding practice:** Eleesha Lockett, "Grounding: Exploring Earthing Science and the Benefits Behind It," *HealthLine.com*, August 30, 2019.

180 **Workplace empathy research:** Tracy Brower, "Empathy Is the Most Important Leadership Skill According to Research," *Forbes*, September 19, 2021.

181 **Harvard Business Review:** Belinda Parmar, "The Most Empathetic Companies, 2016," *Harvard Business Review*, December 20, 2016.

181 **Businesssolver:** 2022 State of Workplace Empathy: Executive Summary, *Businesssolver*.

182 **HeartMath:** HeartMath Institute, https://www.heartmath.org.

182   **Vulnerability means wounded:** Dr. Gabor Mate, "How emotions affect our cognitive functioning," YouTube, January 8, 2016, minute 28:50.

187   **Only 3 percent of the world's ecosystems remain intact:** Damian Carrington, "Just 3% of the World's Ecosystems Remain Intact, Study Suggests," *The Guardian*, April 15, 2021.

190   **Ho'oponopono prayer:** "Ho'oponopono, Mantra Meditation, Hawaiian Prayer, Theta Binaural Beats, Hooponopono," posted on Jason Stephenson—Sleep Meditation Music YouTube channel, January 13, 2014, video, 45:04.

Chapter 10: Listen by Uncovering Feelings and Needs

193   **Dr. Albert Mehrabian's 7-38-55 nonverbal communication research:** "Albert Mehrabian," *British Library*, article featured in "All Management Thinkers."

See also Albert Mehrabian's website at www.kaaj.com/psych.

197   **Mystic Jiddu Krishnamurti on real change:** Jiddu Krishnamurti, *The Book of Life: Daily Meditations with Krishnamurti* (USA: Harper San Francisco, 1995), October 23 entry.

198   **Plutchik's Wheel of Emotions:** "Plutchik's Wheel of Emotions: Exploring the Emotion Wheel," *Six Seconds: The Emotional Intelligence Network*.

198   **Dr. Daniel Goleman defines EI:** Ben Cole, "Emotional Intelligence (EI)," *TechTarget*, May 2019.

See also: Daniel Goleman, *Emotional Intelligence* (USA: Bantam Books, 1995).

200   **Research about the correlation between anger and heart attacks:** British Heart Foundation, "Does Getting Angry Put You at Risk of a Heart Attack?," *Heart Matters magazine*, www.bhf.org.uk.

200   **Chronic Pain:** "Arthritis and Mental Health," *Arthritis Foundation*, arthritis.org.

201   **Dr. Brené Brown, you can't numb hard feelings:** Brené Brown, "How to Navigate the Emotions You're Unwilling to Feel" (an interview with Tim Ferriss), posted on *The Time Ferriss Show* YouTube channel, February 8, 2020, video, minute 7:54.

201   **Barbara Fredickson notes that 75 percent of us live in the left-brain hemisphere:** Bonnie Badenoch, "Nurturing the Heart with the Brain

in Mind" (interview with Liam O Mahony), posted on the Professional Counselling and Psychotherapy Seminars Ireland (PCPSI) YouTube channel October 29, 2021, video, 57:50.

See also Bonnie Badenoch, *The Heart of Trauma: Healing the Embodied Brain in the Context of Relationships* (New York: W.W. Norton & Company, 2017).

201 Ibid.

202 **US Healthcare relationship-centered communication:** Krista Hirschmann, Greta Rosler and Auguste H. Fortin VI, "'For Me, This Has Been Transforming': A Qualitative Analysis of Interpersonal Relationship Centered Communication Skills Training," National Library of Medicine, *Journal of Patient Experience* 7, no. 6 (October 16, 2020), 1007-1014, www.ncbi.nlm.nih.gov, doi: 10.1177/2374373520962921.

202 **Dr. David Hawkins on letting go:** David Hawkins, *Letting Go: The Pathway to Surrender* (USA: Hay House Publishing, 2012), pages 22-23.

204 **Global White Lion Protection Trust:** whitelions.org.

209 **Tokyo's Nippon Medical School research on forest bathing:** Qing Li, "Effect of Forest Bathing Trips on Human Immune Function," *Environmental Health and Preventive Medicine* 15, no. 1 (March 25, 2009), 9 17, doi: 10.1007/s12199-008-0068-3.

Chapter 11: Appreciate by Welcoming Different Perspectives

213 **Defining groupthink:** Daniel M. Mayton II and M. Zachary Brink, "Groupthink," *Wiley Online Library*, November 13, 2011.

214 **Space Shuttle Challenger disaster:** Wayne Gerber, "Decisive History Volume 1: Challenger Explosion and Groupthink," *Powernoodle.com*.

214 **Dr. Daniel Goleman and Richard Boyatzis write about social intelligence:** Daniel Goleman and Richard Boyatzis, "Social Intelligence and the Biology of Leadership," *Harvard Business Review*, September 2008.

218 **Terri Cole on boundaries:** Terri Cole, "Becoming a Boundary Boss" (interview with Tami Simon), posted on the *Sounds True* podcast channel April 20, 2021, audio, 1:01:55.

See also: Terri Cole, *Boundary Boss: The Essential Guide to Talk True, Be Seen and (Finally) Live Free* (Colorado: Sounds True, 2021).

220 **John Welwood's Fourfold Truth:**, John Welwood, *Love and Awakening: Discovering the Sacred Path of Intimate Relationship* (USA: Harper Perennial, 1997), 104.

225 **Inter-Being:** "Thich Nhat Hanh on interbeing," posted on the Zen in the City, YouTube channel video, June 6, 2014, video, 2:53.

Chapter 12: Trust by Speaking Authentically

233 **Attachment styles:** Kendra Cherry, "The Different Types of Attachment Styles," *verywell mind*, May 26, 2022.

238 **Buy-in and enrollment conversations:** Inspired by the teachings of Allan Henderson, GHJ Consulting, Seattle, USA.

239 **Four Horsemen of the Apocalypse:** Ellie Lisitsa, "The Four Horsemen: Criticism, Contempt Defensiveness and Stonewalling," *The Gottman Institute*.

241 **Holding onto anger is like drinking poison**: A quote from Buddha, *Sanvello website*.

See also: Pema Chodron, *Start Where You Are: A Guide to Compassionate Living* (Boston: Shambhala, 2004).

247 A. H. Amas, *Diamond Heart Book One: Elements of the Real in Man* (Boston: Shambala, 1987), 140.

Chapter 13: Equalize by Valuing Process and Outcome

252 **For more information on Focusing:** The International Focusing Institute, *focusing.org*.

253 **Aikido:** Wikipedia.org.

265 **Art Costa and Bena Kallick 3 P's Exercise**: Bena Kallick and Allison Zmuda, "Pauses That Lead to Deeper Thinking," *Learning Personalized*.

Chapter 14: Flying on the Wings of Inner Growth and Outer Engagement

276 **Over 900 species have been lost in the past five centuries:** Hannah Ritchie and Max Roser, "Extinctions," *Our World in Data*.

278 **Law of resonance:** Michael Bernard Beckwith, "Why the Law of Resonance Is More Important than the Law of Attraction" (presentation), posted on the Mindvalley YouTube channel, November 24, 2019, video, 12:10.

280 **Becoming a "belonging activist":** john a. powell, "Building Belonging: Being an Ambassador to the Earth" (interview with Tami Simon), posted on the *Sounds True* podcast channel May 18, 2021, audio, 1:06:42.

ADDITIONAL RESOURCES

Block, Peter. *Community: The Structure of Belonging.* San Francisco: Berrett-Koehler Publishers, 2008.

Brown, Brené. *The Power of Vulnerability: Teachings on Authenticity, Connection & Courage.* Colorado: Sounds True, 2012.

Goodchild, Melanie. "Relational Systems Thinking: That's How Change is Going to Come, From our Earth Mother." *Journal of Awareness-Based Systems Change 1*, no. 1 (2021), doi: https://doi.org/10.47061/jabsc.v1i1.577.

Grenny, Joseph, Kerry Patterson, Ron McMillian, Al Switzler, and Emily Gregory. *Crucial Conversations: Tools for Talking When Stakes Are High, Third Edition.* USA: McGraw Hill, 2021.

Hansen, Morten. *Collaboration: How Leaders Avoid the Traps, Build Common Ground and Reap Big Results.* Boston: Harvard Business School Publishing, 2009.

Hawkins, David. *Power vs Force: The Determinants of Human Behavior.* USA: Hay House Publishing, 2012.

Hendricks, Gay, *Ten-Second Miracle: Creating Relationship Breakthroughs*, USA: HarperCollins Publishers, 1998.

Johnson, Morten. *Emotional Intelligence: Build Strong Social Skills and Improve Your Relationships by Raising Your EQ with Proven Methods and Strategies.* USA: Kindle, 2020.

Kahane, Adam. *Collaborating with the Enemy: How to Work with People You Don't Agree with or Like or Trust.* California: Berrett-Koehler Publishers, 2017.

Killian, Dian, and Jane Marantz Connor. *Connecting Across Differences.* New York: Hungry Duck Press, 2005.

Kimmerer, Robin Wall, *Braiding Sweetgrass, Indigenous Wisdom, Scientific Knowledge, and the Teachings of Plants,* Canada: Milkweed Editions, 2013.

Miyashiro, Marie R. *The Empathy Factor.* USA: PuddleDancer Press, 2011.

Villoldo, Alberto. *The Heart of the Shaman: Stories and Practices of the Luminous Warrior.* USA: Hay House Publishing, 2018.

Wheatley, Margaret, *Turning to One Another: Simple Conversations to Restore Hope to the Future.* San Francisco: Berrett-Koehler Publishers, 2009.

ABOUT ELIZABETH

Elizabeth Soltis is the Founder/Director of Bridges Global, a social enterprise that supports leaders and groups with inner empowerment and outer bridge-building. By elevating the art of collaboration, people are better able to sense-make complex issues and discover creative, sustainable solutions. Her purpose is catalyzing transformation.

In all sectors, Elizabeth has served as an organizational development practitioner, collaboration specialist, learning consultant, group facilitator and workshop/retreat space-holder. When coaching change-makers, she is awe-inspired by the synergy of teamwork, the courage of vulnerable expression, the uplift of new perspectives, the choice towards alignment and the liberation that comes from living one's heart truth.

For many years, Elizabeth has supported United Nations teams to strengthen their processes of learning, change and effectiveness. As a global citizen and advocate of social and eco-justice, Elizabeth has had the privilege of traveling to, working in or volunteering in over 80 countries.

Elizabeth's global experience is complemented by a Master of Arts (International Relations) degree, a diploma in Human Resource Management and certificates in Adult Education, Empowerment Coaching, Life Skills Facilitation and Shamanic Wisdom. She resides in Southwestern Ontario, Canada.